THE FEDERALIZATION OF CRIMINAL LAW

James A. Strazzella
Reporter

Task Force on the Federalization of Criminal Law
American Bar Association
Criminal Justice Section

1998

TABLE OF CONTENTS

PREFACE

The Criminal Justice Section of the American Bar Association created this Task Force in response to widespread concern about the number of new federal crimes being created annually by Congress. Its initial objectives were to look systematically at whether there has been, in fact, an increase in federal crimes which duplicate state crimes, and, if so, to determine whether that development adversely affects the proper allocation of responsibility between the national and state governments for crime prevention and law enforcement.

The members of the Task Force were selected with the explicit goal of including persons with diverse political and philosophical backgrounds. It was important that the Task Force's conclusions and recommendations be the product of a consensus among respected persons whose views on criminal justice issues generally would vary widely.

The Chair of the Task Force is a former Attorney General of the United States. Its members include a former United States Senator, a former Congressman, a former Deputy Attorney General of the United States, a former Chief Executive of the Law Enforcement Assistance Administration of the United States Department of Justice, former State Attorneys General, present and former federal and state prosecutors, state and federal appellate judges, a police chief, private practitioners who specialize in criminal defense, and scholars. (Fuller biographies of the members of the Task Force appear in APPENDIX D.)

With the skillful guidance of Professor James Strazzella of Temple University Law School, who served as reporter for the Task Force and who is the principal author of its report, and the invaluable research assistance of Barbara Meierhoefer, Ph.D., the Task Force undertook to examine the United States Code, data available from public sources, the body of scholarly literature on the subject, the views of professionals in state and federal criminal justice systems, and the experience of the Task Force members themselves.

The Task Force concluded that the evidence demonstrated a recent dramatic increase in the number and variety of federal crimes. Although it may be impossible to determine exactly how many federal crimes could be prosecuted today, it is clear that of all federal crimes enacted since 1865, over forty percent have been created since 1970. The Report explains in more detail how the catalog of federal crimes grew from an initial handful to the several thousand which exist today.

The Task Force also concluded that much of the recent increase in federal criminal legislation significantly overlaps crimes traditionally prosecuted by the states. This area of increasing overlap lies at the core of the Task Force study.

The federalization phenomenon is inconsistent with the traditional notion that prevention of crime and law enforcement in this country are basically state functions. The Task Force was impressed with nearly unanimous expressions of concern from thoughtful commentators, including participants within the criminal justice system and scholars, about the impact of federalization. The Task Force was also impressed that new federal crimes duplicating state crimes became part of our law without requests for their enactment from state or federal law enforcement officials.

The Task Force was told explicitly by more than one source that many of these new federal laws are passed not because federal prosecution of these crimes is necessary but because federal crime legislation in general is thought to be politically popular. Put another way, it is not considered politically wise to vote against crime legislation, even if it is misguided, unnecessary, and even harmful.

As the size of the national government has grown, it is reasonable to expect that there would be some expansion of federal crimes, if, for no other reason, than to protect new federal programs. That is quite a different matter, however, from the indiscriminate federalization of local crime for no reason other than that it is serious.

In this Report, the Task Force explains the process it followed, the data it examined, and the consensus which emerged. It looked systematically at whether new federal criminal laws, which were popular when enacted, are being enforced. It determined, based on obvious data, that in many instances they are not. While there are more people in federal prisons than ever before and they are serving longer sentences, that condition is not the result of increased federal prosecution of crimes formerly prosecuted by states. It is principally a function of increased resources devoted to federal law enforcement, particularly for drug offenses, and the impact of the sentencing guidelines.

The Task Force believes that the Congressional appetite for new crimes regardless of their merit is not only misguided and ineffectual, but has serious adverse consequences, some of which have already occurred and some of which can be confidently predicted.

The Task Force did not attempt to identify the limits of the power of the national government under the Commerce Clause to criminalize conduct which is already, or which could be, prosecuted by states. It noted, of course, the recent decision of the Supreme Court striking down a criminal statute which exceeded that power. The Court observed in that case that the Constitution withholds "from Congress a plenary police power that would authorize enactment of every type of legislation."[1] Even if the Commerce Clause would permit Congress to subject its citizens to federal prosecution for common-law-type crimes, the exercise of that power to its fullest extent would be, at best, wasteful, and, at worst, destructive of the relationship between state and federal law enforcement. As the distinguished Police Executive Research Forum wrote, federalization "diverts federal authorities from what they do best and puts more distance between law enforcers and local community residents — in direct conflict with community policing objectives."[2]

The Report identifies a trend and counsels against its continuation. It does not recommend a reduction or limitation on the national role in fighting crime, but rather a refocusing of that role. It is precisely because federal law enforcement is so necessary in dealing with indisputable federal interests that a legislative instruction to federal prosecutors to

---

[1] Noted in the Report at p. 25.

[2] Quoted in the Report at p. 41.

utilize their time and resources to prosecute relabeled common law crimes ought to be restrained. Moreover, federal financial support of state law enforcement is crucial and ought not to be curtailed.

Finally, the Task Force attempts to articulate general principles which ought to guide the national legislature in determining whether to create new crimes.

It remains the case that federal efforts account for only five percent of all prosecutions nationwide. State law enforcement is still the critical component in dealing with the crime which threatens most people. The Task Force is firmly of the view that state governments are neither incapable nor unwilling to exercise their traditional responsibility to protect the lives and property of citizens, and that the Congress ought to reflect long and hard before it enacts legislation which puts federal police in competition with the states for the confidence of its citizenry and limited law enforcement resources.

Edwin Meese III
Chair, Task Force

William W. Taylor, III
Chair, Criminal Justice Section, 1996-97

REPORT

The fundamental view that local crime is, with rare exception, a matter for the states to attack has been strained in practice in recent years. Congressional activity making essentially local conduct a federal crime has accelerated greatly, notably in areas in which existing state law already criminalizes the same conduct. This troubling federalization trend has contributed to a patchwork of federal crimes often lacking a principled basis.

I. THE FEDERALIZATION TREND: THE GROWTH OF THE FEDERAL CRIMINAL JUSTICE SYSTEM AND CURRENT ACTIVITY

An Overview of the Growth of Federal Crimes

For years following the adoption of the Constitution in 1789, the states defined and prosecuted nearly all criminal conduct. The federal government confined its prosecutions to less than a score of offenses. As one scholar described these offenses, they generally:

> dealt with injury to or interference with the federal government itself or its programs. The federal offenses of the time included treason, bribery of federal officials, perjury in federal court, theft of government property, and revenue fraud. Except in those areas where federal jurisdiction was exclusive (the District of Columbia and the federal territories) federal law did not reach crimes against individuals. Crimes against individuals — such as murder, rape, arson, robbery, and fraud — were the exclusive concern of the states. State law defined these offenses, which were prosecuted by state or local officials in the state courts.[3]

---

[3] Sara Sun Beale, *Federalizing Crime: Assessing the Impact on the Federal Courts*, 543 ANNALS AM. ACAD. POL. & SOC. SCI. 39, 40 (1996). *See also* Beale, *Too Many and Yet Too Few: New Principles to Define the Proper Limits for Federal Criminal Jurisdiction*, 46 HASTINGS L.J. 979 (1995). Detailed accounts of the general growth in

Crime was seen as a uniquely local concern and the power to prosecute rested almost exclusively in the states, whose law enforcement activities covered nearly all the activity believed worthy of criminal sanction.[4] Crime did not become a national issue in Presidential campaigns until 1928,[5] but today it is a resonating staple of federal as well as state electoral politics.[6]

The last third of the nineteenth century saw a significant increase in the assertion of federal jurisdiction, marked initially by a series of Congressional statutes dealing with the misuse of the mails and asserting federal jurisdiction in connection with interstate commerce. For the first time, federal crimes began to cover activity that dealt with subjects clearly also within the ambit of the states' police powers. The steady continuation of this trend into the twentieth century sparked significant debate about the constitutional limits of federal jurisdiction. The expansion of federal jurisdiction was generally premised on an assertion of Congressional power to regulate interstate commerce, and the expansion of federal law on this basis was closely contested in the Supreme Court.[7]

---

the amount of conduct criminalized by federal law can be found in the literature collected in the BIBLIOGRAPHY, APPENDIX A. For purposes of this Report, that general growth need only be briefly stated.

[4] *See* Kathleen F. Brickey, *The Commerce Clause and Federalized Crime: A Tale of Two Thieves,* 543 ANNALS AM. ACAD. POL. & SOC. SC. 27, 28 (1996); Brickey, *Criminal Mischief: The Federalization of American Criminal Law*, 46 HASTINGS L.J. 1135 (1995).

[5] JAMES D. CALDER, THE ORIGIN AND DEVELOPMENT OF FEDERAL CRIME CONTROL POLICY 25 (1983).

[6] *See, e.g.,* N.Y. TIMES, Sept. 25, 1998, at B1 (describing U.S. Senate candidates as trying to "out-tough each other on crime"); N.Y. TIMES, Aug. 27, 1998, at A12 (reporting on a debate between candidates for the U.S. Senate and describing the candidates' positions on death penalty issues).

[7] Champion v. Ames, 188 U.S. 321 (1903) (upholding, by a sharply divided Supreme Court vote, the constitutionality of a statute making it a crime to transport lottery tickets across state lines). For a sense of the debate on the proper extent of constitutional power under the Commerce Clause, *compare* John S. Baker, Jr., *Nationalizing Criminal Law: Does Organized Crime Make It Necessary or Proper?*, 16 RUTGERS L.J. 495 (1985), *with* Tom Stacy & Kim Dayton, *The Underfederalization*

In the twentieth century, increasing federal programs also correspondingly multiplied the criminal sanctions that were attached to these programs, but other factors such as Prohibition ushered in further federal criminal law-making. In the 1960s and 1970s, however, concern with organized crime, drugs, street violence, and other social ills precipitated a particularly significant rise in federal legislation tending to criminalize activity involving more local conduct, conduct previously left to state regulation. With concern about crime mounting in the 1980s and 1990s, the trend to federalize crime has continued dramatically, covering more conduct formerly left exclusively to state prosecution.[8]

The Current High Level of Congressional Activity

The Task Force's research reveals a startling fact about the explosive growth of federal criminal law: *More than 40% of the federal criminal provisions enacted since the Civil War have been enacted since 1970.*[9]

An indication of the legislative activity federalizing crime is seen in the following charts. The first chart indicates the annual legislative activity in the 132-year period between 1864 and 1996. The second chart

---

of Crime, 6 CORNELL J.L. & PUB. POL'Y 247 (1997).

[8] *See* Sara Sun Beale, *Federalizing Crime: Assessing the Impact on the Federal Courts*, 543 ANNALS AM. ACAD POL. & SOC. SCI. 39, 41 (1996) (tracing the rise of federal legislation); *see also* Beale, *Too Many and Yet Too Few: New Principles to Define the Proper Limits for Federal Criminal Jurisdiction*, 46 HASTINGS L.J. 979 (1995); John S. Baker, Jr., *Nationalizing Criminal Law: Does Organized Crime Make It Necessary or Proper?*, 16 RUTGERS L.J. 495 (1985). The Senate report accompanying the 1995 federal budget asserted that the country was faced with a "law enforcement emergency." SEN. REP. NO. 103-309 (1994), at p. 29, as discussed in Kathleen F. Brickey, *The Commerce Clause and Federalized Crime: A Tale of Two Thieves*, 543 ANNALS AM. ACAD. POL. & SOC. SCI. 27, 28 (1996).

[9] Much, though not all, of this surge has occurred in the last two decades. Even excluding provisions enacted in the last Congress (see APPENDIX C), more than a quarter of the federal criminal provisions enacted since the Civil War have been enacted within a sixteen year period since 1980. Both this estimate and the 40% figure in the text are derived from a review of statutory provisions referred to in Chart 2 (contained in the text of this Report and showing the percentage of statutory sections enacted by time period).

shows the percentage of statutory sections enacted by time period. The charts demonstrate the dramatic increase in federal criminal statutes, particularly in the last two decades.

NUMBER OF STATUTORY SECTIONS ENACTED BY YEAR

Average Number of Statutory Sections Enacted Per Year=7.7 (shown as horizontal line). The 414 sections added in 1948 as part of the Title 18 recodification are excluded.

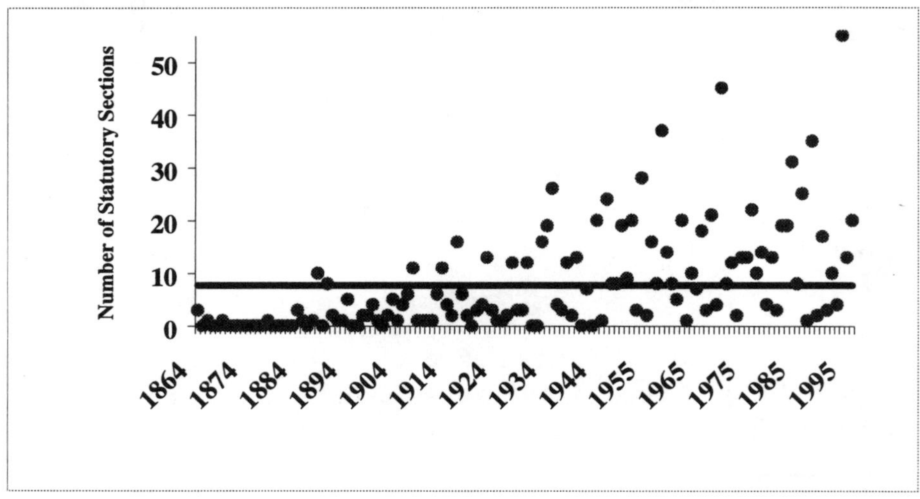

Chart 1.[10] TF on Federalization (ABA)

[10] The year 1948 has been excluded from this graph. In that year, Title 18 of the U.S. Code was recodified. Many of the previous statutory sections were blended together in the recodification, resulting in a disproportionate number of sections that were not entirely new. Adding 1948 to the graph by counting these "new" sections would, therefore, create a potentially misleading picture of new crimes. At the same time, it should be noted that because 1948 is not counted, the existing law does contain sections not counted in the graph.

The counts in Charts 1 and 2 were derived from the date of enactment of each section charted and described in APPENDIX C, without counting subsections. The count does not include enactments which were subsequently repealed, nor does it include amendments which might have substantially expanded or otherwise changed presently existing statutory provisions after initial enactment. If counted, these excluded statutory actions would further expand the amount of legislative activity reflected in the charts.

PERCENT OF STATUTORY SECTIONS ENACTED BY TIME PERIOD
Number excluding 1948 recodification=1,020

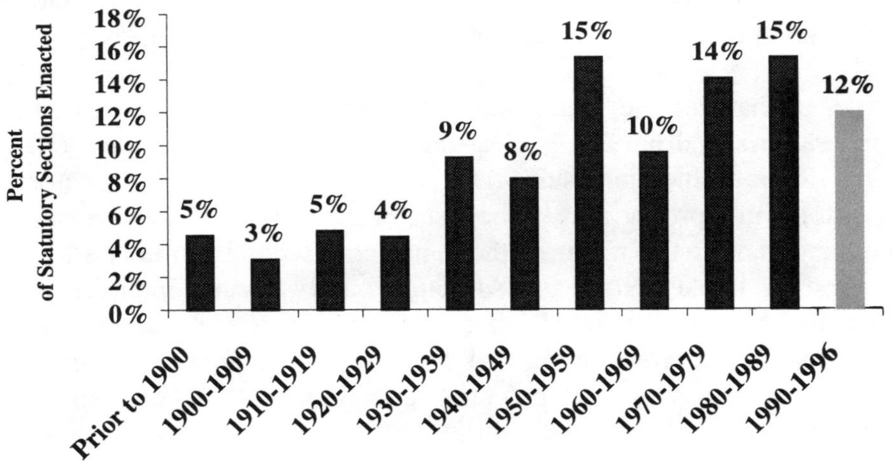

Notes:
(a) The "Prior to 1900" category includes 1864 - 1889.
(b) The 414 sections added or modified as part of the 1948 recodification are excluded from the 1940s.
(c) The "1990-1996" category includes only 7 years.

Chart 2. TF on Federalization (ABA)

So large is the present body of federal criminal law that there is no conveniently accessible, complete list of federal crimes.[11] Criminal

[11] An exact count of the present "number" of federal crimes contained in the statutory sections and the administrative regulations is difficult to achieve and the count is subject to varying interpretations. In part, the reason is not only that the criminal provisions are now so numerous and their location in the books so scattered, but also that federal criminal statutes are often complex. One statutory section can comprehend a variety of actions, potentially multiplying the number of federal "crimes" that could be enumerated. (For example, the language of 18 U.S.C. § 2113 encompasses bank

sanctions are dispersed in places other than the statutory codes (for example, rules of court[12]) and therefore can not be located simply by reading statutes. A large number of sanctions are dispersed throughout the thousands of administrative "regulations" promulgated by various governmental agencies under Congressional statutory authorization. Nearly 10,000 regulations mention some sort of sanction, many clearly criminal in nature, while many others are designated "civil."[13]

Whatever the exact number of crimes that comprise today's "federal criminal law," it is clear that the amount of individual citizen behavior now potentially subject to federal criminal control has increased in astonishing proportions in the last few decades. The Task Force has collected and listed many of the significant federal criminal statutory provisions in APPENDIX C. Although our list is not intended to be exhaustive,[14] the annotated list conveys the sweep of current federal criminal law. It provided the Task Force with an insight into the breadth of activity now subject to potential federal control. It bears emphasis that, in our review of these and subsequently enacted statutory provisions, the Task Force recognizes that not all, or even most, of the federal statutory increase is due to crimes federalizing essentially local conduct. Nevertheless, that portion of the increase which does cover historically state-prosecuted areas (including essentially local conduct and sometimes

---

robbery, extortion, theft, assaults, killing hostages, and storing or selling anything of value knowing it to have been taken from a bank, etc.) Depending on how all this subdivisible and dispersed law is counted, the true number of federal crimes multiplies. While a figure of "approximately 3,000 federal crimes" is frequently cited, that helpful estimate is now surely outdated by the large number of new federal crimes enacted in the 16 years or so years intervening since its estimation. Especially considering both statutory and administrative regulations, the present number of federal crimes is unquestionably larger. *See* APPENDIX C, pp. 93-94.

[12] For example, under the Rules of Criminal Procedure, certain violations of federal grand jury rules may be punished as a contempt of court. FED. R. CRIM. P. 6(e).

[13] The vast percentage specify ways in which a general Congressional statutory prohibition (for example, perjury) is a crime in the context of the regulations, e.g., by setting out forms and providing for perjury in connection with various particular forms. A handful of regulations purport to criminalize conduct without connecting the prohibition to a Congressional statute.

[14] See the limitations of the statutory list, stated at the outset of Appendix C.

street crime) is certainly significant, troubling, and gives rise to the concerns addressed in this Report.

All signs indicate that the federalization trend is growing, not slowing, in fact as well as perception. Highly publicized criminal incidents are frequently accompanied by calls for proposed Congressional responses, although, of course, most of these proposals do not become law. An estimated 1,000 bills dealing with criminal statutes were introduced in the most recent Congress.[15] These bills included, for example, proposals to enhance federal law regarding juvenile crime — an area long at the center of state criminal justice legislation and an area in which most states have recently toughened their laws. Some of these new federal proposals dismayed many who are concerned about the federalization trend, including the Chief Justice of the United States.[16] Many see this federal attention to juvenile crime as likely to produce adverse effects[17] or dangerous consequences,[18] and view it as an example

---

[15] The estimate is based on information provided through the Congressional Research Service approximating the number of bills introduced in the 105th Congress by the end of July 1998. While these bills sought to add to or alter the federal criminal statutes in one way or another, most were not considered major pieces of crime legislation. For information on statutes adopted in the last Congress, *see* APPENDIX C.

[16] William H. Rehnquist, *Address to the American Law Institute*, REMARKS AND ADDRESSES AT THE 75TH ANNUAL ALI MEETING, MAY 1998, at 15-19 (1998), also excerpted in *Chief Justice Raises Concerns on Federalism*, 30 THE THIRD BRANCH, June 1998, at 1.

[17] Consider, for example, the suggestions made to the Task Force by a leader of the ABA Criminal Justice Section's effort in the area of juvenile law. In essence, he notes the following: The federal system is not equipped to handle juvenile offenders. Unlike state systems, the federal system has no juvenile detention programs, no treatment options, no trained juvenile probation or parole officers, no prosecutors or defense attorneys who are specially trained to deal with children. Federal prosecutions waste valuable judicial time — cases are tried before judges who have neither the expertise nor resources for juvenile cases; there is no obvious benefit from trying these cases in federal court. There is no gain in public protection from using the federal system — only 250 or so juveniles each year are prosecuted in the federal system, so it is hardly a deterrence. Indeed, every federal prosecution of a juvenile could also have been brought in state court (despite the requirement in federal law that the Attorney General certify that the state system is inappropriate for this particular defendant — a provision that is used in cases of drug sales and carjackings). The federal sentencing guidelines

of enhanced federal attention where the need is neither apparent nor demonstrated. A recently charged heinous crime in which several defendants are accused of dragging a victim to his death prompted widely publicized calls before a Senate committee to federalize such hate crimes — even though state officials had already charged the accused defendants with a capital offense in state court.[19] In the face of serious and offensive incidents, it is becoming more and more frequent for citizens and legislators to simply urge that Congress should make the conduct a federal crime.[20]

---

were not designed with children in mind, and so take no account of adolescent development. Finally, at a time when almost every state has significantly toughened its juvenile code (by requiring increased incarceration and increased transfer to adult criminal court), it is hard to imagine that any added value will come from federal prosecutions. March 20, 1998, Comments of Robert G. Schwartz, Co-Chair of the ABA Criminal Justice Section's Juvenile Justice Committee. *See also* Washington Report, *Getting Tougher on Kids*, 84 A.B.A. J. 95 (1998) (noting concerns of ABA).

Some of the juvenile federal jurisdiction relates to areas falling within federal territorial jurisdiction.

[18] In a letter to the Task Force (Feb. 25, 1998), the Director of the National Prison Project, American Civil Liberties Union Foundation, discussed pending juvenile legislation and expressed the view that it "is particularly dangerous that Congress is now considering another major federalization of crime control." She argues that "[b]efore the nation embarks on another major federalization of the criminal justice system there should be consensus about the circumstances under which the federal interest is paramount so that the displacement of state policy is appropriate" and that no such consensus exists with regard to juveniles.

[19] *See* July 8, 1998 testimony before the Senate Judiciary Committee on S. 1529, 105 Cong., the bill proposing "The Hate Crimes Prevention Act of 1998," 1998 Westlaw 12762068; PHILADELPHIA INQUIRER, July 9, 1998, at A15. *See also* 1998 WL 12762060 through 12762071 for other testimony on S. 1529, and 12763004 through 12763008 for July 22, 1998 testimony on the related House bill, H.R. 3081, 105 Cong., 1st Sess.

[20] *See, e.g., Mother Rages Against Indifference*, N.Y. TIMES, Aug. 24, 1998, at A10, describing an incident in which a person did not report another person's assault on a child (resulting in the child's death) and the fact that the state where the incident occurred (like most states) does not criminalize a failure to report crimes; a group protesting the status of the law is described as intending to seek a federal law criminalizing the failure to report certain crimes.

Growth in Segments of the Federal Criminal Justice System

As dramatic as it is, the increase in the sheer number of federal crimes — including the amount of national *legislative* activity subjecting a growing amount of essentially local conduct to federal jurisdiction — reveals only one facet of the issue. Beyond the increase in the number of federal laws, the last few decades have seen a significant growth in the size of the overall federal criminal justice system, with attendant costs. Caution about inappropriate federalization, therefore, also includes caution about the addition of federal investigative and prosecution personnel beyond what is needed for offenses of a truly federal nature.

Congress's decision to create a federal crime confers jurisdiction upon other federal entities and results in the involvement of others in different federal government branches — prosecutors, investigators, administrative agencies, courts, and prison authorities — as well as federal public defenders. Federal Executive departments (including, but not limited to, the Department of Justice) assume broad supervisory responsibility and power over newly created crimes. This activates powerful federal investigatory agencies (such as the FBI, Treasury Department agencies, or Postal Inspectors) to investigate citizen activity for possible federal criminal violations. The scope of federal prosecutors' interest widens, resulting in power to act in a broader range of citizen conduct and intervene in more local conduct. The priorities of the Department of Justice may be changed or diluted, requiring consideration of a different set of goals and programs beyond those entailed in concentrating on traditional federal crimes.

Another important effect of federal criminal legislation is felt by the federal courts, which become forums for new classes of cases, many of which would otherwise be tried only in state courts. Convictions lead to federal imprisonment, burdening the federal prison system with all the attendant consequences of such expansion.

Empirical Data on the Growth of the Federal Criminal Justice System. Empirical data verifies a growing federal presence in the criminal justice system. Although part of this growth may be explained by greater societal attention to crime, the increase in federal expenditures is disproportionately greater than comparable increases in state criminal justice costs, indicating that at least some part of the federal growth is attributable to an expanding federal role. For example, between 1982 and 1993, overall federal justice system expenditures increased at twice the rate of comparable state and local expenditures, increasing 317% as compared to 163%.[21] The number of federal justice system personnel increased by 96% from 1982 to 1993, while state personnel increased at a significantly lesser rate, 42%.[22] Over a twelve year period, the number of federal prison inmates rose by 177%, as compared to a lower increase in state prison inmates, 134%.[23] Putting aside personnel at the Department of Justice headquarters in Washington, the regional U.S. Attorneys' Offices (which litigate the bulk of federal criminal cases) have grown in just the past 30 years from approximately 3,000 prosecutors to about 8,000.[24]

Reasons for Continuing Legislative Federalization

A striking phenomenon emerges from the Task Force's consideration of the numerous studies examining the federalization trend (BIBLIOGRAPHY, APPENDIX A). Writer after writer has noticed the absence of any underlying principle governing Congressional choice to criminalize conduct under federal law that is already criminalized by state law. What accounts for this continuing federalization in the face of such concerns and the warnings about its dangers?

New crimes are often enacted in patchwork response to newsworthy events, rather than as part of a cohesive code developed in

---

[21] See Chart 8, APPENDIX B, SECTION 1.

[22] See Chart 9, APPENDIX B, SECTION 1.

[23] See Chart 10, APPENDIX B, SECTION 1. For a sampling of the major types of crimes for which federal prisoners are actually jailed and a related discussion of that data, see Franklin E. Zimring & Gordon Hawkins, *Toward a Principled Basis for Federal Criminal Legislation*, 543 ANNALS AM. ACAD. POL. & SOC. SCI. 15, 18-19 (1996).

[24] *See* Sara Sun Beale, *Federalizing Crime: Assessing the Impact on the Federal Courts*, 543 ANNALS AM. ACAD POL. & SOC. SCI. 39, 45 (1996), citing statistics from THE CRIMINAL CASELOAD: THE NATURE OF CHANGE (Manuscript, Administrative Office of U.S. Courts: 1994).

response to an identifiable federal need. Observers have recognized that a crime being considered for federalization is often "regarded as appropriately federal because it is serious and not because of any structural incapacity to deal with the problem on the part of state and local government."[25] There is widespread recognition that a major reason for the federalization trend — even when federal prosecution of these crimes may not be necessary or effective — is that federal crime legislation is politically popular. For example, police executives noted in communications to the Task Force that despite recognized problems with federalization,

> the trend has not declined, in part because federalization is politically popular. Because relatively little hard research on effective crime control has been conducted or disseminated to lay people, they are easily convinced that making an offense a federal crime means we are taking a tougher stance against such actions. Most citizens believe that by federalizing crimes, we will somehow rid our communities of violence. Herein lies the greatest danger in federalization: creating the illusion of greater crime control, while undermining an already over-burdened criminal justice system.[26]

Others note that particularly notorious conduct receiving widespread media attention frequently prompts Congressional criminalization[27] and

---

[25] Franklin E. Zimring & Gordon Hawkins, *Toward a Principled Basis for Federal Criminal Legislation*, 543 ANNALS AM. ACAD. POL. & SOC. SCI. 15, 20-21 (1996). *See also* Chief Justice Rehnquist's observation about recently enacted federal statutes that have expanded federal jurisdiction: "the question of whether the states are doing an adequate job" in the area under consideration "was never seriously asked." William H. Rehnquist, *Address to the American Law Institute*, REMARKS AND ADDRESSES AT THE 75TH ANNUAL ALI MEETING, MAY 1998, at 18 (1998).

[26] "*Position on Federalism*," Police Executive Research Forum (transmitted to the Task Force, December 1997).

[27] *See, e.g.,* JAMES D. CALDER, THE ORIGIN AND DEVELOPMENT OF FEDERAL CRIME CONTROL POLICY 20-24, 198-203 (1983) (describing events that led to enactment of legislation in the late 1920s and early 1930s); Kathleen F. Brickey, *The Commerce Clause and Federalized Crime: A Tale of Two Thieves,* 543 ANNALS AM. ACAD POL. & SOC. SCI. 27, 30 (1996) (recounting Congressional enactment of carjacking statute

attribute the passage of much of this legislation to its popularity among constituents.[28]

The observations that the recent federalization is too frequently driven by political popularity, and not federal need, accord with the experience of Task Force members.

There is no question about the overall need for reasonable measures to deal with violent crime: The safety of citizens is a core interest of government, an important matter for meaningful governmental attention. Crime breeds genuine concern among our citizens, with violent street crime generating particular alarm. Crime also tends to generate legislative response. Public desire for safety fuels a corresponding desire in legislators to deal with citizen concern for protection. Some of these

---

following a widely publicized incident successfully prosecuted as state robbery and homicide); Constance Johnson, U.S. NEWS & WORLD REPORT, vol. 116, March 28, 1994, p.35 (noting Congressional federal kidnapping response to the Lindbergh baby kidnapping, as well as the federal bank robbery statute enactment in the wake of a streak of notorious bank robberies); Franklin E. Zimring & Gordon Hawkins, *Toward a Principled Basis for Federal Criminal Legislation*, 543 ANNALS AM. ACAD. POL. & SOC. SCI. 15 (1996) (arguing that federal criminal jurisprudence lacks discernable principles and noting backdrop of intense publicity against which the carjacking statute was enacted).

[28] The recurring view communicated to the Task Force is basically that expressed by a President of the National Conference of State Legislatures: "[T]he expansion of federal criminal jurisdiction and resources is totally the result of political popularity of crime legislation." The federalization is, for example, attributed by those in the law enforcement field to a desire for policy makers to be "tough on crime" (*Position on Federalism,* Police Executive Research Forum, transmitted to the Task Force December 1997) and to political expediency, following "the first rule of politics: get re-elected," rather than "a 'demonstrated need'. . . ." (Correspondence to Task Force from an Ohio county prosecutor). *See also* THE REAL WAR ON CRIME: REPORT OF THE NATIONAL CRIMINAL JUSTICE COMMISSION 68-71, 79-80 (1996); Franklin E. Zimring & Gordon Hawkins, *Toward a Principled Basis for Federal Criminal Legislation*, 543 ANNALS AM. ACAD. POL. & SOC. SCI. 15, 20-21 (1996) (noting that crime arouses citizen fear and arguing that in practice the argument for creation of a federal crime typically "stresses the considerable resources of the federal government and the need to proceed on all fronts against the troublesome and uncontrolled threats. The problem is regarded as federal because it is serious and not because of any structural incapacity to deal with the problem on the part of state and local government.").

legislative proposals may stem from a genuine, if often misguided, perception that federal law enforcement efforts are necessary or appropriate to deal with a particular law enforcement problem. However, no matter what the party, "[p]oliticians often use crime issues to 'enhance their popularity and electability.'"[29] Indeed, some of the recent pieces of federal legislation have been characterized as "feel-good, do-something" federal criminal bills[30] and "window dressing,"[31] recognized as only "symbolic gestures to appease the public rather than actual attempts to reduce crime."[32]

II. THE REALITIES OF FEDERAL PROSECUTION AS IT AFFECTS LOCAL CRIME

For much of our national history, the deeply rooted principle that the general police power resides in the states — and that federal law enforcement should be narrowly limited — was recognized in practice as well as in principle. At least until recently, the constitutional vision that the federal government should play a narrowly circumscribed role in defining and investigating criminal conduct was reflected in cautious limitations on the types of behavior that federal lawmakers addressed through criminal law. The Task Force's work leads it to the clear conviction that there has been a significant growth in federal crime legislation (much of it recent) and that a sizeable portion of it deals with

---

[29] NANCY E. MARION, A HISTORY OF FEDERAL CRIME CONTROL INITIATIVES 13 (1994) (citing Erika S. Fairchild & Vincent J. Webb, *Crime, Justice and Politics in the United States Today*, in FAIRCHILD & WEBB, eds., THE POLITICS OF CRIME AND CRIMINAL JUSTICE 8 (1985), and RALPH BAKER & FRED A. MEYER JR., THE CRIMINAL JUSTICE GAME 46 (1980)).

[30] *See* William N. Eskridge, Jr. & Philip P. Frickey, *The Supreme Court 1993 Term —Foreword: The Law as Equilibrium*, 108 HARV. L. REV. 26, 71 (1994).

[31] Sara Sun Beale, *What's Law Got To Do With It? The Political, Social Psychological and Other Non-Legal Factors Influencing the Development of (Federal) Criminal Law*, 1 BUFF. CRIM. L. REV. 23, 30 (1997), citing Fox Butterfield, *"Three Strikes" Rarely Invoked in Courtrooms*, N.Y. TIMES, Sept. 10, 1996, at A1.

[32] NANCY E. MARION, A HISTORY OF FEDERAL CRIME CONTROL INITIATIVES 244 (1994).

localized matters earlier left to the states. A complex layer is being added to the overall criminal justice scheme, dramatically superimposing federal crimes on essentially localized conduct already criminalized by the states.

As a result of these conclusions, the Task Force sought to determine whether the trend could somehow be justified as having a demonstrable, significant impact on public safety, the argued basis for much of the federalization. We conclude that persuasive evidence is lacking.

The Limited Impact of Federal Criminal Law on Local Crime

The important point that emerges from a review of the effects of the recent legislation is this: *Increased federalization is rarely, if ever, likely to have any appreciable effect on the categories of violent crime that most concern Americans, because in practice federal law enforcement can only reach a small percent of such activity.*

Due to limited resources — investigative personnel, federal prosecutors, and court facilities — federal criminal law can realistically respond to only a relatively small number of local crimes at any given time. The actual use and particular application of the expansive body of federal law is necessarily constrained by resources. The selection of which crimes to investigate and prosecute therefore requires a decision-making process which reflects highly selective prioritizing by investigative agencies and federal prosecutors.[33]

The present relatively infrequent federal prosecution of local conduct is likely to remain the norm absent a massive (and unlikely) infusion of federal money into the federal criminal justice system. "It is," police executives have noted, "unrealistic to expect that federal authorities will have the resources and inclination to investigate and

[33] It is difficult to measure the impact of federalization on actual investigations, except by identifying the growing number of federal law enforcement personnel. Many investigations are never disclosed and most are not statistically recorded in any way that leads to meaningful study. Many investigations (undertaken at potentially substantial cost to both the federal government and the individual investigated) do not result in criminal charges.

prosecute traditionally state and local offenses."[34] In a related vein, state judges have expressed the view that indiscriminate federalization of crimes

> creates an illusion by enacting new criminal law without providing the resources required for the federal government to enforce that law; and . . . disrupts funding of state criminal processes by favoring police and corrections with federal funds while disregarding the need this creates for commensurate resources for courts, prosecutors and defense attorneys . . . .[35]

Before reaching these conclusions about the limited value of federalization, the Task Force studied the actual prosecutions of federal crimes.

The Frequency of Prosecution of Selected Federalized Crimes

To assess the extent to which federalization of criminal law has the potential to impact crime in general and local crime in particular, the Task Force first examined available data to assess the comparative frequency of federal and state prosecutions. The key point is that federal prosecutions comprise less than 5% of all the prosecutions in the nation. The other 95% are state and local prosecutions.[36]

---

[34] *Position on Federalism*, Police Executive Research Forum (transmitted to the Task Force, December 1997).

[35] *Id.* (opposing provisions of the federal Violent Crime Control and Law Enforcement Act of 1994 which would federalize traditional areas of ordinary street crime traditionally prosecuted only in state courts). *See also* Resolution XVI, Conference of Chief Justices, August 3, 1995 (opposing federal enactment of laws dealing with homicides and other violent state felonies if firearms are involved); Resolution IV, Conference of Chief Justices, July 17, 1983 (opposing federal enactment of laws authorizing federal prosecution of persons who had two prior state convictions for armed robbery or burglary felonies).

[36] In 1994, there were a reported 872,218 state felony convictions, compared to 39,624 federal felony convictions (accounting for 4% of all felony convictions). Bureau of Justice Statistics, *Felony Sentences in the United States, 1994*, Bulletin NCJ-1651-49 (Washington, D.C., DOJ, July 1997), p.2.

We then did a statistical analysis of the frequency of the use of some selected federal criminal statutes, primarily street crimes, plus a few other traditionally local offenses for comparative purposes.[37] This analysis, coupled with the relative low number of federal prosecutions in general, produced some interesting and useful insights. Even the most frequently prosecuted federal offense, domestic drug trafficking, which constituted 28% of all federal filings in fiscal year 1997, accounts only for less than an estimated 2% of all prosecutions (federal and state) in the nation. Drug cases of all types now occupy one-third of the federal court caseload, yet the overall percentage of federal prosecutions of all drug arrests is still very small: Of the million-plus drug arrests in the country, approximately 1.5% were federally prosecuted in FY97.[38]

Perhaps of greater significance, several recently enacted federal statutes, championed by many because they would have a claimed impact on crime, have hardly been used at all. Two of the most publicized recent violent federalizations, drive-by shooting and interstate domestic violence, were not cited in a single prosecution in fiscal year 1997. Both federal statutes have been in effect since 1994. As the accompanying table and charts show, many other recently enacted federal criminal statutes have been used rarely or not at all.

---

[37] A full description of the process for selecting these statutes and data sources appears in APPENDIX B, SECTION 2.

[38] The U.S. Department of Justice reported a total of 1,506,200 arrests for drug abuse violations in 1996. See SOURCEBOOK OF CRIMINAL JUSTICE STATISTICS ON LINE, albany.edu/sourcebook/1995/tost_4.html, Table D.1. The federal courts, however, handled only 22,276 drug crimes. Administrative Office of U.S. Courts, *Judicial Business of the United States Courts, Report of the Director, 1997*, Table D-4, p. 214. These figures would indicate that less than 2% (approximately 1.5%) of the number of 1996 arrests are handled in federal court.

See also Franklin E. Zimring & Gordon Hawkins, *Toward a Principled Basis for Federal Criminal Legislation*, 543 ANNALS AM. ACAD. POL. & SOC. SCI. 15, 18-19 (1996) (discussing the large percentage that drug cases represent in federal prosecutions, even among robbery, weapons and other street crimes).

FY 1997 FEDERAL FILINGS/SENTENCINGS

Activity	#Filings	#Sentencings
All Federal Criminal Statutes	59,242	47,677
Selected Street or Domestic Violence Crime Statutes		
Domestic Drug Trafficking	16,629	16,082
Use or carrying of firearm during a crime of violence or drug trafficking crime	1,830	1,305
Simple Possession of Drugs	1,104	686
Carjacking	164	117
Transfer of a firearm across state lines	58	8
Drive-by shootings	0	1
Interstate domestic violence	0	5
Endangering lives by the manufacture of drugs	4	1
Failure to report child abuse	0	0
Murder by escaped prisoners	0	0
Selected Non-violent Local Crime Statutes		
Obstruction of state or local law enforcement	2	5
Animal Enterprise Terrorism	3	1
Theft of Livestock	1	0
Odometer Tampering	0	0

Chart 3. Task Force on Federalization of Criminal Law (ABA)

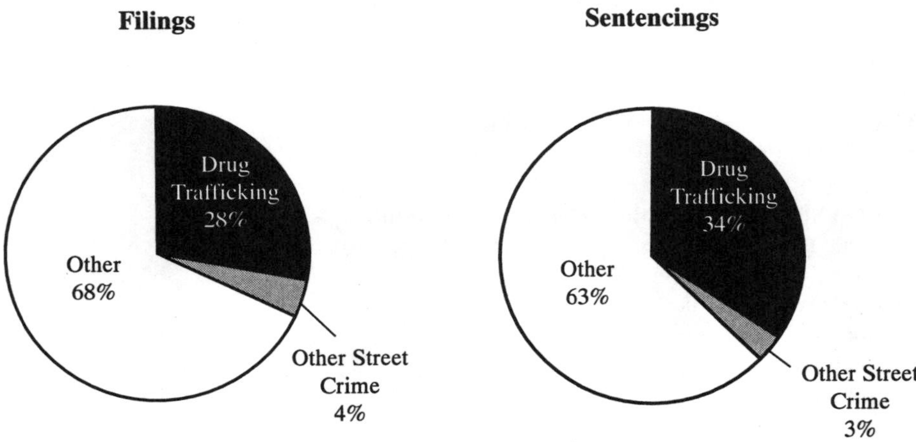

Charts 4 & 5. TF on Federalization of Criminal Law (ABA)

This rare use of many federalization statutes calls into question the belief that federalization can have a meaningful impact on street safety and local crime. But the presence of these federalized crimes on the books does present a possible opportunity for both selective prosecution with its inherent disparity and for shifting prosecutorial priorities that, without open political debate, can alter the traditionally limited federal presence in local matters.

A comparison of the type of cases handled from 1947 through 1997 reflects changing priorities of the crimes selected for federal prosecution. Federal theft and forgery cases have declined; federal fraud cases have increased. The largest increase has been in the number of federal drug cases (some of which are essentially local in nature). Federal dispositions for crimes of violence has remained fairly constant for at least the last 30 years. The following chart shows the changing federal criminal caseload.

Change in the Federal Criminal Caseload Over 50 Year Period

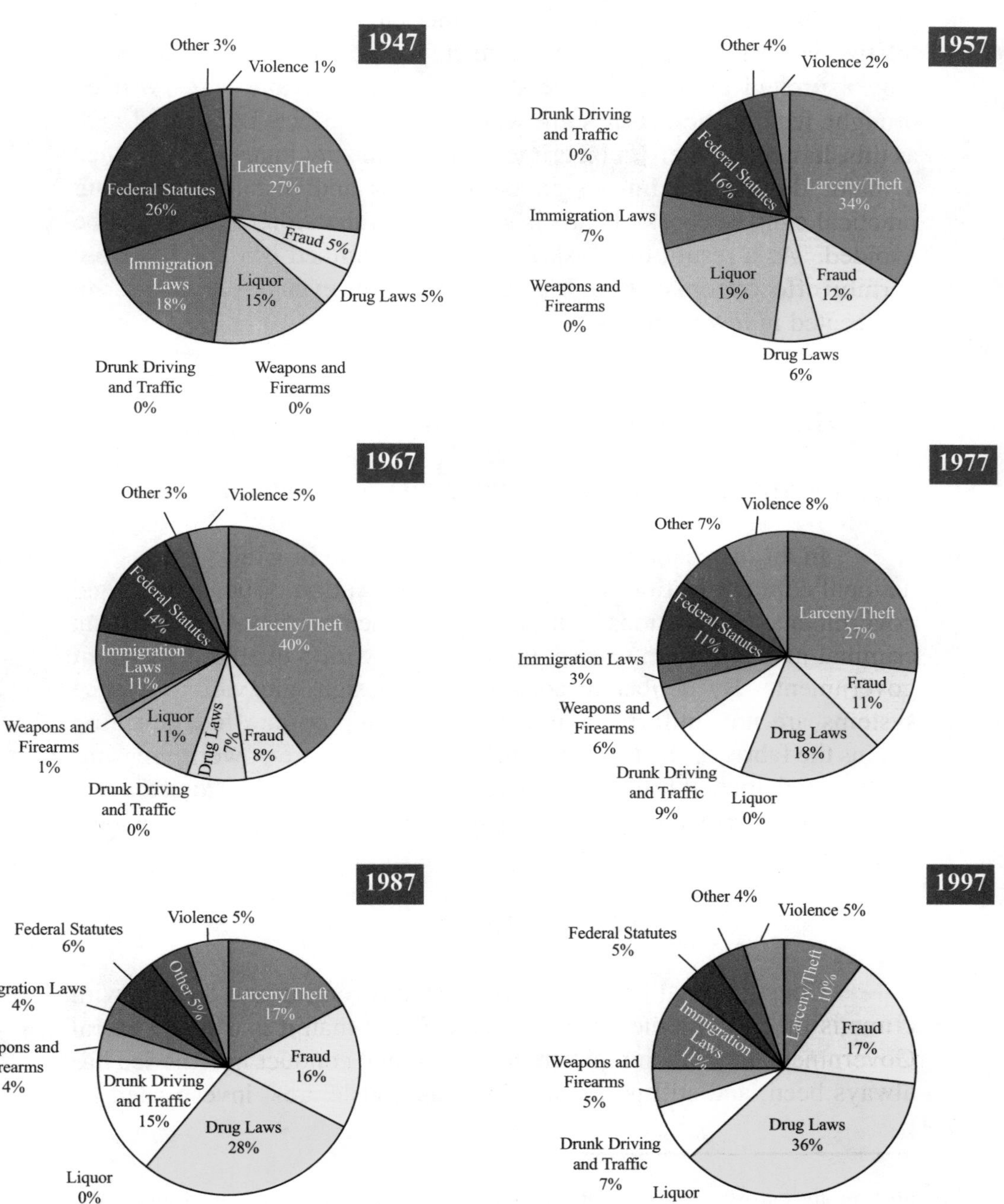

Chart 6.[39] **TF on Federalization of Criminal LAW (ABA)**

[39] The graphs in this chart are based on the *Annual Reports of the Director of the Administrative Office of the U.S. Courts*, Table D-4, for the years 1947, 1957, 1967, 1977, 1987, 1997. (See APPENDIX B, SECTION 3, for additional source information and for the tables on which these graphs are based.) The "Federal Statutes" category is a category used by the Administrative Office of the United States Courts in its reports to group criminal statutes that have no direct state or local counterpart. The category addresses crimes such as agriculture, antitrust, civil rights, food and drug, migratory

Considering the Significance of Low Prosecution Rates. At first glance, the point that federalized crimes are actually prosecuted in relatively low numbers may appear to cut in two different directions: If only a limited number of federal local or street crime cases will be brought, federalization is in some ways limited in effect. But a trend such as this, having little effect on crime control, can simultaneously produce a major detrimental impact on basic values and result in troubling practical consequences. If this is so, the federalization trend should be avoided. As a result, the Task Force next examined whether there are harmful effects from inappropriate federalization, even if such crimes are prosecuted in low numbers.

III. THE DUAL AMERICAN CRIMINAL JUSTICE SYSTEM & THE ADVERSE COSTS OF INAPPROPRIATE FEDERALIZATION

In an increasingly mobile America — one in which the ease of national communications can blur public perception of boundaries and governmental distinctions — it is vital to remember that the American criminal justice system was set up to operate within distinct spheres of government. By deliberate constitutional design, the various justice systems are not uniform or monolithic. Inappropriate federalization strains the fabric of the federal-state system. There are powerful reasons for the fundamental limitations on federal criminal law, reasons that are rooted in the constitutional makeup of the nation and in practical experience.

The Constitutional Framework

Constitutional law recognizes that "preventing and dealing with crime is much more the business of the States than it is of the Federal Government . . . ."[40] In practice, most criminal conduct in America has always been, and still is, defined by state legislatures, investigated by

---

bird, motor carriers, national defense, postal law, and others such as criminal acts committed by or against federal employees.

[40] Patterson v. New York, 432 U.S. 197, 201 (1977).

state agents, prosecuted by state prosecutors, tried in state courts, and punished in state prisons. This accords with the historical American principle that the general police power lies with the states and not with the federal government, although there clearly is an appropriate sphere for federal criminal legislation.

The concept that the general police power resides with the states is a basic consequence of the deliberate constitutional design setting up a dual federal/state system but assigning only limited powers to the federal government, a limitation that applies to federal criminal legislation. As the Supreme Court recently reminded, the Constitution withholds "from Congress a plenary police power that would authorize enactment of every type of legislation. See Art. I, § 8."[41] The Constitution sets up a dual sovereignty system and, the Court has underscored, confers upon Congress "not all governmental powers, but only discrete, enumerated ones,"[42] leaving to the states "all those other subjects which can be separately provided for . . . . "[43] As the Supreme Court observed, the great innovation envisioned in the dual system

> was that "our citizens would have two political capacities, one state and one federal, each protected from incursion by the other" — "a legal system unprecedented in form and design, establishing two orders of government, each with its own direct relationship, its own privity, its own set of mutual rights and obligations to the people who sustain it and are governed by it."[44]

---

[41] United States v. Lopez, 514 U.S. 549, 566 (1995).

[42] Printz v. United States, 521 U. S. ___, ___, 117 S. Ct. 2365, 2376 (1997).

[43] "[I]t is to be remembered," James Madison assured his fellow citizens, "that the general government is not to be charged with the whole power of making and administering laws. Its jurisdiction is limited to certain enumerated objects, which concern all the members of the republic, but which are not to be attained by the separate provisions of any. The subordinate governments, which can extend their care to all those other subjects which can be separately provided for, will retain their due authority and activity." THE FEDERALIST No. 14, at 102 (James Madison) (Clinton Rossiter ed., 1961).

[44] Printz v. United States, 521 U. S. ___, ___, 117 S. Ct. 2365, 2377 (1997), quoting U.S. Term Limits, Inc. v. Thornton, 514 U.S. 799, 838 (1995) (Kennedy, J., concurring).

Inappropriate federalization can undermine the strength of the states, which are an independent, intrinsic component of the American governmental system. The dual system envisioned by the Constitution produces a complex and delicate set of attributes in American criminal law, and a disruption of the delicate balance creates significant dangers. A constitutional strain is not only significant in theory; there are also important, practical, adverse consequences to inappropriate federalization. Federalization, one writer has noted, is not "cost-free" even if it appears to be.[45]

Adverse Consequences in Practice

Impact on the States and Their Courts. Inappropriate federalization undermines the critical role of the states and their courts, which are constitutionally given the primary role of dealing with crime and which, after all, carry the overwhelming criminal case workload. This can lead to a notable diminution of the stature of the state courts in the perception of citizens. There is a discernable perception that federal law enforcement often gravitates toward prosecuting only highly visible incidents of local crime, leaving the vast percentage of less glamorous prosecutions to the states. The unfortunate premise — sometimes express, sometimes implicit — is that the states are not capable of adequately handling important matters, a premise belied by the everyday disposition of tens of thousands of cases in the state systems. The premise also flies in the face of the fact that, federalization notwithstanding, the vast majority of criminal prosecutions will continue to be tried in state courts. Although federalization relieves the state courts of hearing some cases, the reduction is actually small, as discussed elsewhere in this Report.

Concentration of Policing Power. The Constitution's separation of American government into federal and state spheres, the Supreme Court has observed, is considered:

> one of the Constitution's structural protections of liberty. "Just as the separation and independence of the coordinate branches of the

[45] *See* John B. Oakley, *The Myth of Cost-Free Jurisdictional Reallocation*, 543 ANNALS AM. ACAD. POL. & SOC. SCI. 52 (1996).

> Federal Government serve to prevent the accumulation of excessive power in any one branch, a healthy balance of power between the States and the Federal Government will reduce the risk of tyranny and abuse from either front."[[46]] To quote Madison . . . : "a double security arises to the rights of the people. The different governments will control each other, at the same time that each will be controlled by itself."[47]

Historically, centralization of criminal law enforcement power in the federal government has been perceived as creating potentially dangerous consequences and has therefore been avoided. There has always been an innate American distrust for the concentration of broad police power in a national police force, and citizens have long resisted the evolution of such a broadly powerful national police force, as distinguished from specialized national police agencies. (One indication of this concern is the general prohibition against using the military to execute the laws.[48]) Enactment of each new federal crime bestows new federal investigative power on federal agencies, broadening their power to intrude into individual lives. Expansion of federal jurisdiction also creates the opportunity for greater collection and maintenance of data at the federal level in an era when various databases are computerized and linked. Increased and centralized federal power to investigate is, in effect, subject to limited oversight beyond that imposed by the federal Executive Branch itself. Expanding, unreviewed federal power, when no strong case can be made for its existence, is contrary to the American wisdom against concentrating policing power in any one governmental entity.

Disparate Results for the Same Conduct. A long-recognized feature of our dual governmental system is that criminalized behavior

---

[46] Printz v. United States, 521 U.S. ___, ___, 117 S. Ct. 2365, 2378 (1997), quoting Gregory v. Ashcroft, 501 U.S. 452, 458 (1991).

[47] *Id.*, quoting THE FEDERALIST No. 51, at 323 (James Madison) (Clinton Rossiter ed., 1961).

[48] 18 U.S.C. § 1385 (1994) (prohibiting use of Army or Air Force to act as a posse comitatus or to otherwise execute the law without express constitutional or Congressional authorization).

may violate the law of more than one sovereign. The result is that any one of these jurisdictions may choose to prosecute conduct, or that several jurisdictions might possibly punish for essentially the same conduct. For example, a crime might be committed in such a way that the law of two different states might be violated. More to the point here, behavior might violate both the law of a state and the federal government, leading to concurrent jurisdiction to prosecute the conduct in several forums. Many bank robberies, for example, will constitute both the state crime of robbery and the robbery of a federally insured bank; theft of a motor vehicle will usually violate both state theft-based law and federal interstate transportation of stolen vehicle law. Because the conduct offends two different sovereigns — the individual state and the federal government — the Supreme Court has consistently held that, although the offenses involve the same conduct, they are not the "same offense" for constitutional purposes, with the result that the federal Double Jeopardy Clause does not prohibit either two separate prosecutions or two separate punishments.[49] Some state laws, or occasionally a federal statute, will offer protection from some double prosecution or punishment in such situations,[50] but these restrictions are neither universal nor all-encompassing. In practice, the amount of double prosecution/punishment is likely small, and so, rather than double punishment, the more salient feature of overlapping dual prosecution is that it affords the opportunity for selective prosecution of the same conduct in different ways.

---

[49] The U.S. Department of Justice has devised an internal policy setting out for federal prosecutors the limited circumstances in which a dual federal prosecution should be brought following a state prosecution. The dual federal-state "*Petite* Policy" (found in the DOJ's U.S. ATTORNEYS' MANUAL) deals with federal prosecutions subsequent to a state prosecution; the reverse situation is generally within the discretionary decision-making power of state officials. The DOJ policy is discussed in Harry Litman and Mark Greenberg, *Dual Prosecutions: A Model for Concurrent Federal Jurisdiction*, 543 ANNALS AM. ACAD. POL. & SOC. SCI. 72 (1996), which also notes relevant Supreme Court cases on the double jeopardy issue.

[50] *See, e.g.*, the authorities discussing such state laws, collected in NORMAN ABRAMS & SARA SUN BEALE, FEDERAL CRIMINAL LAW AND ITS ENFORCEMENT 743 (1993); George C. Thomas III, *A Blameworthy Act Approach to Double Jeopardy Same Offense Problems*, 83 CAL. L. REV. 1027, 1057 (1995); 18 U.S.C. § 2117 (1994) (dealing with breaking or entering carrier facilities, and providing that a "judgment of conviction or acquittal on the merits under the laws of any State shall be a bar to any prosecution under this section for the same act or acts").

A citizen prosecuted for a state crime is subject to a set of consequences appreciably different than one prosecuted for a federal crime. For a particular defendant, these consequences are sometimes better, sometimes worse, but they are nevertheless disparate. Although every defendant will receive a minimum set of federal constitutional protections, additional procedures and rules of evidence will differ significantly between state and federal systems. For example, the agency which investigates the conduct will usually vary, involving either state, local, or county police on the one hand, or a federal investigating agency on the other. The selection, supervision, confining power, practices, and accountability of these officials will differ between state and federal. Prosecutors who decide which crimes and which persons to prosecute — prosecutors differently selected, differently accountable, and differently restrained by state or federal law and internal policies — will also vary. The proximity of the trial court to defendants' and witnesses' homes, the nature of court procedures and evidentiary rules, and the availability of state protections beyond the minimum offered by the federal Constitution will also differ. Which judge tries the case and which appellate judges review the trial proceedings will likewise be different, with judges selected by different methods.

Of particular importance is the fact that sentencing options (including the length of sentence, as well as the location and nature of confinement) will often be greatly disparate in the different systems, as will be the opportunity for parole and the conditions of probation. A graphic picture of the varying sentence consequences is depicted by a comparison of the different state and federal penalties for offense categories.

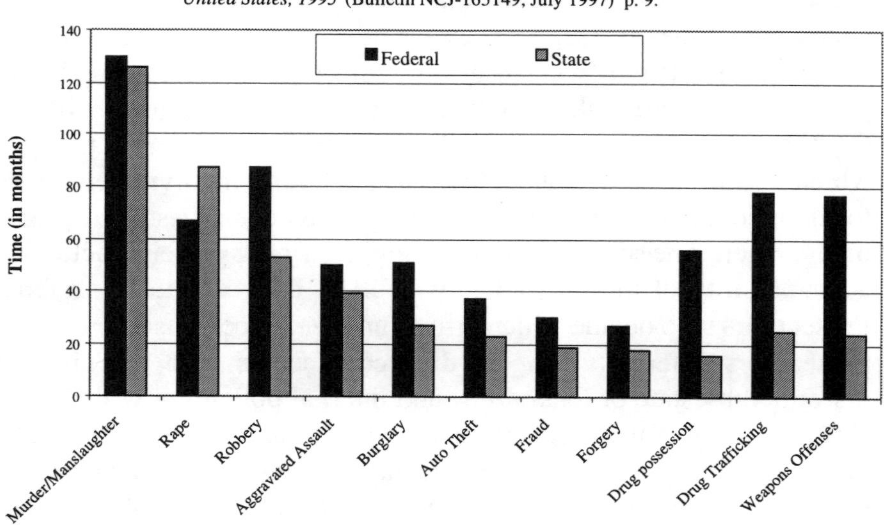

Chart 7.[51] TF on Federalization of Criminal Law (ABA)

A certain amount of disparity is inherent in any system that relies on human decision makers. Police, prosecutors, judges, juries, and defense counsel can all have a substantially disparate impact on the outcomes of individual cases. Whenever possible, however, we should seek to avoid introducing new sources of disparity without carefully considering the benefits and costs. In the case of federalization of the criminal law, this principle has too often been ignored.

Diminution of a Principled Basis for Selecting a Case as a Federal or Local Crime With Its Different Consequences. As a consequence of federalization, essentially local conduct — for example, a street corner assault — may be prosecutable differently without any

---

[51] Many of the generic crime categories in this chart may cover a wide range of behaviors deserving of different sentences. However, others (e.g., drug possession) are more circumscribed as to the type of offenses they include.

persuasive reason why it should trigger one set of consequences rather than another for essentially similar conduct. The federal legislative decision that makes possible these varying results is often premised on the idea that some particular object involved usually travels in interstate commerce in the manufacturing and distribution process. If, for example, the assault involves a simple knife, it will typically be a state crime only, but if a gun is used instead, in some circumstances the incident may be treatable as a federal crime because of modern federal law.[52] Similarly, a street corner robbery will often be only a state crime, but if a car is the object of the robbery, the crime might be both state robbery and federal carjacking.[53] Likewise, drug activity comprises a large category of activity that now violates both state and federal law.

In most such cases, state interest in pursuing the offending conduct is not lacking.

The power to criminally prosecute and punish citizens' behavior is one of the most important and awesome powers of government. As one leading voice of American criminal law put it, penal law is not only "the law on which people place their ultimate reliance for protection against all the deepest injuries that human conduct can inflict on individuals and institutions" but, "by the same token, penal law governs the strongest force that we permit official agencies to bring to bear on individuals."[54] A dual system that affords the opportunity to prosecute essentially the same conduct as a federal crime rather than a state crime, with starkly differing consequences, should be as rational and principled as possible, and cogent reasons should justify federal criminalization. Such reasons have been absent in many instances of recent federalization of local crime.

In practice, the different consequences inherent in the choice between overlapping local federal or state crimes are triggered by a prosecutorial decision, not necessarily by the essential nature of the

---

[52] *See* 18 U.S.C.A. App. § 1202 (West Supp.).

[53] *See* 18 U.S.C.A. § 2119 (West Supp.).

[54] Herbert Wechsler, *The Challenge of a Model Penal Code*, 65 HARV. L. REV. 1097, 1098 (1952).

conduct. Federal prosecutors sometimes institute federal charges involving the same conduct which is already the object of similar state charges, and state charges may then be dropped.[55] In any event, greater overlap between federal and state criminal statutes creates greater potential for increased federal police powers, varying prosecutorial standards and decisions, divergent trial options, and significantly different sentences for essentially the same conduct. Some disparity between consequences inevitably results from the dual system and may be tolerated if carefully considered, principled, and limited in amount; an expansive amount of unprincipled overlap in which very large amounts of conduct are susceptible to selection for prosecution as either federal or state crime is intolerable.

Increased Power at the Federal Prosecutorial Level. Congress's decision to make conduct a federal crime confers on federal prosecutors the authority to decide whether to prosecute particular conduct, moving more power to the federal level. All prosecutors exercise critical discretion in choosing what crimes and which people to prosecute, a discretion largely beyond judicial control. Broadening prosecutorial jurisdiction authorizes more decision-making on the part of federal prosecutors.

From jurisdiction to jurisdiction, the manner in which prosecutors are chosen varies. Some state prosecutors are appointed by governors but, more typically, state citizens have a direct say in the selection of prosecutors by electing local (usually county-wide) prosecutors who are subject to electoral monitoring and the limits set by state legislators, as well as (when appropriate) by the state courts. In contrast, federal prosecutors are part of the Department of Justice, generally under the ultimate direction of the Attorney General who is appointed by the President, with Senate confirmation. While some federal prosecutions are directly brought by attorneys based at the main Department of Justice office in Washington, D.C., the vast majority of federal prosecutions are brought by U.S. Attorneys, who are Presidentially appointed to cover

---

[55] *See, e.g.*, United States v. Lopez, 514 U.S. 549, 551 (1995) (dealing with the constitutionality of the federal Gun-Free School Zones Act under the affecting commerce power) (state prosecution dropped after federal charges filed).

specific regions of the country. Ninety-four in number, the various U.S. Attorneys operate under the ultimate direction of the Department of Justice and its policies, but there is considerable discretion granted to each of these U.S. Attorneys (and their 8,000 or so Assistants) about which federal crimes will be prosecuted, under what circumstances each federal statute will be used, and which defendants will be targeted. Some federal prosecution practices will vary among U.S. Attorneys' offices.[56]

Given the parallel systems of state and federal prosecution that can cover essentially the same conduct, new federal crimes dealing with local conduct place additional (and essentially unreviewable) power in the hands of federal prosecutors, prompting questions about diverse treatment, sentences, and other issues related to the basis for selecting one defendant for federal prosecution while others are prosecuted by the state. In the absence of a distinct federal interest, the decision to prosecute can lack a guiding federal principle. A federal prosecutor is under no legal requirement to state why any particular defendant has been selected to be prosecuted in the federal system and receive a significant federal sentence, and why the many other similar defendants are left to state prosecution. Restraint is essentially left to self-imposed prosecutorial discretion.

In practice, the federal prosecution option is employed in different ways. In some instances, federal and state law enforcement authorities can work cooperatively to attack local crime problems through a coordinated effort that involves both federal and state prosecutions. This permits law enforcement to make use of the particular tools available in federal investigations and prosecutions, including immunity, nationwide subpoena power and increased sentences, while at the same time bypassing rights conferred by local law, such as rights to separate trials for multiple defendants, to transcripts of prior trials and discovery, to evidentiary limitations, to different sentences, and to possible parole

---

[56] *See, e.g.*, NORMAN ABRAMS & SARA SUN BEALE, FEDERAL CRIMINAL LAW AND ITS ENFORCEMENT 91-105 (1993) (collecting some of the pertinent prosecutorial policy statements and describing some of the prosecutorial coordinating devices).

rights.[57] Similarly, in plea negotiations, local prosecutors can use possible federal prosecution, with its likely harsher punishments, as a threat.[58]

These practices may be viewed as helpful to public safety (by enabling the conviction and incarceration of dangerous individuals), or as raising troubling possibilities, including the possibility of disparate treatment. Some have argued that a wide body of overlapping federal law does not create a problem as long as there is wisely exercised prosecutorial discretion in deciding to invoke federal law against some defendants.[59] Indeed, one significant feature of a broadening body of

---

[57] See the testimony of a state county prosecutor regarding the proposed "Hate Crimes Prevention Act." 1998 Westlaw 12762066 (July 8, 1998 testimony before Senate Judiciary Committee regarding S. 1529, 105 Cong., 1st Sess.) and describing such a federal prosecution as having the effect of avoiding such local rights. The prosecutor also noted that avoidance of multiple trials prevented the witnesses from having to testify in several trials. *See also* N.Y. TIMES, Oct. 8, 1998, at B4 (attributing federal prosecution of two young defendants for an interstate kidnapping and subsequent homicide to federal prosecutor's decision based, in part, on fact that state law would have permitted sentencing considerations such as defendants' ages and education that could have reduced sentence, compared to the more severe federal sentence).

[58] *See* Testimony of William J. Stunts, July 8, 1998, before Senate Judiciary Committee regarding S. 1529, 105 Cong., 1st Sess., the proposed "Hate Crimes Prevention Act." 1998 Westlaw 12762070. Professor Stunts notes that this potential is particularly common in drug cases. A frequently cited example of an executed threat of this nature is recounted in Dennis E. Curtis, *The Effect of Federalization on the Defense Function*, 543 ANNALS AM. ACAD. POL. & SOC. SCI. 85 (1996). A state drug defendant was offered a guilty plea which would have led to a 4-8 year sentence. When the defendant declined and wanted a trial, a federal drug prosecution was brought, leading to a mandatory life sentence. *Id.* at 96, citing Jim Smith, *Petty Pusher Goes Out Big Time*, PHILADELPHIA DAILY NEWS, July 17, 1992.

[59] For discussions of the exercise of prosecutorial discretion in the context of the federalization problem, *see, e.g.*, G. Robert Blakey, *Federal Criminal Law: The Need, Not for Revised Constitutional Theory or New Congressional Statutes, but the Exercise of Responsible Prosecutive Discretion*, 46 HASTINGS L.J. 1175 (1995); Jamie S. Gorelick & Harry Litman, *Prosecutorial Discretion and the Federalization Debate*, 46 HASTINGS L.J. 967 (1995); Harry Litman & Mark D. Greenberg, *Federal Power and Federalism: A Theory of Commerce-Clause Based Regulation of Traditionally State Crimes*, 47 CASE W. RES. L. REV. 921 (1997); Litman & Greenberg, *Dual*

federal law is that it allows federal prosecutors (as well as investigative agencies) to pick from a wider set of target activity and defendants, choosing to concentrate from time to time on particular conduct and subjecting to federal investigation and prosecution those thought to be most dangerous. On the other hand, others note that this approach has obvious potential for disparate results in a system in which prosecutorial discretion is basically unreviewable, especially in the current absence of articulated standards for the selection of crimes and defendants from among a very long (and lengthening) list of candidates.

Whatever the law enforcement merits of such an approach, the members of the Task Force agree that it presents serious concerns for a federal system in which state and local law enforcement is intended to be the first line of protection for public safety.

Adverse Impact on the Federal Judicial System. Inappropriate federalization also has an adverse effect on federal courts. The disparity between the increase in the number of federal judges, when compared to the far greater increase in federal criminal justice personnel, indicates some of the impact that increased federal legislation can have in numerical terms: Federal justice personnel almost doubled between 1982 and 1993, but the number of authorized federal judgeships in the district courts increased by only 26%.[60] More importantly, an increase in the volume of federal criminal cases, driven primarily by additional cases that could as well be tried in state courts, diminishes the separate and distinctive role played by federal courts.

This is an era of increasingly complex (and correspondingly more lengthy) federal cases, many involving already traditional federal criminal law prosecutions and many entailing increasingly complicated federal civil suits. All of these cases compete for scarce court attention. Thrusting additional crimes into federal court places demands on an

---

Prosecutions: A Model for Concurrent Federal Jurisdiction, 543 ANNALS AM. ACAD. POL. & SOC. SCI. 72 (1996).

[60] See Chart 11, APPENDIX B, SECTION 1. The resource difference is more acute when the overall growth in personnel is compared to the number of sitting judges, which, because of unfilled vacancies, increased by only 14% over the same time period.

already strained federal court system and threatens the quality of essential federal justice. Additional federal crimes mean not only federal trials, but also additional ancillary proceedings, sentencings, post-sentence matters, and appeals. As a result, there is a danger that scarce court resources will have to be shared with those needed to adjudicate offenses for which there is little, if any, need for a federal forum, instead of being devoted primarily to offenses with a clear need for adjudication in a federal court.

For a number of reasons (including laws requiring the prompt disposition of criminal indictments), federal criminal cases generally are given priority over civil cases (whether between an individual and the government, or between individuals).[61] Civil litigants therefore suffer because of the priority that must be given to any increase in federal prosecutions. The Judicial Conference of the United States, representing the views of federal judges, notes that the federalization trend "will negatively impact on the ability of the federal courts to hear federal criminal prosecutions, as well as carry out vital civil responsibilities in a timely manner."[62] And, emphasizing the traditional balance that has previously existed between state and federal jurisdiction, the Chief Justice of the United States has more than once expressed concern about some federal legislative responses to the growing crime apprehension that lead to unwise expansion of the federal courts' role in the administration of criminal justice.[63]

A significant increase in federal court caseloads, driven in part by increasing numbers of criminal cases, poses a serious threat to the proper

---

[61] *See* Sara Sun Beale, *Federalizing Crime: Assessing the Impact on the Federal Courts*, 543 ANNALS AM. ACAD POL. & SOC. SCI. 39, 50 (1996).

[62] *September 1992 Report of the Proceedings of the Judicial Conference of the United States*, p. 57; *see also March 1993 Report of the Proceedings of the Judicial Conference of the United States*, p.13; *September 1990 Report of the Proceedings of the Judicial Conference of the United States*, pp. 70, 72; LONG RANGE PLAN FOR THE FEDERAL COURTS (1995).

[63] *See, e.g.*, 1997 YEAR-END REPORT ON THE FEDERAL JUDICIARY; 1993 YEAR-END REPORT ON THE FEDERAL JUDICIARY; William H. Rehnquist, *Address to the American Law Institute*, REMARKS AND ADDRESSES AT THE 75TH ANNUAL ALI MEETING, MAY 1998, at 15-19 (1998), excerpted in *Chief Justice Raises Concerns on Federalism*, 30 THE THIRD BRANCH, June 1998, at 1.

functioning of the federal courts.[64] On the one hand, rising caseloads lead to a disquieting choice of either greatly increasing the number of judgeships, with adverse short and long term consequences at both the trial and appeal level, or maintaining the current size of the federal judiciary and accepting unsatisfactory shortcuts in the disposition of cases. Adding a significant number of judges, especially in the courts of appeals, threatens the coherence of circuit law, risks reduction in the quality of appointments as the degree of individual scrutiny given to the selection and confirmation of large numbers of candidates declines, and impairs the close working relationships essential to the deliberations within multi-judge courts. On the other hand, processing increased caseload volume without significant increases in judgeships risks unacceptable short-cuts, such as the severe restriction or virtual elimination of oral arguments, a marked increase in the percentage of appeals disposed of without a published opinion, and greater reliance on expanded central staffs. A likely consequence of permitting essentially state and local offenses to swell federal court caseloads will be some combination of both sets of adverse consequences — the number of federal judgeships will grow to an unacceptable size and the federal courts will function far less efficiently and far less effectively.

It would be a tragic irony if ill-considered placement of state offenses in federal courts led to such an erosion of the quality of federal criminal justice that the historic reasons for having a distinct system of federal courts no longer justified their existence. The federal courts should play the distinctive and complementary role envisioned for them in the Constitution's federal scheme, and not simply duplicate the functions of the state courts.

---

[64] *See, e.g., September 1992 Report of the Proceedings of the Judicial Conference of the United States*; Jon O. Newman, *Restructuring Federal Jurisdiction: Proposals to Preserve the Federal Judicial System,* 56 U. CHI. L. REV. 761, 761-66 (1989). *See also* the Federal Bar Association views offered in considering stress on the federal courts: "[C]rimes that adequately are addressed in state courts do not belong in federal courts." *Comments of the Federal Bar Association on the Tentative Draft Report of the Commission on Structural Alternatives for the Federal Courts of Appeals, October 1998,* at 4 (Nov. 5, 1998) (urging Congress's attention to the substantial impact on federal court caseloads caused by Congressional actions in regard to the federalization of state crimes).

Nearly all of those who have examined the impact of federalization have concluded that the federal courts are being overburdened with cases traditionally handled in state courts. However, a few scholars have argued the contrary position: that the federal courts are now bearing less than their proportionate share of criminal jurisdiction, and accordingly that federal prosecutions for traditional state crimes can be increased.[65] This view is based on a marshaling of statistical evidence measuring (among other factors) the percentage of all prisoners held in federal and state prisons, federal criminal filings as compared to total population, and filings per judge in the federal and the state systems. Assuming that this data is correct, it fails to take account of the true toll the current criminal caseload is placing on the federal courts and the serious future consequences. For example, in 1997, while criminal cases constituted 16% of the *filings* in federal court, they took up a far greater share of court *time* (even excluding time to hear contested motions). Criminal cases accounted for 39% of the trials, and 62% of those trials lasting 20 days or more.[66] In recent years, more than half of the trial docket in many districts has been devoted to criminal cases.[67] Furthermore, comparisons with earlier statistics can be misleading,

---

[65] *See* Tom Stacy & Kim Dayton, *The Underfederalization of Crime*, 6 CORNELL J.L. & PUB. POL'Y 247 (1997).

Several pieces of the BIBLIOGRAPHY literature offer interesting insights concerning federal judge case load, in addition to the literature cited in this section of the Report. *See, e.g.*, Franklin E. Zimring & Gordon Hawkins, *Toward a Principled Basis for Federal Criminal Legislation*, 543 ANNALS AM. ACAD. POL. & SOC. SCI. 15 (1996); Rory K. Little, *Myths and Principles of Federalization*, 46 HASTINGS L.J. 1029 (1995).

[66] Administrative Office of the U. S. Courts, *Judicial Business of the United States Courts: 1997 Report of the Director*, Table T-2 (U.S. District Court — Length of Civil and Criminal Trials Resulting in a Verdict or Judgment by District, for the Twelve-Month Period ending September 30, 1997) (table excludes hearings on contested motions).

[67] By 1992, 38 of the 94 federal judicial districts devoted more than 50% of their trial time to criminal cases. Sara Sun Beale, *Reporter's Draft for the Working Group on Principles to Use When Considering the Federalization of Criminal Law*, 46 HASTINGS L.J. 1277, 1285 (1995) (citing Administrative Office of the U.S. Courts, *The Criminal Caseload: The Nature of Change* 1 (1994)). In 1994 it was estimated that criminal cases took up 48% of federal judges' time. *Id.* at 1285 (citing Statement of Kathleen Sullivan)).

because changes in both the kinds of federal prosecutions being brought and the applicable procedures require more judicial resources for each case. This is most apparent in the sentencing process, due to the adoption of the federal Sentencing Guidelines, but it is also true at the pretrial and trial stage, where motions practice in criminal cases has expanded significantly, requiring longer responses and more frequent (and longer) pre- and post-trial hearings. The present imbalance in the allocation of prosecutorial and judicial resources underscores the fact that the federal judiciary can not reasonably take on an ever-increasing number of cases. Between 1980 and 1994, for example, the number of federal prosecutors grew by 125%, while the number of federal judges in the district and appellate courts grew by the far lesser rate of 17%.[68]

Although the number of federal prosecutions has not increased in proportion to the growth in the population of the United States, the federal courts cannot and should not grow indefinitely. This is most apparent in the case of the Supreme Court which, due to its size and the nature of its decision-making process, cannot greatly increase the number of cases it decides on the merits. The same point is relatively true of all the federal courts. As noted earlier, it would be equally unwise to indefinitely expand the size of the federal judiciary in proportion to the size of the population, because it would fundamentally alter the character of the federal courts.[69] It would, of course, be possible simply to spread the same resources more thinly over an ever-increasing docket, as many states have been forced to do, laboring under crushing caseloads. There is, however, no rational justification for treating any overburdened court as the model for other courts.

Adverse Implications for the Federal Prison System. A significant portion of the expansion of the federal prison system can be attributed to increased sentence lengths for existing crimes, but the increased number

---

[68] Administrative Office of the U.S. Courts, *The Criminal Caseload: The Nature of Change* 1 (1994) (which also notes that the number of prosecutors per judicial officer had doubled in the previous ten years).

[69] These issues have been more fully addressed in the REPORT OF THE FEDERAL COURTS STUDY COMMITTEE 35-38 (1990) and in the LONG RANGE PLAN FOR THE FEDERAL COURTS (adopted by the Judicial Conference December 1995).

of federalized crimes may also have an impact on federal prisons. Even if the number of persons prosecuted under these federalizing statutes is relatively small (as discussed elsewhere in this Report), among its other costs, federalization still tends to increase the number of prisoners and to strain the capacity of the federal prison system. The point is not that persons who commit the crimes discussed in this Report ought to be free; it is whether they ought to be in federal prisons.

Adverse Implications for Local Law Enforcement Efforts. Members of the Task Force and others who have examined the subject have warned of another adverse result of federalization as lines of responsibility between state and federal agencies blur. Some caution that the increasing presence of the federal government in the criminal law field can often (though not always) lead to counterproductive competition and friction. Law enforcement in ferreting out crime is competitive, as Justice Jackson (a former Attorney General) once observed.[70] This competition may sometimes manifest itself between federal and state officials, notably in our nation's large metropolitan areas. Most state prosecutors are elected; all federal prosecutors are appointed. Many in each group have aspirations for higher office. The potential for competition to detect and prosecute crime increases in direct proportion to the number of overlapping federal statutes which criminalize conduct that has traditionally been prosecuted locally. The overlap can create "turf wars between local district attorneys and U.S. Attorneys, as each tries to claim jurisdiction over cases that catch the public eye. These turf wars do not add to the system's ability to fight crime; they simply waste time and energy."[71]

More widely, others caution that the blurring of responsibility for the same conduct can lead to an unhealthy, diminishing local presence, and may have the ironic and unfortunate effect of discouraging or

---

[70] Johnson v. United States, 333 U.S. 10, 14 (1948) (Jackson, J., writing for a majority of the Court).

[71] Professor William J. Stunts, testifying about the potential of the proposed "Hate Crimes Prevention Act," including its likely effect of federalizing all rape cases. 1998 Westlaw 12762070 (July 8, 1998 testimony before Senate Judiciary Committee regarding S. 1529, 105 Cong., 1st Sess.).

confusing local law enforcement efforts. In light of federal assumption of jurisdiction, some state entities may hesitate in pursuing the conduct in question. Such a hesitation or withdrawal by local law enforcement would undermine the primary role played by state law enforcement.

While federal support of local agencies can have a salutary effect, inappropriate federalization creating abundant concurrent jurisdiction can raise problems for law enforcement officials. The Police Executive Research Forum identifies the problems often associated with unwarranted federalization as including:

> uncertainty about investigative authority, omission of local expertise, additional burdens on the federal system with commensurate resources, promotion of disparate sentencing, and creation of expectations that will further disillusion victims and the electorate if federal laws cannot be enforced or are not applied. Federalization may also undermine efforts to better coordinate local, state, and federal enforcement efforts. Federalization also diverts federal authorities from what they do best and puts more distance between law enforcers and local community residents — in direct conflict with community policing objectives.[72]

Additional reasons argue for the principled allocation of roles to federal and state law enforcement. "One is that it is far more efficient for each jurisdiction to know for what it is responsible and for what it can held accountable. The second is that, with a principled division of responsibility, each set of agencies can build specialized capabilities, at least if the allocation of jurisdiction is functional rather than simply geographic."[73]

The Conference of Chief Justices (reflecting the views of the

---

[72] "*Position on Federalism*," Police Executive Research Forum (transmitted to the Task Force December 1997).

[73] Philip B. Heymann & Mark H. Moore, *The Federal Role in Dealing With Violent Street Crime: Principles, Questions, and Cautions*, 543 ANNALS AM. ACAD. POL. & SOC. SCI. 103, 108 (1996).

nation's state judges) has on several occasions decried much of the recent federalization as resulting in "the needless disruption of effective state and local enforcement efforts."[74] Similarly, the National Governors Association has expressed concern that "some attempts to expand federal criminal law into traditional state function would have little effect in eliminating crime, but could undermine state and local anticrime efforts."[75] Variations of this common view were echoed by other state officials corresponding with the Task Force. For example, state judicial officials see the indiscriminate federalization of crimes as "contravening principles of federalism and further flawed because it: (1) assumes without foundation that states have been unresponsive and ineffective in addressing crime; [and] (2) fails to enact plausible solutions for violence, drugs, weapons or gangs . . . ."[76]

Citizen Perception and Diffused Citizen Power. A lessening of citizens' perception about their power to have an impact on critical crime issues should be avoided. Confusion of state and federal authority can leave citizens uncertain about who bears the responsibility for dealing with crime, while at the same time dissipating accountability for one governmental authority or the other to seriously confront the problem.

---

[74] Resolution IX, Conference of Chief Justices, Feb. 10, 1994 (transmitted to the Task Force December 1997). In correspondence with the Task Force, the Conference president noted that the "federalization of criminal law is a mounting concern of the state judiciary . . . . Congress has for more than a decade shown a strong tendency to denigrate the state role in addressing crime and to inject federal agencies into the realm of state criminal law. Some of these initiatives have been ameliorated, but the threat to the fundamentals of American federalism is clear." Letter of Chief Justice Thomas Phillips, December 11, 1997.

[75] National Governors Association Policy HR-19, "Federalism and Criminal Justice" (revised 1996; transmitted to the Task Force January 1998). The Governors Association policy emphasizes that, "[t]raditionally, state and local governments are on the front lines of crime control. Virtually all planning of criminal justice activities, as well as the prosecution and incarceration of violent criminals, occurs at the state level." The policy perceives that the "federal government has served largely in a supporting role in this effort, providing research, data, analysis, material, and human resource assistance for state and local governments" and states that the "nation's Governors recognize and welcome the federal government's unique capabilities and resources in the fight against crime."

[76] *Id.*

On the whole, state law is easier to modify (and so more easily accommodates new local conditions) than is national legislation. Public accountability in the state and local segments of government is higher. As a result, the movement of the crime debate to the federal level may leave local citizens with the belief that they have less power to influence the debate about the response to crime and therefore less control over crime's immediate impact upon them.

Allocation of Resources. Inappropriate federalization scatters, rather than focuses, the resources needed to combat crime. In practice, efforts to combat crime compete for resources. The application of limited federal resources to one problem can deplete their use where they might be utilized better. Inappropriate use of federal investigators on local problems, for example, deprives federal authorities of time to address truly federal problems which only they investigate. Likewise, overburdening federal courts with essentially local cases lessens their ability to take up cases in which there is a distinctly federal stake, while at the same time undermining a vibrant system of state criminal justice. As federal judges have put it, "Congress should be encouraged to conserve the federal courts as a distinctive judicial forum of limited jurisdiction in our system of federalism. . . . [C]riminal jurisdiction should be assigned to the federal courts only to further clearly defined and justified national interests, leaving to the state courts the responsibility for adjudicating all other matters."[77]

All these adverse consequences strongly argue against inappropriate federalization of crime, particularly given the lack of actual gain it realistically can produce in combating crime.

IV. CONCLUSIONS

The current federalization trend presents a troubling picture with far-reaching consequences. It reflects a phenomenon capable of altering and undermining the careful decentralization of criminal law authority that has worked well for all of our constitutional history. It also raises

---

[77] LONG RANGE PLAN FOR THE FEDERAL COURTS 23 (1995).

questions about what kind of American criminal justice system will evolve if the trend continues.

The dual federal-state system of criminal law enforcement is constitutionally established. It is important in principle and should be maintained in practice. Each governmental system constantly makes, interprets, and embodies decisions about what citizen conduct should merit criminal investigation and possible sanctions. These varied systems, in turn, produce long-valued experimentation and thereby increase the likelihood of improvements in all systems.

A federal crime applies uniformly throughout all the states, yet local values concerning what conduct should be subjected to criminal sanctions (as distinguished from subjecting that conduct only to non-criminal law suits or other forms of condemnation) vary from state to state.[78] Local crimes involve local values and should be handled by state law. Each state's criminal justice system embodies a series of state decisions about what conduct should be subjected to governmental control and criminal sanctions (prison or fine) and about what socially unacceptable conduct should be left outside those criminal prohibitions (left perhaps to private social pressures, to moral restraints, or perhaps to non-criminal suits between individuals or between governmental agencies and individuals). Community views also differ from state to state on related issues: the appropriate limits on police investigative practices, acceptable prosecutorial discretion, the locale of trials, suitable court procedures and rules of evidence, the exact penal consequences that should accompany conviction, and the wisest allocation of limited resources to confront the important problem of crime. In the participatory democracy of our large nation, with varying local values, citizen views about such matters are more likely to be felt and acted upon through representatives at the local level, rather than at the federal level where most of those in power are more removed from the affected local values and more preoccupied with issues of national and international concern.

The diminution of local autonomy inherent in the imposition of

---

[78] *See generally* Neil H. Cogan, *The Rules of Everyday Life*, 543 ANNALS AM. ACAD. POL. & SOC. SCI. 97 (1996).

national standards, without regard to local community values and without regard to any noticeable benefits, requires cautious legislative assessment. The appropriate balance affords room for truly national interests to be protected by federal law while reserving most criminal law enforcement to the states.

In concluding, we emphasize three points about the problem of inappropriate federalization. First, federal legislative power to create new crimes should be used with great caution. Second, in areas involving essentially local crime, the adverse consequences of inappropriate federalization should be recognized and avoided. Finally, Congress should consider several steps to limit federalization of local crime.

The Use of Federal Criminal Legislative Power

Congressional power to make conduct a federal crime is constitutionally limited. The power is more clear in some circumstances than in others.[79] Without attempting to describe in this Report the exact limits of Congressional power, it is useful to note the bases upon which Congress typically premises federal criminal legislation:[80]

---

[79] *See* U.S. CONST. art. I, § 8 (expressly allocating Congressional power to "provide for the Punishment of counterfeiting the Securities and current Coin of the United States" and to "define and punish Piracies and Felonies committed on the high Seas, and Offense against the Law of Nations"); U.S. CONST. art. III, § 3 (defining treason against the United States, granting Congress the power to declare the punishment for treason, and affording certain related protections).

[80] Professor Louis B. Schwartz, one of the earliest scholars to recognize the deficiencies of the federal criminal law and a leader in the effort to make it rational, helpfully defines the jurisdictional premises in *Reform of the Federal Criminal Laws: Issues, Tactics, and Prospects*, 41 LAW & CONTEMP. PROBS. 1, 16 (1977): "The problems of federal penal jurisdiction may be analyzed under four main headings: (1) the core of the federal government's power to preserve itself and carry out federal functions (therein are treason, espionage, tax and customs violations, etc.); (2) the territorial scope within which federal legislative power is plenary (federal enclaves, American vessels on the high seas) and where the federal penal code would be, in principle, as comprehensive as that of an ordinary state; (3) the question of "assimilated crimes" — state-defined offenses which Congress adopts by reference for application in federal enclaves; and (4) the question of the extent to which Congress should, by using its constitutional power (for example, over interstate commerce or the mails),

- *Crimes interfering with the core functions of the federal government.* Treason, controlling national borders, and protecting government currency are examples;

- *Legislation essentially based on a federal relationship to the site of the crime.* In such matters, the federal government basically operates as its own state, in general acting to control behavior in certain areas where only the federal government can effectively legislate (such as dealing with certain crimes on the high seas) or out of concern for certain federal premises (Congressional assimilation of state law to apply standards for certain federal lands and American Indian reservations located within state boundaries); and

- *Criminalization of conduct on a Commerce Clause basis.* Drive-by shootings and carjackings are recent examples of Congress's assertion of jurisdiction on this basis.

Of these jurisdictional bases, the earliest federal crimes reflected a Congressional attention to protecting core federal functions; in contrast, more recently a legislative basis is often asserted on the last-mentioned interstate commerce power.[81] In the process, the recent legislation frequently makes federal crimes out of local crime (sometimes violent street crime) that has been long penalized by state law — crime which is predominately local in most of its manifestations but the type of crime which most alarms citizens. Of course, simply because there is a Commerce Clause basis for asserting jurisdiction does not mean that in a particular case the conduct actually prosecuted has much, if any, real connection to, or impact upon, interstate commerce. There is general agreement that the federal government can and must act in those areas that are within its exclusive control and unique sphere. On the other hand, there is considerable disagreement about how far Congress should go in criminalizing matters that touch on interstate commerce, in part

---

make federal crimes out of behavior that is already penalized by state law." (Footnote omitted.)

[81] U.S. CONST. art. I, § 8 grants Congress the power to "regulate Commerce with foreign Nations and among the several States, and with the Indian Tribes . . . ."

because this creates a problematic overlap with local interests and threatens other values discussed in this Report.

What criminal activity falling within Congress's power should be made a federal crime? Some commonly agreed upon answers are detailed in the studies collected in the BIBLIOGRAPHY. From these common grounds the jurisdictional spectrum stretches out to areas of lesser agreement. The Task Force has not set out to define these areas with precision, not only because others have done so,[82] but because we are concerned with one part of this issue: those areas of essentially local conduct traditionally left to state control but now being made the subject of expanding federalization. Nevertheless, brief reference should be made as to the scope of the jurisdictional spectrum.

It is of some value to first underscore what is not generally problematic. We take it as clear that the concerns exhibited in this Report generally are not present when Congress addresses crime that intrudes upon federal functions, harming entities or personnel acting in a federal capacity, or when it addresses offenses committed on sites where the federal government has territorial responsibility, or when it addresses matters of international crime. Without serious debate, all agree that the federal government can, for example, appropriately criminalize counterfeiting and federal tax offenses. Likewise, the appropriateness of federal territorial oversight is not problematic for our purposes (crimes on federal lands, for example). Nor is the Task Force's concern generally with federal law addressing truly national and international interests. Only the federal government can vindicate truly national interests, and it certainly has the vital role to play in adequately addressing problems of transnational crimes (e.g., international terrorism), especially because of the nature of related investigations and prosecutions. In an era of evolving international activity, this complicated arena is likely to require more and more federal attention.

---

[82] *See, e.g.*, LONG RANGE PLAN FOR THE FEDERAL COURTS (1995) ; Franklin E. Zimring & Gordon Hawkins, *Toward a Principled Basis for Federal Criminal Legislation*, 543 ANNALS AM. ACAD. POL. & SOC. SCI. 15, 22-23, 25 (1996) (arguing for a distinct federal interest); Rory K. Little, *Myths and Principles of Federalization*, 46 HASTINGS L.J. 1029 (1995); Adam H. Kurland, *First Principles of American Federalism and the Nature of Criminal Jurisdiction*, 45 EMORY L.J. 1 (1996).

More disagreement surrounds the appropriate role of federal criminalization in the multistate activity area, frequently described as interstate commerce jurisdiction. The accelerating federalization which concerns the Task Force largely tracks Congressional reliance on an expansive definition of the Commerce Clause power.

Most students of the problem agree that truly interstate activity implicates national interests, sometimes requiring the resources of federal investigative agencies and justifying federal prosecution. There is, however, a highly debatable issue as to what conduct should be targeted for federal prosecution in the interstate commerce category. Conduct that involves a substantial and truly multistate activity presents a generally acceptable basis for federal legislation. Nevertheless, this is an area for substantial legislative caution because legislating on this basis without hard inquiry into the actual nature of the conduct and the need for federal criminalization (in addition to state criminalization) can give rise to tenuous federalization with all its adverse consequences. The respond to citizen concern can produce a contrived or tenuous interstate basis that is not really distinctly federal in nature. Such responses can intrude into areas of traditional state control and be counterproductive, producing a federal crime not likely to have any demonstrable impact and one which will risk detrimental consequences. The overwhelming opposition widely expressed by front-line police, state governors, district attorneys, state and federal judges, as well as groups concerned primarily with citizen liberties, is strong testimony to the great caution needed in the face of proposals for new federal crimes.

Others would include still other areas as candidates for federalization because they deem them areas in which state enforcement is ineffectual. For example, some would include situations in which investigative resources and certain skills are beyond the usual capacity of local police — situations such as complex financial investigations or activity calling for complicated surveillance capability. Still others would include situations that require prosecution of certain local officials (political officials or local police, for example) where local pressures, it is argued, may otherwise make needed prosecution politically difficult and unlikely. Others would include certain types of organized criminal activity where federal resources might supplement local law enforcement.

No matter what the theoretical extent of Congressional power, there is overwhelming agreement within the Task Force on one principle concerning the creation of a federal crime: *To create a* federal *crime, a strong federal interest in the matter should be clearly shown, that is, a distinctly federal interest beyond the mere conclusion that the conduct should be made criminal by* some *appropriate governmental entity.* Federal law enforcement for criminal activity that is essentially local in character generally should not be undertaken, at least not without clearly considered Congressional articulation of principles which has so far been absent. The near unanimity of concern and agreement among those who have studied the problem should be a powerful danger signal to the public, to the press, and to legislators.

Recognizing the Adverse Consequences of Inappropriate Federalization

As noted earlier and underscored here, the Task Force recognizes that there is a surface inconsistency between its identification of the risks of undue federalization of criminal law and our data showing the infrequency with which some recently enacted federal criminal laws have been used. If the recent laws are rarely used, some might wonder why there is any appreciable concern about those particular crimes. There are several answers to this: First, added federal criminal laws, even if not widely used initially, may well be used more frequently in the future. To take two notable examples, federal drug laws and the federal RICO statute were rarely used when first enacted, but eventually became widely used because of shifting federal Executive Branch priorities or other reasons.[83] Second, even though some recent federal criminal laws have been rarely used, the total federal legislative framework now authorizes broad use of federal investigative and prosecutive activity with all the attendant risks identified in this Report. Even if the recent statutes continue to be used rarely, those with responsibility for setting funding levels for federal law enforcement and for determining priorities for use of appropriated funds would still have a heavy obligation to consider carefully the risks of inappropriate uses of federal law enforcement authority.

---

[83] *See, e.g.*, Chart 6 in text and APPENDIX B, SECTION 3.

The Task Force believes that inappropriately federalized crime causes serious problems to the administration of justice in this country. Even when prosecuted only occasionally, inappropriately federalized crimes threaten fundamental allocations of responsibility between state and federal authorities. While a single unsuitable proposal, intended as a well-meaning antidote for criminal ills, may be thought to do little damage, it is therefore important to keep in mind the detrimental long-term effects of unwarranted federal intrusions.

- It generally undermines the state-federal fabric and disrupts the important constitutional balance of federal and state systems.
- It can have a detrimental impact on the state courts, state prosecutors, attorneys, and state investigating agents who bear the overwhelming share of responsibility for criminal law enforcement.
- It has the potential to relegate the less glamorous prosecutions to the state system, undermine citizen perception, dissipate citizen power, and diminish citizen confidence in both state and local law enforcement mechanisms.
- It creates an unhealthy concentration of policing power at the federal level.
- It can cause an adverse impact on the federal judicial system;
- It creates inappropriately disparate results for similarly situated defendants, depending on whether their essentially similar conduct is selected for federal or state prosecution.
- It increases unreviewable federal prosecutorial discretion.
- It contributes, to some degree, to costly and unneeded consequences for the federal prison system.
- It accumulates a large body of law that requires continually increasing and unprofitable Congressional attention in monitoring federal criminal statutes and agencies.
- It diverts Congressional attention from a needed focus on that criminal activity which, in practice, only federal prosecutions can address.
- Overall, it represents an unwise allocation of scarce resources needed to meet the genuine issues of crime.

In light of these considerations, the Task Force believes that Congress should seriously consider the following recommendations for limiting inappropriate federalization.

Specific Recommendations for Limiting Inappropriate Federalization of Local Crimes

In formulating our recommendations for the issues identified in this Report, we recognize that the excessive federalization of criminal law cannot be countered effectively by a neatly packaged blueprint for action. On the contrary, what is required has more to do with how the Congress and the public *think* about these issues — more to do with a careful approach rather than any specific proposal for mechanical action or line-drawing. If the legitimate concern to deal effectively with criminals is met only by a generalized response of passing more federal criminal laws and funding more federal law enforcement resources, then the serious risks we have identified will only increase. That is why the Task Force's most fundamental plea is for all who are concerned with effective law enforcement — legislators and members of the public alike — to think carefully about the risks of excessive federalization of the criminal law and to have these risks clearly in mind when considering any proposal to enact new federal criminal laws and to add more resources and personnel to federal law enforcement agencies.

Because inappropriate federalization produces insubstantial gains at the expense of important values, it is important to legislate, investigate and prosecute federal criminal law only in circumstances where limited legislative time and law enforcement efforts can most realistically deal with the serious problem of crime and do so without intruding on long-standing values. Congress should not bring into play the federal government's investigative power, prosecutorial discretion, judicial authority, and sentencing sanctions unless there is a strong reason for making wrongful conduct a federal crime — unless there is a distinct federal interest of some sort involved.

The opportunity to limit the excessive federalization of local crimes rests entirely with Congress. It is conceivable that at some point the Supreme Court might adopt a more narrow construction of the Commerce Clause that would inhibit Congress's authority to federalize local crimes (a matter on which the Task Force expresses no view). For now, the extent to which new federal laws will federalize local crimes and the extent to which added federal funds will permit increased federal prosecution of such local crimes as are already covered by federal statutes rests entirely with Congress.

There are several steps Congress should consider in order to limit the federalization of local crime.

(1) *Recognizing How Best to Fight Crime Within the Federal System.* The first step is a frank recognition that the understandable pressure to respond to constituent concerns about public safety can be met by taking constructive steps that aid law enforcement without incurring the risks inherent in excessive federalization of criminal law. While recognizing the pressure placed upon members of Congress, there must also be recognition that a refusal to endorse a new federal crime is not a sign that a legislator is "soft on crime." On the contrary, it means that the legislator wants to strengthen law enforcement within the traditional federal structure of this nation by leaving local crime to local authorities. The press, the public, and Congress itself must recognize these important truths.

(2) *Focused Consideration of the True Federal Interests in Crime Control and the Risks of Federalization of Local Crime.* Congress can avoid inappropriate federalization by recognizing its limited constitutional authority to criminalize conduct and by exercising restraint in passing new criminal laws dealing with essentially local conduct. Congress should insist on focused debate about what criminal conduct should and should not be federalized. This is especially true given the scarcity of funds to meet all needs. In the usually piecemeal debates over what to do about crime, it is critical in allocating federal resources that Congressional attention focus on areas that most appropriately fit long-understood federal values and those most likely to produce practical, demonstrable benefits in dealing with crime.

If the goal is to meet the dangers of local crimes, it is important for Congress to recognize that federalization has limited crime control effect on local crime and significant negative effect on important federal and local interests. A telling fact for Congressional consideration is that, despite the existing federal capacity to prosecute certain local crimes, only a small portion of crimes committed across America are prosecuted by the federal government. This particularly holds true for the local conduct which is the focus of this Report and which now all too frequently qualifies as both federal and state crime.

If the increasing federalization were to have a demonstrable practical impact on crime, it would be expected that there would be a significant number of prosecutions, prosecutions that might act as a deterrent or have an incapacitating effect on criminals. This does not seem to be the case. The new waves of federal statutes often stand only as symbolic book prohibitions with few actual prosecutions. This means that whatever the reasons for any recent crime reduction, the reduction can not realistically be attributed to the creation of more localized federal crimes. There is no persuasive evidence that federalization of local crime makes the streets safer for American citizens.

Where a clear federal interest is demonstrated, especially to meet a public safety need not being adequately dealt with by the states, the federal interest should be vindicated — if needed, by new laws and new resources. Otherwise, the federal response should be limited to aiding state and local law enforcement, not duplicating their efforts.

(3) *Institutional Mechanisms to Foster Restraint on Further Federalization.* Congress should consider mechanisms to assist its analysis of proposed crime legislation and proposed federal law enforcement funding to provide the systematic, coherent analysis that is needed. One possible mechanism, for example, might require that the costs to the federal/state system of any new federal crime law be the subject of concrete, Congressionally supervised analysis before passage — perhaps by an impact statement of the sort provided by Congressional Budget Office assessment or by Congressional Research Service analysis. Such an analysis would provide Congress with objective data upon which to base legislative decisions. It could discern federal/state comparative costs, as well as the real need and the extent of benefits, and the risk of adverse impacts of the legislation. The use of such analysis in the highly charged debate about crime could be particularly useful in light of the reasons that account for most of the legislation at issue in this Report.

Beyond an impartial, technical staff analysis, Congress might consider institutionalizing an impartial public policy analysis by its own members, perhaps through the mechanism of a joint Congressional committee on federalism. Such a committee could assess proposed crime legislation and other proposals with significant impact on federal/state jurisdictional relationships. In any event, the federalization aspect of proposed crimes calls for close, on-going scrutiny in those standing Congressional committees with criminal law jurisdiction, as well as those with oversight responsibilities.

A federalization assessment, by Congressional staff and by a select joint committee, could usefully be made both as to proposed new federal crime bills and proposed new funding for federal law enforcement personnel.

(4) *Sunset Provisions.* When, after careful analysis, new federal criminal laws are thought warranted, the new legislation should include a fairly short "sunset provision," perhaps no more than five years. Congress has found the sunset safeguard acceptable in other contexts and it would seem particularly valuable in this arena. Use of this safeguard will afford future Congresses an opportunity to assess claims made prior to enactment about what a particular statute might accomplish in dealing with crime. The use of a sunset provision might also be of value where the claimed need for federal legislation has to do with a perceived state deficiency in dealing with certain crimes; in due time, that deficit may be cured at the state level.

(5) *Responding to Public Safety Concerns with Federal Support for State and Local Crime Control Efforts.* Congress can significantly respond to public safety concerns without enacting new *federal* statutes or adding new funds for *federal* law enforcement. Virtually all of the criminal behavior that most concerns citizens is already a state crime. Congressional allocations of funds to state systems in support of state criminal justice efforts have, in modern times, been one of the alternative techniques used by the federal government in assisting with crime problems without duplicating efforts. That approach to combating crime is believed by many to be an appropriate technique which avoids many of the undermining effects of legislating a federal crime in areas properly left to the states.[84] Federal funding for crime control can take the form of

---

[84] *See* Philip B. Heymann & Mark H. Moore, *The Federal Role in Dealing With Violent Street Crime: Principles, Questions, and Cautions*, 543 ANNALS AM. ACAD.

block grants, of specifically targeted program funds, or a combination of the two.

The understandable public pressure to "do something" about crime can, in most circumstances, be more effectively met by providing resources — financial and technical — to state and local law enforcement agencies than by adding federal statutes and federal personnel. Such state-aiding responses can combat crime without risk of impairing the proper functioning of our federal system.

- O -

The expanding coverage of federal criminal law, much of it enacted in the absence of a demonstrated and distinctive federal justification, is moving the nation rapidly toward two broadly overlapping, parallel, and essentially redundant sets of criminal prohibitions, each filled with differing consequences for the same conduct. Such a system has little to commend it and much to condemn it.

The principles of federalism and practical realities provide no justification for the duplication inherent in two criminal justice systems if they perform basically the same function in the same kinds of cases. There are no persuasive reasons why both federal and state police agencies should be authorized to investigate the same kind of offenses, federal and state prosecutors should be directed to prosecute the same kinds of offenses, and federal and state judges should be empowered to try essentially the same kind of criminal conduct. When the consequences of these parallel legal systems can be so different, increases in the scope of federal criminal law and the areas of concurrent jurisdiction over local crime make it increasingly difficult, if not impossible, to treat equally all persons who engaged in the same conduct and these increases multiply the difficulty of adequately regulating the discretion of federal prosecutors. Moreover, it makes little sense to invest scarce resources indiscriminately in a separate system of slender federal prosecutions

---

POL. & SOC. SCI. 103 (1996), for a discussion of the differing implications of a federal financial role supporting state law enforcement, compared to a direct federal operational role involving the prosecution of essentially local street crime as a federal offense.

rather than investing those resources in already existing state systems which bear the major burden in investigating and prosecuting crime.

In the important debate about how to curb crime, it is crucial that the American justice system not be harmed in the process. The nation has long justifiably relied on a careful distribution of powers to the national government and to state governments. In the end, the ultimate safeguard for maintaining this valued constitutional system must be the principled recognition by Congress of the long-range damage to real crime control and to the nation's structure caused by inappropriate federalization.

APPENDICES

APPENDIX A

BIBLIOGRAPHY

LAW REVIEW ARTICLES & COMMENTS:

George Allen, *A Federalist Perspective on the Crime Problem*, 4 CORNELL J.L. & PUB. POL'Y 535 (1995).

Gerald G. Ashdown, *Federalism, Federalization and the Politics of Crime*, 98 W. VA. L. REV. 789 (1996).

John S. Baker, Jr., *Nationalizing Criminal Law: Does Organized Crime Make It Necessary or Proper?*, 16 RUTGERS L.J. 495 (1985).

Sara Sun Beale, *Federalizing Crime: Assessing the Impact on the Federal Courts*, 543 ANNALS AM. ACAD. POL. & SOC. SCI. 39 (1996).

______________, *Reporter's Draft for the Working Group on Principles to Use When Considering the Federalization of Criminal Law*, 46 HASTINGS L.J. 1277 (1995) (discussing the adverse effect on the federal prison system relative to the increased number of federal crimes).

______________, *Too Many and Yet Too Few: New Principles to Define the Proper Limits for Federal Criminal Jurisdiction*, 46 HASTINGS L.J. 979 (1995) (arguing, among other points, that the concurrent nature of criminal law may involve sizable differences in sentences for essentially the same conduct, thereby raising justifiable concern for the potential disparity of results among similarly situated citizens; also arguing that federal civil cases suffer because of the priority that must be given to the ncreased number of complex federal criminal cases).

_____________, *What's Law Got To Do With It? The Political, Social, Psychological and Other Non-Legal Factors Influencing the Development of (Federal) Criminal Law*, 1 BUFF. CRIM. L. REV. 23 (1997).

G. Robert Blakey, *Federal Criminal Law: The Need, Not for Revised Constitutional Theory or New Congressional Statutes, but the Exercise of Responsible Prosecutive Discretion*, 46 HASTINGS L.J. 1175 (1995).

Kathleen F. Brickey, *Crime Control and the Commerce Clause: Life After* Lopez, 46 CASE W. RES. L. REV. 801 (1996).

________________, *Criminal Mischief: The Federalization of American Criminal Law*, 46 HASTINGS L.J. 1135 (1995) (noting that the increasing presence of the federal government in the criminal law field is likely to lead to a diminishing local presence and may discourage local law enforcement efforts).

________________, *The Commerce Clause and Federalized Crime: A Tale of Two Thieves*, 543 ANNALS AM. ACAD. POL. & SOC. SCI. 27 (1996).

________________, *Federal Criminal Code Reform: Hidden Costs, Illusory Benefits*, 2 BUFF. CRIM. L. REV. 161 (1998).

Jay S. Bybee, *Insuring Domestic Tranquility:* Lopez, *Federalization of Crime and the Forgotten Role of the Domestic Violence Clause*, 66 GEO. WASH. L. REV. 1 (1997).

Steven G. Calabresi, *"A Government of limited and Enumerated Powers": In Defense of* United States v. Lopez, 84 MICH. L. REV. 752 (1995).

Paul D. Carrington, *Federal Use of State Institutions in the Administration of Justice*, 49 SMU L. REV. 557 (1996).

Mary M. Cheh, *Constitutional Limits on Using Civil Remedies to Achieve Criminal Law Objectives: Understanding and Transcending the Criminal-Civil Law Distinction*, 42 HASTINGS L.J. 1325 (1991).

Harry A. Chernoff, Christopher M. Kelly & John R. Kroger, *The Politics of Crime*, 33 HARV. J. ON LEGIS. 527 (1996).

Stephen Chippendale, Note, *More Harm Than Good: Assessing Federalization of Criminal Law*, 79 MINN. L. REV. 455 (1994).

Steven D. Clymer, *Unequal Justice: The Federalization of Criminal Law*, 70 S. CAL. L. REV. 643 (1997).

Neil H. Cogan, *The Rules of Everyday Life*, 543 ANNALS AM. ACAD. POL. & SOC. SCI. 97 (1996) (expressing view that state law appropriately accommodates different citizen values from state to state).

Cynthia R. Cook, Comment, *The Armed Career Criminal Act Amendment: A Federal Sentence Enhancement Provision*, 12 GEO. MASON L. REV. 99 (1989).

Anne M. Coughlin, *Rethinking Federal Criminal Law: Of White Slaves and Domestic Hostages*, 1 BUFF. CRIM. L. REV. 109 (1997).

Dennis E. Curtis, *Congressional Powers and Federal Judicial Burdens*, 46 HASTINGS L.J. 1019 (1995).

_____________, *The Effect of Federalization on the Defense Function*, 543 ANNALS AM. ACAD. POL. & SOC. SCI. 85 (1996).

Victoria Davis, Note, *A Landmark Lost: The Anemic Impact of* United States v. Lopez *on the Federalization of Criminal Law*, 75 NEB. L. REV. 117 (1996).

Deanne Dissinger, Note, *Carjacking: Congressional Authority Under the Commerce Clause To Federalize Crimes*, 69 TEMP. L. REV. 507 (1995).

Robert F. Drinan, Michael E. Ward & David W. Beier III, *The Federal Criminal Code: The Houses are Divided*, 18 AM. CRIM. L. REV. 509 (1981).

Julian Epstein, *Evolving Spheres of Federalism After* U.S v. Lopez *and Other Cases*, 34 HARV. J. ON LEGIS. 525 (1997).

William N. Eskridge, Jr. & Philip P. Frickey, *The Supreme Court 1993 Term — Foreword: The Law as Equilibrium*, 108 HARV. L. REV. 26 (1994).

Sam J. Ervin, III, *The Federalization of State Crimes: Some Observations and Reflections*, 98 W. VA. L. REV. 761 (1996).

Barry Friedman, *Legislative Findings and Judicial Signals: A Positive Political Reading of* Lopez v. United States, 46 CASE W. RES. L. REV. 757 (1996).

Matthew T. Fricker & Kelly Gilchrist, Case Comment, United States v. Nofziger *and the Revision of 18 U.S.C. § 207: The Need for a New Approach to the Mens Rea Requirements of Federal Criminal Law*, 65 NOTRE DAME L. REV. 803 (1990).

Ronald L. Gainer, *Federal Criminal Code Reform: Past and Future*, 2 BUFF. CRIM. L. REV. 46 (1998).

_____________, *Report to the Attorney General on Federal Criminal Code Reform*, 1 CRIM. L. FORUM 99 (1989).

Larry E. Gee, Comment, *Federalism Revisited: The Supreme Court Resurrects the Notion of Enumerated Powers by Limiting Congress's Attempt to Federalize Crime*, 27 ST. MARY'S L. J. 151 (1995).

Ethan B. Gerber, Note, *"A RICO You Can't Refuse": New York's Organized Crime Control Act*, 53 BROOK. L. REV. 979 (1988).

Jamie S. Gorelick & Harry Litman, *Prosecutorial Discretion and the Federalization Debate*, 46 HASTINGS L.J. 967 (1995).

Sandra Guerra, *The Myth of Dual Sovereignty: Multijurisdictional Drug Law Enforcement and Double Jeopardy*, 73 N.C. L. REV. 1159 (1995).

Robert Heller, Comment, *Selective Prosecution and the Federalization of Criminal Law: The Need for Meaningful Judicial Review of Prosecutorial Discretion*, 145 U. PA. L. REV. 1309 (1997).

Peter J. Henning, *Foreword: Statutory Interpretation and the Federalization of Criminal Law*, 86 J. CRIM. L. & CRIMINOLOGY 1167 (1996).

Philip B. Heymann & Mark H. Moore, *The Federal Role in Dealing With Violent Street Crime: Principles, Questions, and Cautions*, 543 ANNALS AM. ACAD. POL. & SOC. SCI. 103 (1996).

Roderick M. Hills, Jr., *The Political Economy of Cooperative Federalism: Why State Autonomy Makes Sense and "Dual Sovereignty" Doesn't*, 96 MICH. L. REV. 813 (1998).

Greg Hollon, Note, *After the Federalization Binge: A Civil Liberties Hangover*, 31 HARV. C.R.-C.L. L. REV. 499 (1996).

John C. Jeffries, Jr. & John Gleeson, *The Federalization of Organized Crime: Advantages of Federal Prosecution*, 46 HASTINGS L.J. 1095 (1995).

Robert H. Joost, *Federal Criminal Code Reform: Is it Possible?*, 1 BUFF. CRIM. L. REV. 195 (1997).

Sanford H. Kadish, *The Folly of Overfederalization*, 46 HASTINGS L.J. 1247 (1995).

Dan M. Kahan, *Is* Chevron *Relevant to Federal Criminal Law?*, 110 HARV. L. REV. 469 (1996).

____________, *Lenity and Federal Common Law Crimes*, 1994 SUP. CT. REV. 345 (1995).

____________, *Three Conceptions of Federal Criminal-Lawmaking*, 1 BUFF. CRIM. L. REV. 5 (1997).

J. Anthony Kline, *Comment: The Politicalization of Crime*, 46 HASTINGS L.J. 1087 (1995).

Herb Kohl, *Response to "The Politics of Crime,"* 33 HARV. J. ON LEGIS. 581 (1996) (response to Chernoff, Kelly & Kroger article, above).

Adam H. Kurland, *First Principles of American Federalism and the Nature of Criminal Jurisdiction*, 45 EMORY L.J. 1 (1996).

Renée M. Landers, *Federalization of State Law: Enhancing Opportunities for Three-Branch and Federal-State Cooperation*, 44 DEPAUL L. REV. 811 (1995).

______________, *Prosecutorial Limits on Overlapping Federal and State Jurisdiction*, 543 ANNALS AM. ACAD. POL. & SOC. SCI. 64 (1996).

Frederick M. Lawrence, *Civil Rights and Criminal Wrongs: The Mens Rea of Federal Civil Rights Crimes*, 67 TUL. L. REV. 2113 (1993).

George Danzig Levine, *The Proposed New Federal Criminal Code: A Constitutional and Jurisdictional Analysis*, 39 BROOK. L. REV. 1 (1972).

Harry Litman & Mark D. Greenberg, *Dual Prosecutions: A Model for Concurrent Federal Jurisdiction*, 543 ANNALS AM. ACAD. POL. & SOC. SCI. 72 (1996).

______________, *Federal Power and Federalism: A Theory of Commerce-Clause Based Regulation of Traditionally State Crimes*, 47 CASE W. RES. L. REV. 921 (1997).

______________, *Reporters' Draft for the Working Group on Federal-State Cooperation*, 46 HASTINGS L.J. 1319 (1995).

Rory K. Little, *Myths and Principles of Federalization*, 46 HASTINGS L.J. 1029 (1995).

Nancy E. Marion, *Symbolic Policies in Clinton's Crime Control Agenda*, 1 BUFF. CRIM. L. REV. 67 (1997).

Tracey L. Meares, *Charting Race and Class Differences in Attitudes Toward Drug Legalization and Law Enforcement: Lessons for Federal Criminal Law*, 1 BUFF. CRIM. L. REV. 137 (1997).

Edwin Meese III, Keynote Address to the Second Annual Lawyers Convention of the Federalist Society: *The Constitution and Federal Criminal Law*, 26 AM. CRIM. L. REV. 1779, 1781 (1989) (noting the historical American recognition that the general police power lies with the states, not the federal government).

______________, *Big Brother on the Beat: The Expanding Federalization of Crime*, 1 TEX. REV. L. & POL. 1 (1997) (arguing, among other points, that concurrent jurisdiction raises substantial questions of redundant punishment for essentially the same conduct; also arguing that the centralization of criminal law enforcement historically has been perceived as creating potentially dangerous consequences and therefore avoided).

Thomas M. Mengler, *The Sad Refrain of Tough on Crime: Some Thoughts on Saving the Federal Judiciary from the Federalization of State Crime*, 43 U. KAN. L. REV. 503 (1995) (noting that state law is less difficult to change so as to accommodate new local conditions).

Deborah Jones Merritt, *Commerce!*, 94 MICH. L. REV. 674 (1995).

______________, *The Fuzzy Logic of Federalism*, 46 CASE W. RES. L. REV. 685 (1996).

Roger J. Miner, *The Consequences of Federalizing Criminal Law: Overloaded Courts and a Dissatisfied Public*, CRIM. JUST. 16 (Spring 1989) (arguing, among other points, that increased federalization reaches only a small percent of the crimes that most concern Americans, and that the removal of crime debate to the federal level is likely to lead to a diminution of citizens' perception about their power to have an impact).

____________, *Crime and Punishment in the Federal Courts*, 43 SYRACUSE L. REV. 681 (1992).

____________, *Federal Courts, Federal Crimes, and Federalism*, 10 HARV. J.L. & PUB. POL'Y 117 (1987).

_____________, *Planning for the Second Century of the Second Circuit Court of Appeals: The Report of the Federal Courts Study Committee*, 65 ST. JOHN'S L. REV. 673 (1991).

Geraldine Szott Moohr, *The Federal Interest in Criminal Law*, 47 SYRACUSE L. REV. 1127 (1997).

Jon O. Newman, Essay, *Restructuring Federal Jurisdiction: Proposals to Preserve the Federal Judicial System*, 56 U. CHI. L. REV. 761 (1989) (arguing that increased federalization has had an adverse effect on federal courts because of the volume of federal criminal cases).

John B. Oakley, *The Myth of Cost-Free Jurisdictional Reallocation*, 543 ANNALS AM. ACAD. POL. & SOC. SCI. 52 (1996).

Greg O'Reilly & Robert Drizin, United States v. Lopez: *Reinvigorating the Federal Balance by Maintaining the States' Role as the "Immediate and Visible Guardians" of Society*, 22 J. OF LEG. 1 (1996).

Robert C. Palmer, *The Federal Common Law of Crime*, 4 LAW & HIST. REV. 267 (1986).

Ellen S. Podgor, *Globalization and the Federal Prosecution of White Collar Crime*, 34 AM. CRIM. L. REV. 325 (1997).

Stephen B. Presser, *The Supra-Constitution, the Courts, and the Federal Common Law of Crimes: Some Comments on* Palmer *and* Preyer, 4 LAW & HIST. REV. 325 (1986).

Kathryn Preyer, *Jurisdiction to Punish: Federal Authority, Federalism and the Common Law of Crimes in the Early Republic*, 4 LAW & HIST. REV. 223 (1986).

Jed S. Rakoff, *The Federal Mail Fraud Statute (Part I)*, 18 DUQ. L. REV. 771 (1980).

Kevin R. Reitz, *The Federal Role in Sentencing Law and Policy*, 543 ANNALS AM. ACAD. POL. & SOC. SCI. 116 (1996) (noting that federal incarceration has important, different consequences when contrasted with state incarceration).

Gary D. Rowe, Note, *The Sounds of Silence*: United States v. Hudson & Goodwin, *The Jeffersonian Ascendancy, and the Abolition of Federal Common Law Crimes*, 101 YALE L.J. 919 (1992).

Andrew St. Laurent, Note, *Reconstituting* United States v. Lopez: *Another Look at Federal Criminal Law*, 31 COLUM. J.L. & SOC. PROBS. 61 (1997).

Bernd Schunemann, *Rethinking Federal Criminal Law: Principles of Criminal Legislation in Post-Modern Society*, 1 BUFF. CRIM. L. REV. 175 (1997).

Louis B. Schwartz, *Federal Criminal Jurisdiction and Prosecutors' Discretion*, 13 LAW & CONTEMP. PROBS. 64 (1948).

_________________, *Reform of the Federal Criminal Laws: Issues, Tactics and Prospects*, 41 LAW & CONTEMP. PROBS. 1 (1977). (The article contains an important history of the National Commission on Reform of the Federal Criminal Laws ("The Brown Commission" 1971) and its work, written by the Commission's Director. An earlier version of this paper was published in 1977 DUKE L.J. 171.)

William W. Schwarzer & Russell R. Wheeler, *On the Federalization of the Administration of Civil and Criminal Justice*, 23 STETSON L. REV. 651 (1994) (noting that increased federalization has had an adverse effect on state courts because it undermines their histroic and important role).

Tom Stacy, *Whose Interests Does Federalism Protect?*, 45 U. KAN. L. REV. 1185 (1997).

Tom Stacy & Kim Dayton, *The Underfederalization of Crime*, 6 CORNELL J.L. & PUB. POL'Y 247 (1997).

Robert L. Stern, *The Commerce Clause Revisited -- The Federalization of Intrastate Crime*, 15 ARIZ. L. REV. 271 (1973).

Jeffrey Standen, *An Economic Perspecive on Federal Criminal Law Reform*, 2 BUFF. CRIM. L. REV. 249 (1998).

Nadine Strossen, *Criticism of Federal Counter-Terrorism Laws*, 20 HARV. J. L. & PUB. POL'Y 531 (1997) (describing increased and centralized federal police power as subject to little oversight or review).

George C. Thomas III, *A Blameworthy Act Approach to Double Jeopardy Same Offense Problems,* 83 CAL. L. REV. 1027 (1995).

Barry C. Toone and Bradley J. Wiskirchen, Note, *Great Expectations: The Illusion of Federalism After* United States v. Lopez, 22 J. LEGIS. 241 (1996).

William Van Alstyne, *Dual Sovereignty, Federalism, and National Criminal Law: Modernist Constitutional Doctrine and the Nonrole of the Supreme Court*, 26 AM. CRIM. L. REV. 1740 (1989).

Vaughn R. Walker, *Comment, Federalizing Organized Crime*, 46 HASTINGS L.J. 1127 (1995).

Charles Warren, *Federal Criminal Laws and the State Courts*, 38 HARV. L. REV. 545 (1925).

Russell L. Weaver, Lopez *and the Federalization of the Criminal Law*, 98 W. VA. L. REV. 815 (1996).

Andrew Weis, Note, *Commerce Clause in the Cross-Hairs: The Use of* Lopez-*Based Motions to Challenge the Constitutionality of Federal Criminal Statutes*, 48 STAN. L. REV. 1431 (1996).

Victor Williams, *A Constitutional Charge and a Comparative Vision to Substantially Expand and Subject Matter Specialize the Federal Judiciary: A Preliminary Blueprint for Remodeling Our National Houses of Justice and Establishing a Separate System of Federal Criminal Courts*, 37 WM. & MARY L. REV. 535 (1996).

Franklin E. Zimring & Gordon Hawkins, *Toward a Principled Basis for Federal Criminal Legislation*, 543 ANNALS AM. ACAD. POL. & SOC. SCI. 15 (1996).

OTHER ARTICLES & MISCELLANEOUS:

Administrative Office of the U.S. Courts, *The Criminal Caseload: The Nature of Change* (1994).

Maryanne Trump Barry, *Don't Make a Federal Case Out of It*, N.Y. TIMES, Mar. 11, 1994, at A31.

Sara Sun Beale, *Federal Criminal Jurisdiction*, *in* 2 ENCYCLOPEDIA OF CRIME AND JUSTICE 775 (Sanford H. Kadish ed., 1983).

Arnold Beichman, Commentary, *Criminal Offenses Going Federal*, WASH. TIMES, June 25, 1997, at A15.

Natalia Bendavid, *How Much More Can Courts, Prisons Take? Its Tempting to Federalize Crimes, But Opponents are Gathering Momentum*, LEGAL TIMES, June 7, 1993, at 1.

Beth M. Bollinger, *Defending Dual Prosecutions: Learning How to Draw the Line*, CRIM. JUST. 16 (Fall 1995).

Stephen Braun & Judy Pasternak, *A Nation with Peril on Its Mind; Crime Has Become the Top Concern of Many People*, L.A. TIMES, Feb. 13, 1994, at A1.

Jim R. Carrigan & Jessica Bolger Lee, *Criminalizing the Federal Courts*, 30 TRIAL 50 (1994).

Kenneth Conboy, *Trouble in Foley Square*, N.Y. TIMES, Dec. 27, 1993, at A17.

Donald A. Dripps, *Don't Make a Federal Case Out of It, Federalizing Additional Crimes*, 31 TRIAL 90 (1995).

Editorial, *Federalizing vs. Federalism; Fighting Crime, Especially Juvenile Crime, is State's Role, as One Might Think House Republicans Would Agree,* HARRISBURG (PA.) PATRIOT & EVENING NEWS, May 16, 1997, at A18.

Getting Tougher on Kids, 84 A.B.A. J. 95 (1998).

Ronald Goldstock, Gerald Lefcourt & William Murphy, *Justice That Makes Sense*, CRIM. JUST. 1 (Winter 1998) (decrying the adverse impact of federalization).

Jamie S. Gorelick, *Federalization of Crime is Focus of Federal Bar Association Panel Discussion*, 58 CRIM. L. REP. (BNA) 1174-75 (Nov. 22, 1995) (comments of Dep. Att'y Gen. Jamie S. Gorelick).

Philip Hager, *Making a Federal Case Out of It - Congressional Supplements to State Crimes Foster Confusion and Waste*, 15 CAL. LAW. 39 (Sept. 1995).

Lorie Hearn, *Trying Times Are Ahead; Justice O'Connor Says Federalization of Crime Could Overwhelm the Court*, SAN DIEGO UNION-TRIB., Aug. 17, 1994, at A4.

Thomas A. Henderson, *Congress Rediscovers Crime*, 17 STATE CT. J. 2 (1993).

Michael Decourcy Hinds, *Citing Caseload, Federal Judges Assail Two Provisions in Crime Bill*, N.Y. TIMES, July 14, 1991, at 19.

Constance Johnson, *Law and Disorder*, U.S. NEWS & WORLD REP., Mar. 28, 1994, at 35.

Kenneth Jost, *A Changing Legal Landscape; Anti-crime and Tort Reform Proposals Likely to Flourish in GOP Congress*, 81 A.B.A.J. 14 (1995).

Judges Irked by Tough-on-Crime Laws, 80 A.B.A. J. 18 (1994).

Judith S. Kaye, *Federalism Gone Wild*, N.Y. TIMES, Dec. 13. 1994, at A29.

Stephen Labaton, *New Tactics in the War on Drugs Tilt Scales of Justice Off Balance*, N.Y. TIMES, Dec. 29, 1989, at A1.

Jim McGee, *The New FBI*, WASH. POST MAGAZINE, July 20, 1997, at 11.

Brigid McMenamin & Janet Novak, *The White-Collar Gestapo*, FORBES MAGAZINE, (Dec. 1, 1997), at 82.

John G. Miles, *Federal Criminal Code Reform: The Jurisdictional Issue*, 23 CRIM. L. REP. (BNA) No. 11 (Supp.) (June 14, 1978).

Roger J. Miner, *Federal Court Reform Should Start at the Top*, 77 JUDICATURE 104 (1993).

Geraldine Szott Moohr, *Don't Make a Federal Case of Everything*, LEGAL TIMES, March 2, 1998, p. 28.

W. John Moore, *The High Price of Good Intentions*, NAT'L L. J., May 8, 1993, at 140.

Otto G. Obermaier, *Crime Legislation of the 104th Congress*, Outside Counsel, N.Y.L.J., Jan. 10, 1997.

________________, *Justice's Vigilant Gatekeeper*, After Hours, LEGAL TIMES, Jan. 29, 1996.

________________, *Revamping the Criminal Law Patchwork*, LEGAL TIMES, Nov. 21, 1994.

________________, *United States Attorneys: Don't Rein 'Em In, In Rebuttal*, LEGAL TIMES, Feb. 8, 1993.

________________, *What United States Attorneys Prosecute*, N.Y.L.J., July 3, 1989.

Otto G. Obermaier & Laraine Pacheco, *Crime Legislation of the 103rd Congress*, Outside Counsel, N.Y.L.J., Oct. 6, 1994.

Otto G. Obermaier & Ronald R. Rossi, *Too Many Federalized Crimes?*, N.Y.L.J., July 6, 1998, at 1.

William C. O'Malley, *Making a Federal Case*, U.S. NEWS AND WORLD REP., Apr. 24, 1994, at 7.

Robert Raven, *Don't Wage War on Crime in Federal Courts*, THE RECORDER, Aug. 11, 1992, at 8.

Lorin L. Reisner, *Criminal Prosecution of Trade Secret Theft*, Outside Counsel, N.Y.L.J., Jan. 10, 1997 (discussing the Economic Espionage Act of 1996 and its impact in an area where there was previously little federal law, and noting that recognition of the danger of prosecutions under the law resulted in period of specific approval of federal prosecution only after high level DOJ approval).

William H. Rehnquist, *Address to the American Law Institute*, REMARKS AND ADDRESSES AT THE 75TH ANNUAL AMERICAN LAW INSTITUTE MEETING, MAY 1998, at 15-19 (ALI: 1998).

Ronald G. Savage, *Federal Drug Cases More than Triple in Last 10 Years*, L.A. TIMES, Jan. 1, 1990, at A29.

Jim Smith, *Petty Pusher Goes Out Big Time*, PHILADELPHIA DAILY NEWS, July 17, 1992.

Jill Smolowe, *When Violence Hits Home*, TIME, July 4, 1994, at 18 (discussing federal Violence Against Women Act).

Garry Sturgess, *Another Clash Over Criminal Caseload*, LEGAL TIMES, Apr. 1, 1991, at 7.

Michael Tackett, *Drug War Chokes Federal Courts; Assembly-line Justice Perils Legal System*, CHI. TRIB., Oct. 14, 1990, at 1.

Tracy Thompson, *Stop Complaining, Stephens Tells Judges; Federal Jurists Bristle When U.S. Attorney Suggests They Don't Work Very Hard*, WASH. POST, June 8, 1991, at B1.

Saundra Torry, *Some Federal Judges Just Say No to Drug Cases*, WASH. POST, May 17, 1993, at F7.

Laura Vozzella, *Criminal Trials Landing on Federal Dockets - Critics Say Efforts to Obtain Longer Sentences by Federalizing Criminal Cases Mock the Constitution,* FT. WORTH STAR-TELEGRAM, Mar. 3, 1997, at 1.

H. Scott Wallace, *The Drive to Federalize Is a Road to Ruin: When Less is More*, CRIM. JUST. 8 (Fall 1993).

J. Clifford Wallace, *Tackling the Caseload Crisis; Legislators and Judges Should Weigh the Impact of Federalizing Crimes*, 80 A.B.A.J. 88 (1994).

J. Harvie Wilkinson III, *We Don't Need More Federal Judges*, WALL STREET JOURNAL, Feb. 9, 1998, at A19.

Victor Williams, *Solutions to Federal Judicial Gridlock*, 76 JUDICATURE 185 (1993).

Rick Wriggliest, *Courts Hint at Clipping Federal Prosecutors' Wings*, OMAHA WORLD-HERALD, May 22, 1997, at 1.

SYMPOSIA:

Symposium, *Federalism and the Criminal Justice System*, 98 W. VA. L. REV. 757 (1996).

Symposium, *Federalism and the Scope of the Federal Criminal Law*, 26 AM. CRIM. L. REV. 1737 (1989).

Symposium, *The Federalization of State Law*, 44 DEPAUL L. REV. 811 (1995).

Symposium, *Federalization of Crime: The Roles of the Federal and State Governments in the Criminal Justice System*, 46 HASTINGS L.J. 965 (1995) (articles and comments from this symposium are also individually indexed in this Bibliography).

Symposium, *Reflections on United States v. Lopez*, 94 MICH. L. REV. 533 (1995).

Symposium, *Rethinking Federal Criminal Law*, 1 BUFF. CRIM. L. REV. 1 (1997) (articles from this symposium are also individually indexed in this Bibliography).

Proceedings of the Middle Altantic State-Federal Judicial Relationships Conference, 162 F.R. D. 177 (1994).

Proceedings of the Western Regional Conference on State-Federal Judicial Relationships, *The Federalization of State Law*, 155 F.R.D. 301 (1994).

BOOKS & REPORTS:

NORMAN ABRAMS & SARA SUN BEALE, FEDERAL CRIMINAL LAW AND ITS ENFORCEMENT (2d ed., West: 1993).

Sara Sun Beale, Reporter, *Draft for the Working Group on Principles to Use When Considering the Federalization of Criminal Law*, 46 HASTINGS L.J. 1277 (1995).

KATHLEEN F. BRICKEY, CORPORATE CRIME AND WHITE COLLAR CRIME (2d ed., Little, Brown: 1995).

PAMELA H. BUCY, WHITE COLLAR CRIME (West: 1992).

Comments of the Federal Bar Association on the Tentative Draft Report of the Commission on Structural Alternatives for the Federal Courts of Appeals, October 1998 (Nov. 5, 1998).

JAMES D. CALDER, THE ORIGINS AND DEVELOPMENT OF FEDERAL CRIME CONTROL POLICY: HERBERT HOOVER'S INITIATIVES (Praeger: 1983).

STEVEN A. DONZIGER ed., THE REAL WAR ON CRIME: THE REPORT OF THE NATIONAL CRIMINAL JUSTICE COMMISSION (Nat'l Center on Institutions and Alternatives/Harper Books: 1996).

MALCOLM M. FEELY & AUSTIN D. SARAT, THE POLICY DILEMMA: FEDERAL CRIME POLICY AND THE LAW ENFORCEMENT ASSISTANCE ADMINISTRATION (Univ. of Minn. Press: 1980).

FEDERAL JUDICIAL CENTER, ON THE FEDERALIZATION OF THE ADMINISTRATION OF CIVIL AND CRIMINAL JUSTICE (1994).

RICHARD F. FENNO, JR., LEARNING TO LEGISLATE (CQ Press: 1991) (describing the history of the 1984 amendment to 18 U.S.C.A. App. § 1202).

HARRY FIRST, BUSINESS CRIME (Foundation: 1990).

LAWRENCE M. FRIEDMAN, CRIME AND PUNISHMENT IN AMERICAN HISTORY (Basic Books: 1994).

KERMIT L. HALL ed., CRIME AND CRIMINAL LAW: MAJOR HISTORICAL INTERPRETATIONS (Garland: 1987).

Hearings on Reform of the Federal Judicial Criminal Laws Before the Subcommittee on Criminal Laws and Procedures of the Senate Comm. on the Judiciary, 92nd Cong., 1st sess, through 94th Cong., 1st Sess. (1971-75).

DWIGHT HENDERSON, CONGRESS, COURTS AND CRIMINALS: THE DEVELOPMENT OF FEDERAL CRIMINAL LAW (Greenwood Press: 1985).

JEROLD H. ISRAEL, ELLEN PODGOR & PAUL D. BORMAN, WHITE COLLAR CRIME (West: 1996).

Renée M. Landers, Reporter, *Draft for the Working Group on the Mission of the Federal Courts*, 46 HASTINGS L.J. 1255 (1995).

LONG RANGE PLAN FOR THE FEDERAL COURTS (adopted by the Judicial Conference December 1995) (Administrative Office of U.S. Courts: 1995).

NANCY E. MARION, A HISTORY OF FEDERAL CRIME CONTROL INITIATIVES (Praeger: 1994) (contains numerous additional citations to a large amount of relevant reference material found in non-legal journals and other books).

KENNETH M. MURCHISON, FEDERAL CRIMINAL LAW DOCTRINES: THE FORGOTTEN INFLUENCE OF NATIONAL PROHIBITION (Duke Univ. Press: 1994).

NATIONAL COMMISSION ON LAW OBSERVANCE & ENFORCEMENT, REPORT OF THE ENFORCEMENT OF THE PROHIBITION LAWS OF THE UNITED STATES, H.R. Rep. No. 722, 71st Cong., 3d Sess. 55-58 (1931).

NATIONAL COMMISSION ON REFORM OF FEDERAL CRIMINAL LAWS ("The Brown Commission"), FINAL REPORT (U.S. Govt. Printing Office: 1971). Also reprinted in *1 Hearings Before the Subcomm. on Criminal Laws and Procedures of the Senate Comm. on the Judiciary*, 92nd Cong., 1st Sess. 129-517 (1971). The work of the Commission is discussed by its Director, Louis B. Schwartz, in *Reform of the Federal Criminal Laws: Issues, Tactics, and Prospects*, 41 LAW & COMTEMP. PROB. 1 (1977). (Former Congressman Robert W. Kastenmeier of Wisconsin, a member of that Commission, was also a member of this ABA Task Force.)

NATIONAL COMMISSION ON REFORM OF FEDERAL CRIMINAL LAW, STUDY DRAFT OF A NEW FEDERAL CRIMINAL CODE (1970), discussed in Louis B. Schwartz, *Reform of the Federal Criminal Laws: Issues, Tactics and Prospects*, 41 L. & CONTEMP. PROB. 1 (1977).

NATIONAL COMMISSION ON REFORM OF FEDERAL CRIMINAL LAW, WORKING PAPERS (1970).

JOHN T. NOONAN, JR., BRIBES, chapt. 18 (MacMillan: 1984).

ELLEN PODGOR, WHITE COLLAR CRIME IN A NUTSHELL (West: 1993).

PRESERVING ACCESS TO JUSTICE: THE IMPACT ON STATE COURTS OF THE PROPOSED LONG RANGE PLAN FOR THE FEDERAL COURTS, Report of the 1995 Forum for State Judges (Roscoe Pound Foundation & Yale Law School: 1996).

William H. Rehnquist, Chief Justice of the United States, *1997 Year-End Report on the Federal Judiciary*, reprinted in 30 THE THIRD BRANCH, Jan. 1998, at 1, and available online at www.usgov/cj97.htlm .

__________________, Chief Justice of the United States, *1993 Year-End Report on the Federal Judiciary*, reprinted in 26 THE THIRD BRANCH, Jan. 1994, at 1, and 17 AM. J. TRIAL ADV. 571 (1994).

REPORT TO THE ATTORNEY GENERAL ON FEDERAL CRIMINAL CODE REFORM, (transmitted to the Attorney General of the United States January 1989), reprinted as Ronald L. Gainer, *Report to the Attorney General on Federal Criminal Code Reform*, 1 CRIM. L. FORUM 99 (1989).

REPORT OF THE FEDERAL COURTS STUDY COMMITTEE (1990).

WILLIAM W. SCHWARZER & RUSSELL R. WHEELER, ON THE FEDERALIZATION OF THE ADMINISTRATION OF CIVIL AND CRIMINAL JUSTICE (Federal Judicial Center: 1994).

JAMES A. STRAZZELLA special ed., THE FEDERAL ROLE IN CRIMINAL LAW (Sage: 1996), also published in periodical form, 543 ANNALS AM. ACAD. POL. & SOC. SCI. 15 (1996) (Westlaw, 543 ANAMAPSS 9 *et seq.*). (Articles and comments from this volume are individually indexed in this Bibliography.)

SARAH WELLINGTON, SARA SUN BEALE & PAM H. BUCY, FEDERAL CRIMINAL LAW AND RELATED ACTIONS (Westgroup: 1998).

FRANKLIN E. ZIMRING & GORDON HAWKINS, CRIME IS NOT THE PROBLEM (Oxford Univ. Press: 1997) (exploring the view that what citizens mainly fear is not theft crimes, but the prospect of lethal violence).

APPENDIX B

TECHNICAL APPENDIX[1]

Section 1 Section 1 of this Appendix contains Charts 8, 9, 10, 11 described in this Report's text.

Section 2 Section 2 contains material related to this Report's textual discussion of the Task Force's study of the frequency of certain prosecutions.

Section 3 Section 3 contains data relating to the changing composition of the federal criminal caseload.

[1] Statistical work for the data contained in the Report and this Appendix was done by Dr. Barbara Meierhoefer.

Appendix B: Technical Appendix
Section 1

Charts 8, 9, 10, 11

Justice system direct and intergovernmental expenditures By level of government, United States, fiscal years 1982-93 (Dollar amounts in millions)
Source: Sourcebook of Criminal Justice Statistics, Table 1.1 available at www.albany.edu/sourcebook

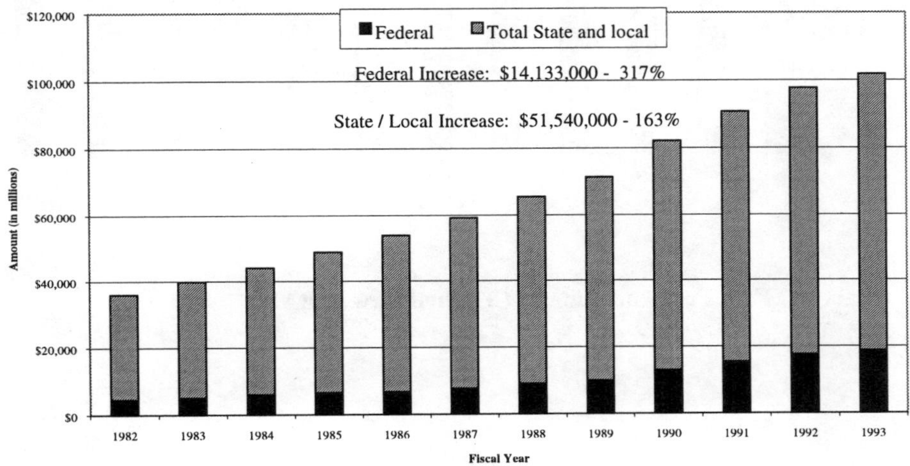

Chart 8. TF on Federalization of Criminal Law (ABA)

Justice system Personnel (Enforcement, Correctional, Judicial) By level of government, United States, fiscal years 1982-93

Source: Sourcebook of Criminal Justice Statistics, Table 1.1 available at www.albany.edu/sourcebook

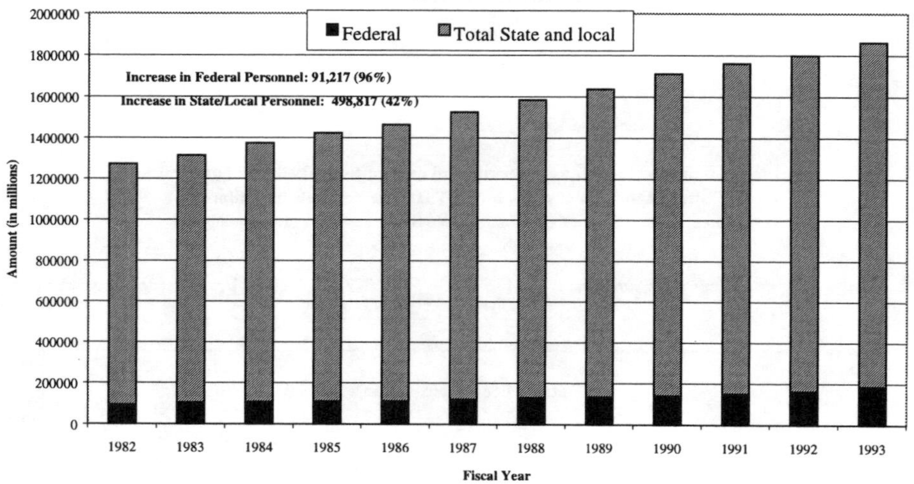

Chart 9. TF on Federalization of Criminal Law (ABA)

Persons held in prisons, 1985, 1990-1997

Source: Bureau of Justics Statistics Bulletin, "Prison and Jail Inmates at Midyear 1997," (U.S. Department of Justice Office of Justice Programs, January 1998)

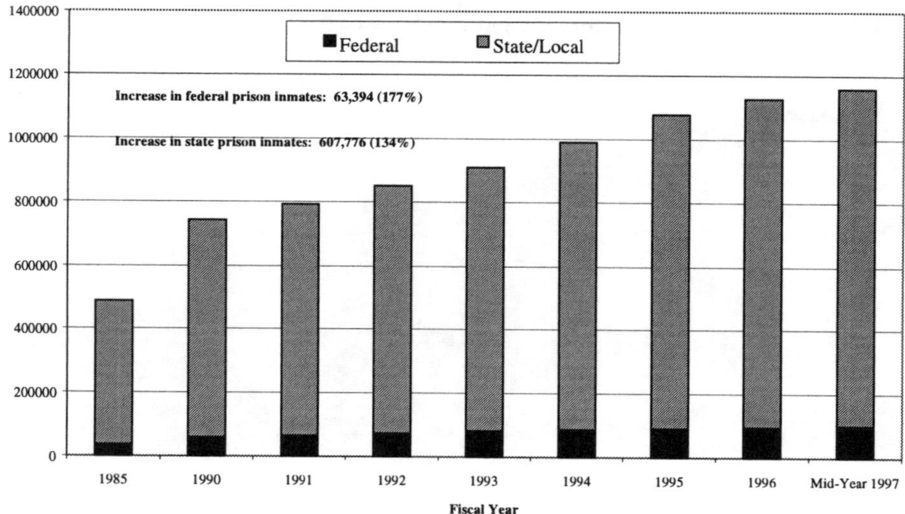

Chart 10. TF on Federalization of Criminal Law (ABA)

Federal Judges vs. All Federal Criminal Justice Personnel Between 1982 - 1993
Sources: Federal Court Management Statistics (judge data) and Sourcebook of Criminal Justice Statistics, Table 1.20

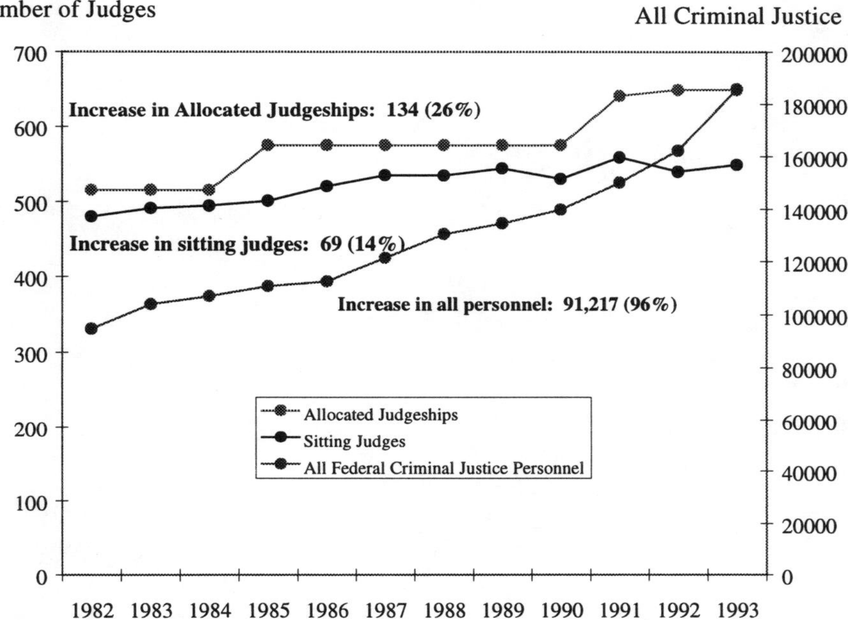

Chart 11. TF on Federalization of Criminal Law (ABA)

The number of sitting judges was computed by subtracting the number of vacant judge months in a particular year from the number of expected judge months (i.e., the number of allocated judgeships multiplied by 12) and dividing by 12.

Appendix B: Technical Appendix
Section 2

FREQUENCY OF FEDERAL CHARGES AND SENTENCINGS UNDER SELECTED STATUTES

Information from two data sources was used to assess how frequently federal statutes proscribing behavior historically prosecuted by state or local authorities were used in the charging and sentencing of federal defendants. (See Report, p. 19.) In the discussion and tables that follow, a case was counted as involving a particular charge if that charge was among any of those listed for the offender.

Selecting Statutes For Closer Examination

The statutes examined in more detail were selected from among those listed in the "Statutory Index" compiled by the United States Sentencing Commission.[2] This listing includes federal felonies and those misdemeanors which are newly enacted or were historically presented for federal sentencing with some frequency. The listing was annotated and reviewed with an eye to identifying examples of federal statutes which proscribe behaviors most commonly prosecuted by state or local authorities, particularly those that have been the subject of discussion in the federalization literature. (See Appendix C for the Task Force's annotated Statutory Index.) Eighteen (18) crimes were selected as examples of common rationales for federal intervention in areas historically under state or local control.

Data Sources Used For Examination

The Filing of Criminal Cases in the Federal Courts: The Federal Judicial Center made available for the Task Force project a subset of items contained in the federal courts criminal database for fiscal year 1997 (October 1, 1996 - September 30, 1997).[3] This is an automated data system which includes a record for each defendant and contains, among other things, information on district, date of filing, date of termination, disposition, and up to five of the statutes which were cited at filing in the

---

[2] Commission information is available online from the United States Sentencing Commission's home page at USSC.gov.

[3] This database, maintained by The Administrative Office of the United States Courts, contains information provided by Clerks of Court in the 94 federal districts.

indictment or information (i.e., the original charges). Where the charges involve more than five statutes, those which carry the longest maximum penalty are included in the database. This source contains information about the 59,242 cases filed during fiscal year 1997. There were an additional 7,088 filings (12%) that included at least one count indicating that federal jurisdiction was asserted under Indian territory, maritime, or assimilated state crime provisions (18 U.S.C. §§ 13, 113, 1152 or 1153). In view of the Task Force's specific inquiry, these cases were eliminated for purposes of counting the frequency of selected statutes.

The Sentencing of Federal Offenders: The United States Sentencing Commission provided a database to the Task Force that contains data from fiscal years 1992 through 1997.[4] In fiscal year 1997 (October 1, 1996 - September 30, 1997), information is available for the sentences imposed on 47,677 offenders. The file includes up to ten (10) statutory sections of conviction, listed in the order in which they appear on the Judgment of Conviction (rather than according to maximum potential sentence or any other way of assessing offense seriousness). The 655 cases which cited assimilated crimes, state, maritime, or territorial statutes were eliminated for purposes of counting the frequency of selected statutes.

Frequency of Use of Statutory Sections

Of the eighteen (18) crimes selected for examination, the following three (3) were never the object of a federal filing or sentence in FY 1997.

Failure to report child abuse (18 U.S.C. § 2258, enacted Nov. 29, 1990).

Murder by escaped prisoners (18 U.S.C. § 1120, enacted Sept. 13, 1994).

Odometer tampering (18 U.S.C. §§ 1983, 1984, enacted Oct. 15, 1970 - moved to 49 U.S.C. § 32703).

There were six (6) other of the selected offenses that were rarely the object of a federal filing or sentence. These are:

Animal enterprise terrorism (18 U.S.C. § 43, enacted Aug. 26, 1992). Three (3) cases were filed, all in CA-E; and one (1) was sentenced in DC.

---

4 Commission data with up to eight (8) statutory cites (and a wealth of additional information) are available through the internet at ICPSR@umich.edu.

Theft of livestock (18 U.S.C. § 667, enacted Oct. 12, 1984). One (1) case was filed in TX-N. There were no sentencings in FY 1997.

Drive-by shooting (18 U.S.C. § 36, enacted Sept. 13, 1994). There were no criminal filings and one (1) sentencing (in NM).

Interstate domestic violence (18 U.S.C. § 2261, enacted Sept. 13, 1994): Five (5) cases were sentenced during fiscal year 1997 (1 each in LA-M, TX-N, and UT; and 2 in NY-S). There were no criminal filings in FY 1997.

Endangering lives by the manufacture of drugs (21 U.S.C. § 858, enacted Nov. 18, 1988): One(1) case was sentenced in PA-E; and four (4) cases were filed, 1 each in GA-M and SC, and 2 in TN-W.

Obstruction of state or local law enforcement (18 U.S.C. § 1511, enacted Oct. 15, 1970). In fiscal year 1997, there were two (2) filings (1 each in OK-N and PA-M); and there were five (5) sentencings, (1 each in LA-E and PA-M, and 3 in OK-N).

The following statutes were more frequently the subject of a federal filing or sentence. These are:

Use or carrying of a firearm during a crime of violence or drug trafficking (18 U.S.C. § 924(c) or (j) [causes death through same])*	*FY '97 Cases Filed: 1,830* *FY '97 Offenders Sentenced: 1,305*
Simple possession of drugs (21 U.S.C. § 844, enacted Oct. 27, 1970)	*FY '97 Cases Filed: 1,104* *FY '97 Offenders Sentenced: 686*
Theft of motor vehicle by force, violence or intimidation with intent to cause death or serious bodily injury [Car Jacking] (18 U.S.C. § 2119, enacted Oct. 25, 1992)	*FY '97 Cases Filed: 164* *FY '97 Offenders Sentenced: 117*
Violation of Civil Rights (18 U.S.C. §§ 241 [conspiracy], 242 enacted Mar. 4, 1909, or 245(b) [under color of law], enacted Apr. 11, 1968)	*FY '97 Cases Filed: 107* *FY '97 Offenders Sentenced: 105*

* Section 924 was enacted June 19, 1968.

Transfer of a firearm with knowledge that it will be used in a crime (18 U.S.C. §924 (h))*

FY '97 Cases Filed: 58
FY '97 Offenders Sentenced: 8

Racketeering (18 U.S.C. §§ 1951, 1952 [travel or transportation in aid of], enacted Jun. 18, 1934, 1958 [murder for hire] enacted Sep. 13, 1961, 1959 [violent crimes in aid of] enacted Oct. 12, 1984)

FY '97 Cases Filed: 1,098
FY '97 Offenders Sentenced: 558

Racketeer Corrupt and Influenced Organizations (18 U.S.C. §§ 1962, 1963, enacted Oct. 15, 1970)

FY '97 Cases Filed: 236
FY '97 Offenders Sentenced: 279

Mail Fraud (18 U.S.C. §§ 1341, 1342, enacted Mar. 4, 1909)

FY '97 Cases Filed: 1,849
FY '97 Offenders Sentenced: 1,266

Wire Fraud (18 U.S.C. § 1343, enacted Jul. 16, 1952)

FY '97 Cases Filed: 998
FY '97 Offenders Sentenced: 715

---

* Section 924 was enacted June 19, 1968.

APPENDIX B
Section 3

CATEGORIZING PRIMARY OFFENSE TYPES

The Changing Nature of the Federal Criminal Caseload

The data to generate the Chart 6 snapshot graphs of the changing composition of the federal criminal caseload were taken from table D-4 of the Annual Report of the Director of the Administrative Office of the U.S. Courts for the years 1947, 1957, 1967, 1977, 1987, and 1997. The table displays the number of criminal defendants disposed of by type of disposition and offense during the fiscal year. For classification purposes, the "Nature of Offense" for defendants with multiple charges is determined by the charge carrying the highest maximum penalty.

Year # Terminated Defendants	**1947 38,180**	**1957 31,284**	**1967 31,020**	**1977 53,168**	**1987 54,103**	**1997 63,148**	**% Change in Actual Numbers**
Violence	**1.4%**	**2.3%**	**5.3%**	**7.8%**	**5.1%**	**5.1%**	**489%**
Homicide	0.0%	0.0%	0.2%	0.3%	0.3%	0.5%	Not a category in 1947
Robbery	0.3%	0.7%	2.6%	4.4%	2.5%	2.5%	1430%
Assault	0.2%	0.2%	0.9%	1.4%	1.3%	0.8%	783%
Burglary	0.3%	0.5%	0.9%	1.0%	0.2%	0.1%	-43%
Sexual Offenses	0.7%	0.9%	0.4%	0.4%	0.6%	0.9%	132%
Kidnapping	0.0%	0.0%	0.3%	0.3%	0.1%	0.2%	Not a category in 1947
Larceny/Theft	**26.0%**	**33.2%**	**39.5%**	**26.6%**	**17.1%**	**10.3%**	**-35%**
Larceny/Theft	5.2%	9.1%	8.6%	10.7%	7.4%	5.8%	84%
Embezzlement	1.8%	3.0%	4.3%	4.0%	4.2%	1.9%	74%
Auto Theft	13.1%	12.6%	16.6%	3.0%	0.7%	0.4%	-94%
Forgery	5.7%	8.1%	8.8%	7.3%	3.6%	0.4%	-87%
Counterfeiting	0.2%	0.4%	1.2%	1.5%	1.1%	1.7%	1022%
Fraud	4.6%	11.7%	8.3%	10.9%	16.4%	17.1%	514%
Drug Laws	4.9%	6.1%	7.3%	18.3%	28.0%	35.3%	1085%
Liquor	14.9%	19.5%	10.9%	0.4%	0.0%	0.0%	-100%
Drunk Driving & Traffic	0.0%	0.0%	0.2%	8.9%	14.6%	7.3%	Not a category in 1947

Weapons & Firearms	0.0%	0.0%	0.9%	5.9%	4.1%	5.3%	Not a category in 1947
Immigration Laws	18.5%	7.3%	10.7%	3.0%	4.4%	10.7%	-4%
"Federal Statutes:"*	26.4%	15.9%	14.4%	11.2%	5.8%	4.6%	-71%
Agriculture Acts	0.0%	0.0%	0.4%	0.7%	0.7%	0.5%	Not a category in 1947
Antitrust	1.1%	0.5%	0.2%	0.4%	0.2%	0.1%	-92%
Civil Rights	0.0%	0.0%	0.2%	0.2%	0.3%	0.2%	Not a category in 1947
Food and Drug	1.9%	1.2%	1.9%	0.3%	0.2%	0.1%	-90%
Migratory Bird	1.7%	2.3%	2.2%	1.5%	0.1%	0.0%	-96%
Motor Carrier Act	1.0%	1.1%	3.0%	0.2%	0.1%	0.0%	-97%
National Defense	12.9%	1.7%	3.7%	4.3%	0.0%	0.0%	-100%
Postal Laws	0.6%	0.7%	0.3%	1.8%	0.6%	0.3%	-25%
Other Federal Statutes*	7.4%	8.5%	2.5%	1.9%	3.5%	3.4%	-24%
Other	3.2%	4.0%	2.6%	7.1%	4.5%	4.4%	129%
Escape	0.5%	0.5%	1.1%	2.2%	1.4%	0.9%	185%
Extorting/ Racketeering	0.3%	0.4%	0.4%	1.3%	1.3%	1.8%	1015%
Gambling/ Lottery	0.2%	0.0%	0.5%	1.2%	0.4%	0.1%	-46%
Bribery	0.0%	0.0%	0.2%	0.6%	0.4%	0.3%	Not a category in 1947
Perjury	0.1%	0.2%	0.1%	0.4%	0.3%	0.3%	437%
Other General	2.1%	2.9%	0.3%	1.5%	0.7%	1.0%	-23%

* Notes:

The "Federal Statutes" category is a category used by the Administrative Office of the United States Courts in its reports to group criminal statutes that have no direct state or local counterpart. The category addresses crimes such as agriculture, antitrust, civil rights, food and drug, migratory bird, motor carriers, national defense, postal law, and others such as criminal acts committed by or against federal employees.

1545 (47) & 1559 (57) prosecutions under the Juvenile Delinquency Act. (Counted as "Other Federal Statutes.")

APPENDIX C

STATUTORY GRID

For the purposes discussed in the body of the Report, the Task Force assembled statutory information contained in this appendix. The appendix contains an annotated grid listing many, but not all, of the present federal criminal statutes and was devised early in the Task Force's work. The grid contains the statutory title, section, and (in many cases) subsections numbers of federal crimes, including both felonies and misdemeanors, with brief descriptive annotations added. It contains only statutory criminal provisions, and does not contain any regulations dealing with criminal acts.

The statutory section and subsection numbers in the grid came from one of two sources: (1) a selective U.S. Sentencing Commission list, devised by the Commission for use in connection with sentencing; and (2) a computer generated list devised by the Task Force.

The list generated by the Federal Sentencing Commission was obtained early in the Task Force's work. That list contained 778 section numbers, many of which were further divided into a list of subsections. Unless subsequently repealed, all the sections and subsections on that list were included in this appendix's grid. The statutory section numbers generated from the second source, a computer word search, were also included in the grid after eliminating subsequently repealed statutes and after a comparison that eliminated duplications with the Sentencing Commission list.[1]

The grid thus contains all the statute section numbers representing federal crime provisions on the Sentencing Commission's selective list at

---

[1] The computer search used the key words "fine" and "imprison" (including any variations of those words such as "imprisonment"). The computer search generated a list of nearly 1,500 section numbers. Of those section numbers, nearly 90 have now been repealed in whole or in part. Specific subsections were not identified by the computer search.

the time that list was obtained, complimented by the non-duplicative sections located through the computer search, with the exception of those statutes that have been repealed. Nevertheless, the grid does have limitations derived both from the fact that it was created for a limited purpose and from the fact that the computer search had practical limitations.[2] Given the Task Force's limited purpose in studying statutory provisions, it could not and did not undertake a section by section review of every printed federal statutory section. Such a massive review was unnecessary for our purposes.

Additional statutes were enacted after the grid was devised. We note that between 1996 and 1998, the last Congress (the 105th) passed a number of criminal statutes, adding more than a dozen criminal sections not included in the grid constructed for the Task Force's original study.[3]

---

[2] As performed, the Westlaw computer search did not produce a complete list of federal crimes. For example, if the penalty for the crime is not listed in the actual statute number, the section does not appear in the computer word search. (*E.g.,* 16 U.S.C. § 973c, dealing with South Pacific Tuna fishing, is a criminal offense but does not use the words "fine," "imprisonment," "sentence" or "penalty" anywhere in the statutory text; the penalty is contained in another statutory provision within the chapter.) For practical reasons, the search could be performed using only a limited number of key words ("fine" and "imprison," or their variations). Adding key words to the search (such as "unlawful," "prohibited," or "sentence") results in the retrieval of many unnecessary items and an unmanageable volume of information.

[3] *See* The Taxpayer Browsing Protection Act, Pub. L. 105-35, enacted August 5, 1997 (amends 26 U.S.C. § 7213 to prohibit the willful, unauthorized inspection of tax returns or tax return information by federal employees and other persons); The Veterans' Cemetery Protection Act of 1997, Pub. L. 105-101, enacted November 19, 1997 (amends 18 U.S.C. § 91 to provide criminal penalties for theft and willful vandalism at national cemeteries); The No Electronic Theft (NET) Act, Pub. L. 105-147, enacted December 16, 1997 (amends 17 U.S.C. § 506(a) to provide for enhanced criminal punishments for willful infringement of copyrights); The Telemarketing Fraud Prevention Act of 1998, Pub. L. 105-184, enacted June 23, 1998 (amends 18 U.S.C. § 982 to provide for forfeiture of any real or personal property used or intended to be used to commit commission of telemarketing fraud, or constituting or derived from gross proceeds obtained through telemarketing fraud, and amends 18 U.S.C. § 2326 to add a conspiracy offense); The Deadbeat Parents Punishment Act of 1998, Pub. L. 105-187, enacted June 24, 1998 (amends 18 U.S.C. § 228 to provide prison terms of up to two years for any person who fails to pay certain child support obligations, or travels in interstate or foreign commerce to evade certain child support obligations, and also

As noted elsewhere in the Report (pp. 9-10), an exact count of the present "number" of federal crimes contained in the statutes (let alone those contained in administrative regulations) is difficult to achieve and the count subject to varying interpretations. In part, the reason is not only that the criminal provisions are now so numerous and their location in the books so scattered, but also that federal criminal statutes are often complex. One statutory section can comprehend a variety of actions, potentially multiplying the number of federal "crimes" that could be enumerated. (For example, the language of 18 U.S.C. § 2113 encompasses bank robbery, extortion, theft, assaults, killing hostages, and storing or selling anything of value knowing it to have been taken from a bank, etc.) Depending on how all this subdivisible and dispersed law is counted, the true number of federal crimes multiplies.

---

provides for mandatory restitution); The IRS Restructuring and Reform Act of 1998, Pub. L. 105-206, enacted July 22, 1998, containing several distinct criminal offenses (prohibits certain issuances of summons to produce or analyze any tax-related computer software source code, and sets penalties for persons who willfully divulge or make known software to any person in violation of act) (prohibits, with exceptions, any executive branch official from requesting the IRS to conduct or terminate an audit or other investigation of any particular taxpayer with respect to the tax liability of such taxpayer, mandates certain persons to report receipt of such a request, and sets penalties for violations); The Higher Education Amendments of 1998, Pub. L. 105-244, enacted October 7, 1998 (§ 517 of act provides penalties for whoever, being an officer director, agent or employee of, or connected in any capacity with, any recipient of federal financial assistance or grant pursuant to the title, embezzles, willfully misapplies, steals or obtains by fraud any of the funds that are the subject of such grant or assistance); The Digital Millennium Copyright Act, Pub. L.105-304, enacted Oct. 28, 1998 (amends 17 U.S.C. to implement the World Intellectual Property Organization (WIPO) Copyright Treaty and Performance and Phonograms Treaty; Section 1204 sets penalties for anyone who violates certain sections of the act willfully and for purposes of commercial advantage or private financial gain); The Identity Theft and Assumption Deterrence Act of 1998, Pub. L. 105-318, enacted October 30, 1998 (amends 18 U.S.C. § 1028(b)(3) to provide penalties for production, possession or transfer of false identification document when committed in connection with a crime of violence or after a prior conviction, and amends 18 U.S.C. § 1028 to add an "attempt and conspiracy" offense); The Migratory Bird Treaty Reform Act of 1998, Pub. L. 105-312, enacted October 30, 1998 (sets penalties for anyone who violates amended § 3(b)(2) of the Migratory Bird Treaty Act and prohibits baiting of migratory birds).

This abbreviated list of activity in the last few years excludes statutory actions that dealt solely with sentencing enhancements and statutes that dealt solely with what are considered to be civil sanctions (e.g., forfeitures).

While a figure of "approximately 3,000 federal crimes" is frequently cited, that helpful estimate is now surely outdated by the large number of new federal crimes enacted in the 16 years or so years intervening since its estimation. The present number of federal crimes is unquestionably larger.

The approximate 3,000 figure is traceable to a January 1989 *Report to the Attorney General on Federal Criminal Code Reform.* The Task Force is informed that the estimate was culled from House of Representative committee documents as well as a review by the Department of Justice's Office of Legal Policy undertaken in the early 1980s and reported in 1983. That DOJ review focused on types of activity prohibited by then-existing statutory provisions. The 1989 report is reprinted as Ronald L. Gainer, *Report to the Attorney General on Federal Criminal Code Reform*, 1 CRIM. L. FORUM 99 (1989). Further discussion of related issues by the same author appears in Gainer, *Federal Criminal Code Reform: Past and Future*, 2 BUFF. CRIM. L. REV. 46 (1998). Speaking of the situation existing today, the author notes: "The federal statutory law today is set forth in the 50 titles of the United States Code. Those 50 titles encompass roughly 27,000 pages of printed text. Within those 27,000 pages, there appear approximately 3,300 separate provisions that carry criminal sanctions for their violation. Over 1,200 of those provisions are found jumbled together in Title 18, euphemistically referred to as the 'Federal Criminal Code,' and the remainder are found scattered throughout the other 49 titles. The judicial interpretations of those provisions, which are necessary for their understanding, are found within the printed volumes reporting the opinions issued by judges in federal cases — volumes which now total over 2,800 and which contain approximately 4,000,000 printed pages." *Id.* at 53.

Title & Section Numbers	Caption of Section (Chapter Headings)	Relates to any persons(s) who...
2 USC 167g	Prosecution and punishment of offenses in Library buildings and grounds (The Congress).	violates any provision of sections 167a to 167e of this title.
2 USC 192	Refusal of witness to testify or produce papers (The Congress).	
2 USC 390	Penalty for failure to appear, testify, or produce documents (The Congress).	
4 USC 3	Use of flag for advertising purposes; mutilation of flag.	
7 USC 6	Restriction of futures trading and foreign transactions.	
7 USC 6b(a)	Contracts designed to defraud, or mislead; bucketing orders (Commodity Exchanges).	cheats or defrauds or attempts to cheat or defraud such other persons or makes or causes to be made by such other person, any false report or statement thereof, or willfully enters or causes to be entered for such person any false record thereof.
7 USC 6b(b)	Buying and selling orders for commodities (Commodity Exchanges).	
7 USC 6c	Prohibited transactions (Commodity Exchanges).	
7 USC 6h	False self-representation as contract market member prohibited (Commodity Exchanges).	
7 USC 6o	Fraud and misrepresentation by commodity trading advisors, commodity pool operators, and associated persons (Commodity Exchanges).	

Title & Section Numbers	Caption of Section (Chapter Headings)	Relates to any persons(s) who...
7 USC 13(a)(1)	Felonies generally (Commodity Exchanges).	embezzles, steals, purloins, or with criminal intent, converts to such person's use any money, securities, or property in excess of a specified amount, and is registered under this chapter, or is any employee or agent thereof.
7 USC 13(a)(2)	Felonies generally (Commodity Exchanges).	manipulates or attempts to manipulate the price of any commodity in interstate commerce, or for future delivery on or subject to the rules of any contract market or to corner or attempt to corner any such commodity or knowingly delivers or causes to be delivered for transmission through the mails or interstate commerce by telegraph, telephone, wireless, or other means of communication false or misleading or knowingly inaccurate reports concerning crop or market information or conditions that affect or tend to affect the price of any commodity in interstate commerce.
7 USC 13(a)(3)	Felonies generally (Commodity Exchanges).	makes, or causes to be made, any false or misleading statement in any application, report, or document required to be filed under this chapter or any rule or regulation thereunder or any undertaking contained in a registration statement required under this chapter.
7 USC 13(a)(4)	Felonies generally (Commodity Exchanges).	willfully to falsify, conceal, or cover up by any trick, scheme, or artifice, a material fact, makes any false, fictitious, or fraudulent statements or representations.
7 USC 13(c)	Transactions by Commissioners and Commission employees prohibited (Commodity Exchanges).	
7 USC 13(d)	Use of information by Commissioners and Commission employees prohibited (Commodity Exchanges).	
7 USC 13(f)	Insider trading prohibited (Commodity Exchanges).	

Title & Section Numbers	Caption of Section (Chapter Headings)	Relates to any persons(s) who...
7 USC 13a	Nonenforcement of rules of government or other violations; cease and desist orders; fines and penalties; imprisonment; misdemeanor; separate offenses (Commodity Exchanges).	
7 USC 13b	Manipulations or other violations; cease and desist orders against persons other than contract markets; punishment; misdemeanor or felony; separate offenses (Commodity Exchanges).	
7 USC 15b	Cotton futures contracts.	knowingly violates any regulation made in pursuance of this section.
7 USC 23	Standardized contracts for certain commodities.	
7 USC 60	Penalties for violations (Cotton Futures).	knowingly violates any provision of sections 52 or 59 of this title.
7 USC 87b	Prohibited acts (Grain Standards).	
7 USC 87c	Criminal penalties (Grain Standards).	
7 USC 87f	Enforcement provisions (Grain Standards).	
7 USC 96	Punishment for violation of prohibition (Naval Stores).	willfully violates any provision of section 95 of this title, dealing with prohibition of acts deemed injurious to commerce in naval stores.
7 USC 136	Definitions (Environmental Pesticide Control).	
7 USC 136h	Protection of trade secrets and other information (Environmental Pesticide Control).	

Title & Section Numbers	Caption of Section (Chapter Headings)	Relates to any persons(s) who...
7 USC 136j	Unlawful acts (Environmental Pesticide Control).	distributes or sells to any person any pesticide that is not registered under section 136a of this title or whose registration has been canceled or suspended, except to the extent that distribution or sale has been authorized by the Administrator under this subchapter.
7 USC 136k	Stop sale, use, removal, and seizure (Environmental Pesticide Control).	
7 USC 136l	Penalties (Environmental Pesticide Control).	
7 USC 149	Regulation, cleaning, etc., of vehicles and materials entering the U.S. (Insect Pests Generally).	
7 USC 150bb	Movement of pests prohibited.	
7 USC 150gg	Violations (Plant Pests).	
7 USC 154	Importation of nursery stock.	
7 USC 156	Notification of arrival at port of entry; forwarding without notification forbidden; inspection before shipment.	
7 USC 157	Marking packages, etc., for entry.	
7 USC 158	Marking packages, etc., for interstate shipment; inspection.	
7 USC 161	Interstate quarantine; shipments or removals from quarantined localities forbidden; regulations by Secretary for shipment, etc., from quarantined localities; promulgation.	
7 USC 163	Violations; forgery, alterations, etc., of certificates; punishment; civil penalty.	

Title & Section Numbers	Caption of Section (Chapter Headings)	Relates to any persons(s) who...
7 USC 499n	Inspection of perishable agricultural commodities.	
7 USC 503	Reports, necessity; by whom made; penalties (Tobacco Statistics).	refuses or willfully neglects to furnish any information required by this chapter or willfully gives answers that are false or misleading.
7 USC 511d	Designation of markets; manner; inspection and related services; fees and charges (Tobacco Inspection).	
7 USC 511i	Offenses (Tobacco Inspection).	
7 USC 511k	Penalty for violations (Tobacco Statistics).	
7 USC 608d	Books and records; disclosure of information; notification of Congressional committees (Commodity Benefits).	
7 USC 610(g)	Officers; dealing or speculating in agricultural products; penalties.	while acting in any official capacity in the administration of this chapter, speculate, directly or indirectly, in any agricultural commodity or product to which this chapter applies, or in contracts relating thereto, or in the stock or membership interest of any association or corporation engaged in handling, processing, or disposing of any such commodity or product.
7 USC 615	Refunds of tax; exemptions from tax; compensating tax; compensating tax on foreign goods; covering into Treasury (Commodity Benefits).	with intent to defraud forges, makes, alters, or counterfeits any taxpayment warrant or any stamp, tag, or other means of indentification provided for by this chapter.
7 USC 620	Falsely ascribing deductions or charges to taxes; penalty (Commodity Benefits).	
7 USC 953	Reports; by whom made; penalties (Peanut Statistics).	

Title & Section Numbers	Caption of Section (Chapter Headings)	Relates to any persons(s) who...
7 USC 195	Punishment for violation of order (Packers Generally).	fails to obey any order of the Secretary issued under the provision of section 193 of this title and is a packer, officer, director, agent, or employee of a packer.
7 USC 207	Schedule of rates (Packers Generally).	fails to comply with the provisions of this section or of any regulation or order of the Secretary made thereunder.
7 USC 221	Accounts and records of business; punishment for failure to keep (Live Poultry Dealers and Handlers).	
7 USC 270	Punishment for violations; reimbursement of owner of products converted (Warehouses).	
7 USC 281	Honeybee importation.	[Authorizing the Secretary of Agriculture to prohibit or restrict the importation or entry of honeybees and honeybee semen into or through the U.S. in order to prevent the introduction and spread of diseases and parasites harmful to honeybees.]
7 USC 282	Punishment for unlawful importation (Honeybees).	
7 USC 472	Information furnished of confidential character; penalty for divulging information (Cotton Statistics and Estimates).	as an employee of the Department of Agriculture, publishes or communicates any information placed in employee's possession by reason of employment.
7 USC 473c-1	Offenses in relation to sampling of cotton for classification.	knowingly samples cotton improperly, or identifies cotton samples improperly, or accepts money or other consideration, directly or indirectly for any neglect or improper performance of duty as a sampler.
7 USC 473c-2	Penalties for offenses relating to sampling of cotton.	
7 USC 491	Destruction or dumping of farm produce received in interstate commerce by commission merchants; penalty.	

Title & Section Numbers	Caption of Section (Chapter Headings)	Relates to any persons(s) who...
7 USC 1314g	Submission of purchase intentions by cigarette manufacturers (Loans, Parity Payments, Consumer Safeguards, Marketing Quotas, and Marketing Certificates).	being an officer or employee of the Department of Agriculture, violates this subsection.
7 USC 1379i	Penalties (Wheat Marketing Allocation).	
7 USC 1471j	Penalties (Emergency Livestock Feed Assistance Act of 1988).	
7 USC 1986	Conflicts of interest (Administrative Provisions).	
7 USC 2018(c)	Approval of retail food stores and wholesale food concerns - Information submitted by applicants; safeguards; disclosure to and use by state agencies.	
7 USC 2024	Violations and enforcement (Food Stamp Program).	
7 USC 2028	Puerto Rico block grant (Food Stamp Program).	knowingly and willfully embezzles, misapplies, steals, or obtains by fraud, false statement, or forgery, any funds, assets, or property provided or financed under this section.
7 USC 2146	Administration and enforcement by Secretary (Transportation, Sale, and Handling of Certain Animals).	forcibly assaults, resists, opposes, impedes, intimidates, or interferes with any person while engaged in or on account of the performance of his official duties under this chapter.
7 USC 2149	Violations by licensees (Transportation, Sale, and Handling of Certain Animals).	being a dealer, exhibitor, or operator of an auction sale subject to section 2142 of this title, knowingly violates any provision of this chapter.
7 USC 2156	Animal fighting venture prohibition (Transportation, Sale, and Handling of Certain Animals).	[Section relates to sponsoring or exhibiting animal in any fighting venture; buying, selling, delivering, or transporting animals for participation in animal fighting venture; use of Postal Service or other interstate instrumentality for promoting or furthering animal fighting venture.]

Title & Section Numbers	Caption of Section (Chapter Headings)	Relates to any persons(s) who...
7 USC 2157	Release of trade secrets (Transportation, Sale, and Handling of Certain Animals).	[Section prohibits release of confidential information; prohibits wrongful use of confidential information.]
7 USC 2276	Confidentiality of information (Department of Agriculture).	publishes, causes to be published, or otherwise publicly releases information collected pursuant to a provision of law referred to in subsection (d) of this section.
7 USC 2619	Assessments (Potato Research and Promotion).	[Section relates to confidential information; disclosure during proceedings; prohibition inapplicable to general statements and publication of violations; penalties; removal from office.]
7 USC 2706	Permissive terms and conditions in order (Egg Research and Consumer Information).	
7 USC 2807	Penalties (Noxious Weeds).	knowingly violates section 2803 or 2804 of this title, or any regulation promulgated under this chapter.
7 USC 2904	Required terms in orders (Beef Research and Information).	
7 USC 3404	Permissive terms and conditions of orders (Wheat and Wheat Foods Research and Nutrition Education).	
7 USC 3806	Criminal penalties (Swine Health Protection).	
7 USC 4004	Food bank special nutrition projects (Agricultural Trade Suspension Adjustment).	receives any remuneration in exchange for food provided under this section.
7 USC 4307	Permissive terms in orders (Floral Research and Consumer Information).	
7 USC 4534	Required terms of order; agreements under order; records (Dairy Research Program).	

Title & Section Numbers	Caption of Section (Chapter Headings)	Relates to any persons(s) who...
7 USC 4810	Permissive provisions (Pork Promotion, Research, and Consumer Information).	
7 USC 4908	Assessment procedures (Watermelon Research and Promotion).	
7 USC 5712	Export reporting and contract sanctity.	knowingly fails to make any report required under this section.
7 USC 6005	Required terms in plans (Pecan Promotion and Research).	
7 USC 6104	Required terms in orders (Mushroom Promotion, Research, and Consumer Information).	
7 USC 6304	Required terms in orders (Soybean Promotion, Research, and Consumer Information).	
7 USC 6407	Required terms in orders (Processor-Funded Milk Promotion Program).	
7 USC 6810	Confidentiality (Fresh Cut Flowers and Fresh Cut Greens Promotion and Information).	[Prohibits making public information on how a person voted in a referendum conducted under this chapter.]
7 USC 7104	Required terms in orders (Sheep Promotion, Research, and Information).	
7 USC 7414	Required terms in orders (Issuance of Orders for Promotion, Research, and Information Activities Regarding Agricultural Commodities).	
7 USC 7444	Required terms in orders (Canola and Rapeseed).	
7 USC 7465	Required terms in orders (Kiwifruit).	
7 USC 7484	Required terms in orders (Popcorn).	

Title & Section Numbers	Caption of Section (Chapter Headings)	Relates to any persons(s) who...
8 USC 1160(b)(7)(a)	Special agricultural workers.	[Pertains to criminal penalties for false statements in application.]
8 USC 1185(a)(1)	Travel control of citizens and aliens - Restrictions and prohibitions.	[Making it unlawful for any alien to depart from or enter or attempt to depart from or enter the U.S. except under such reasonable rules, regulations, and orders, subject to such limitations and exceptions as the President may prescribe.]
8 USC 1185(a)(2)	Travel control of citizens and aliens - Restrictions and prohibitions.	transports or attempts to transport from or into the U.S. another person with knowledge or reasonable cause to believe that the departure or entry of such other person is forbidden by this section.
8 USC 1185(a)(3)	Travel control of citizens and aliens - Restrictions and prohibitions.	knowingly makes any false statement in an application for permission to depart from or enter the U.S. with intent to induce or secure the granting of such permission either for himself or for another.
8 USC 1185(a)(4)	Travel control of citizens and aliens - Restrictions and prohibitions.	knowingly furnishes or attempts to furnish or assists in furnishing to another, permit or evidence of permission to depart or enter not issued and designed for such other person's use.
8 USC 1185(a)(5)	Travel control of citizens and aliens - Restrictions and prohibitions.	knowingly uses or attempts to use any permit or evidence of permission to depart or enter not issued and designed for his use.
8 USC 1252(e)	Apprehension and deportation of aliens - Penalty for willful failure to depart; suspension of sentence.	
8 USC 1253	Penalties related to removal (Aliens and Nationality - Deportation; Adjustment of Status).	

Title & Section Numbers	Caption of Section (Chapter Headings)	Relates to any persons(s) who...
8 USC 1255a	Adjustment of status of certain entrants before January 1, 1982, to that of person admitted for lawful residence.	files an application for adjustment of status under this section and knowingly and willfully falsifies, misrepresents, conceals, or covers up a material fact or makes any false, fictitious, or fraudulent statements or representations.
8 USC 1282	Conditional permits to land temporarily (Special Provisions Relating to Alien Crewmen).	being an alien crewman, willfully remains in the United States in excess of the number of days allowed in any conditional permit issued under subsection (a) of this section.
8 USC 1304	Forms for registration and fingerprinting (Registration of Aliens).	
8 USC 1306	Penalties (Registration of Aliens).	[Relating to willful failure to register; failure to notify change of address; fraudulent statements; counterfeiting.]
8 USC 1324(a)	Criminal penalties - Bringing in and harboring certain aliens.	
8 USC 1324a	Unlawful employment of aliens.	
8 USC 1324c	Penalties for document fraud (Aliens and Nationality).	
8 USC 1325(a)	Improper entry by alien - Improper time or place; avoidance of examination or inspection; misrepresentation and concealment of facts.	
8 USC 1325(c)	Improper entry by alien - Marriage fraud.	knowingly enters into a marriage for the purpose of evading any provision of the immigration laws.
8 USC 1326	Reentry of deported alien; criminal penalties for reentry of certain deported aliens.	
8 USC 1327	Aiding or assisting certain aliens to enter.	

Title & Section Numbers	Caption of Section (Chapter Headings)	Relates to any persons(s) who...
8 USC 1328	Importation of alien for immoral purpose.	imports into the U.S. any alien for the purpose of prostitution, or for any other immoral purpose.
10 USC 847	Refusal to appear or testify (Armed Forces - Trial Procedure).	
10 USC 976	Membership in military unions, organizing of military unions, and recognition of military unions prohibited (Armed Forces).	
12 USC 95	Emergency limitations and restrictions on business of members of Federal reserve system; designation of legal holiday for national banking associations; exceptions; "State" defined (Banks and Banking).	
12 USC 95a	Regulation of transactions in foreign exchange of gold and silver; property transfers; vested interests, enforcement and penalties (Banks and Banking).	
12 USC 378	Dealers in securities engaging in banking business; individuals or associations engaging in banking business; examinations and reports; penalties (Banks and Banking).	
12 USC 617	Engaging in commerce or trade in commodities; price fixing; forfeiture of charter; acts forbidden to directors, officers, agents or employees (Banks and Banking).	
12 USC 630	Offenses by officers of corporation; punishment (Banks and Banking).	

Title & Section Numbers	Caption of Section (Chapter Headings)	Relates to any persons(s) who...
12 USC 631	False representations as to liability of U.S. for acts of corporation; punishment (Foreign Banking).	
12 USC 1141j	Miscellaneous provisions (Agricultural Marketing).	being a director, officer, employee, or member or person acting on behalf of any such association, corporation, or committee, to which or to whom information has been imparted in confidence by the administration, to disclose such information in violation of any regulation of the administration.
12 USC 1457	Prohibited activities; penalties for violations by organizations, officers and members of organizations, and individuals (Federal Home Loan Mortgage Corporation).	
12 USC 1467a	Regulations of holding companies (Federal Savings Associations).	
12 USC 1709-2	Equity skimming; penalty; persons liable; one dwelling exception (Mortgage Insurance).	
12 USC 1715z-19	Equity skimming penalty (Mortgage Insurance).	
12 USC 1785	Requirements governing insured credit insurance (Share Insurance).	
12 USC 1786	Termination of insured credit union status; cease and desist orders; removal or suspension from office; procedure (Share Insurance).	[Section relates to criminal penalty for violation of certain orders.]
12 USC 1818	Termination of status as an insured depository institution (Federal Deposit Insurance Corporation).	being subject to an order in effect under subsection (e) or (g) of this section, knowingly participates, directly or indirectly, in any manner in the conduct of the affairs of any insured depository institution.
12 USC 1829	Penalty for unauthorized participation by convicted individual (Federal Deposit Insurance Corporation).	

Title & Section Numbers	Caption of Section (Chapter Headings)	Relates to any persons(s) who...
12 USC 1847	Penalties (Bank Holding Companies).	knowingly violates any provision of this chapter or, being a company, violates any regulation or order issued by the Board under this chapter.
12 USC 1956	Criminal penalty (Financial Recordkeeping).	willfully violates any regulation under this chapter.
12 USC 1957	Additional criminal penalties in certain cases (Financial Recordkeeping).	willfully violates any regulation under this chapter, section 1829b of this title, or section 1730d of this title, where the violation is committed in furtherance of the commission of any violation of Federal law punishable by imprisonment for more than one year.
12 USC 2269	Further penalties (Enforcement Powers of Farm Credit Administration).	
12 USC 2277a-14	Prohibitions (Farm Credit System Insurance Corporation).	
12 USC 2607	Prohibition against kickbacks and unearned fees (Real Estate Settlement Procedures).	
12 USC 3108	Regulation and enforcement (Foreign Bank Participation in Domestic Markets).	willfully refuses or fails to attend and testify or to answer any lawful inquiry or to produce books, papers, correspondence, memoranda, contracts, agreements, or other records in accordance with any subpoena under this subsection.
12 USC 3111	Criminal penalty (Foreign Bank Participation in Domestic Markets).	with intent to deceive, to gain financially, or to cause financial gain or loss to any person, knowingly violates any provision of this chapter or any regulation or order issued by the appropriate Federal banking agency under this chapter.

Title & Section Numbers	Caption of Section (Chapter Headings)	Relates to any persons(s) who...
13 USC 211	Receiving or securing compensation for appointment of employees (Census).	receives or secures to himself any fee, reward, or compensation as a consideration for the appointment of any person as supervisor, enumerator, clerk, or other officer or employee of the Department of Commerce.
13 USC 213	False statements, certificates, and information (Census).	being an officer or employee referred to in subchapter II of chapter 1 of this title, willfully and knowingly swears or affirms falsely as to the truth of any statement required to be made or subscribed by him under oath by or under authority of this title.
13 USC 214	Wrongful disclosure of information (Census).	
13 USC 221	Refusal or neglect to answer questions; false answers (Census).	
13 USC 222	Giving suggestions or information with intent to cause inaccurate enumeration of population (Census).	
13 USC 224	Failure to answer questions affecting companies, businesses, religious bodies, and other organizations; false answers (Census).	
14 USC 638	Coast Guard ensigns and pennants.	[Section pertains to vessels or aircraft without authority carry, hoist, or display any ensign, pennant, or other identifying insignia prescribed for, or intended to resemble, any ensign, pennant, or other identifying insignia prescribed for Coast Guard vessels or aircraft.]
14 USC 639	Penalty for unauthorized use of words "Coast Guard".	
15 USC 1	Trusts, etc., in restraint of trade illegal; penalty.	

Title & Section Numbers	Caption of Section (Chapter Headings)	Relates to any persons(s) who...
15 USC 2	Monopolizing trade a felony; penalty.	
15 USC 3	Trusts in Territories or District of Columbia illegal; combination a felony.	
15 USC 8	Trusts in restraint of import trade illegal; penalty.	
15 USC 13a	Discrimination in rebates, discounts, or advertising service charges; underselling in particular localities; penalty.	
15 USC 24	Liability of directors and agents of corporation (Commerce and Trade).	
15 USC 50	Offenses and penalties (Federal Trade Commission).	
15 USC 54	False advertisements; penalty (Federal Trade Commission).	
15 USC 68h	Criminal penalty (Labeling of Wool Products).	willfully violates section 68a, 68c, 68f, or 68g(b) of this title.
15 USC 69i	Criminal penalty (Labeling of Fur Products).	willfully violates section 69a, 69d, or 69h(b) of this title.
15 USC 70i	Criminal penalty (Textile Fiber Products Identification).	willfully does an act which by section 70a, 70c, 70d, 70g, or 70h(b) or this title is declared to be unlawful.
15 USC 72	Importation or sale of articles at less than market value or wholesale price (Prevention of Unfair Methods of Competition).	
15 USC 76	Retaliation against restriction of importations in time of war (Prevention of Unfair Methods of Competition).	
15 USC 77	Discrimination against neutral Americans in time of war (Prevention of Unfair Methods of Competition).	

Title & Section Numbers	Caption of Section (Chapter Headings)	Relates to any persons(s) who...
15 USC 77e	Prohibitions relating to interstate commerce and the mails.	[Section pertains to sale or delivery after sale of unregistered securities; necessity or prospectus meeting requirements of section 77j of this title; necessity of filing registration statement.]
15 USC 77q	Fraudulent interstate transactions.	[Making it unlawful for any person in the offer or sale of any securities by the use of any means or instruments of transportation or communication in interstate commerce or by the use of the mails, directly or indirectly to employ any device, scheme, or artifice to defraud, or obtain money or property by means of any untrue statement of a material fact or any omission to state a material fact necessary to make the statements made not misleading.]
15 USC 77x	Penalties (Domestic Securities).	willfully violates any of the provisions of this subchapter.
15 USC 77yyy	Penalties (Trust Indentures).	willfully violates any provision of this subchapter or any rule, regulation, or order thereunder, or willfully, in any application, report, or document filed or required to be filed under the provisions of this subchapter or any rule, regulation, or order thereunder, makes any untrue statement of a material fact.
15 USC 78j	Manipulative and deceptive devices (Securities Exchange).	[Making it unlawful for any person to (a) effect a short sale, or to use or employ any stop-loss order in connection with the purchase or sale, of any security registered on a national securities exchange, in contravention of such rules and regulations as the Commission may prescribe or (b) use or employ, in connection with the purchase or sale of any security registered on a national securities exchange or any security not so registered, any manipulative or deceptive device or contrivance in contravention of such rules and regulations as the Commission may prescribe as necessary or appropriate in the public interest or for the protection of investors.]

Title & Section Numbers	Caption of Section (Chapter Headings)	Relates to any persons(s) who...
15 USC 78u	Investigations and actions (Securities Exchanges).	without just cause, fail or refuse to attend and testify or to answer any lawful inquiry or to produce books, papers, correspondence, memoranda, and other records, if in his power to do so, in obedience to the subpena of the Commission.
15 USC 78dd-1	Prohibited foreign corrupt practices by issuers (Securities Exchange).	
15 USC 78dd-2	Prohibited foreign corrupt practices by domestic concerns (Securities Exchange).	
15 USC 78ff	Penalties (Securities Exchange).	[Section pertains to willful violations; false and misleading statements; failure to file information, documents, or reports; violations by issuers, officers, directors, stockholders, employees, or agents of issuers.]
15 USC 78jjj	Prohibited acts (Securities Investor Protection).	[Section pertains to failure to pay assessment, etc.; engaging in business after appointment of trustee or initiation of direct payment procedure; concealment of assets; false statements or claims.]
15 USC 79r	Investigations, injunctions, and enforcement of law (Public Utility Holding Companies).	without just cause, fail or refuse to attend and testify or to answer any lawful inquiry or to produce books, papers, correspondence, memoranda, and other records, if in his power to do so, in obedience to the subpena of the Commission.
15 USC 79z-3	Penalties (Public Utility Holding Companies).	willfully violates any provision of this chapter or willfully makes any statement or entry in any application, report, document, account, or record filed or kept or required to be filed or kept under the provisions of this chapter.

Title & Section Numbers	Caption of Section (Chapter Headings)	Relates to any persons(s) who...
15 USC 80a-41	Enforcement of subchapter (Investment Companies).	without just cause, fail or refuse to attend and testify or to answer any lawful inquiry or to produce books, papers, correspondence, memoranda, and other records, if in his power to do so, in obedience to the subpena of the Commission.
15 USC 80a-48	Penalties (Investment Companies).	violates any provision of this subchapter or of any rule, regulation, or order hereunder, or willfully in any registration statement, application, report, account, record, or other document filed or transmitted pursuant to this subchapter.
15 USC 80b-6	Prohibited transactions by investment advisers.	
15 USC 80b-9	Enforcement of subchapter (Investment Advisers).	without just cause, fail or refuse to attend and testify or to answer any lawful inquiry or to produce books, papers, correspondence, memoranda, and other records, if in his power to do so, in obedience to the subpena of the Commission.
15 USC 80b-17	Penalties (Investment Advisers).	willfully violates any provision of this subchapter, or any rule, regulation, or order promulgated by the Commission under authority thereof.
15 USC 158	False or fraudulent statements prohibited; penalties (China Trade).	[Providing no stockholder, director, officer, employee, or agent of a China Trade Act corporation shall make, issue, or publish any statement, written or oral, or advertisement in any form, as to the value or as to the facts affecting the value of stocks, bonds, or other evidence of debt, or as to the financial condition or transactions, or facts affecting such condition or transactions, whenever he knows or has reason to believe that any material representation in such statement or advertisement is false.]

Title & Section Numbers	Caption of Section (Chapter Headings)	Relates to any persons(s) who...
15 USC 235	Sale or shipment of barrel of less capacity than standard; punishment (Standard Barrels).	sell, offer, or expose for sale in any State, Territory, or the District of Columbia, or to ship from any State, Territory, or the District of Columbia to any other State, Territory, or the District of Columbia or to a foreign country, a barrel containing fruits or vegetables or any other dry commodity of less capacity than the standard barrels defined in section 234 of this title.
15 USC 293	Penalty for infraction (Falsely Stamped Gold or Silver Goods Manufactured Therefrom).	
15 USC 298	Violations of law (Falsely Stamped Gold or Silver Goods Manufactured Therefrom).	
15 USC 377	Penalties (Collection of State Cigarette Taxes).	
15 USC 645(a)	False statements; overvaluation of securities (Aid to Small Business).	
15 USC 645(b)	Embezzlement, etc. (Aid to Small Business).	
15 USC 645(c)	Concealment, etc. (Aid to Small Business).	with intent to defraud, knowingly conceals, removes, disposes of, or converts to his own use or to that of another, any property mortgaged, pledged to, or held by, the Administration.
15 USC 714m(a)	False statements; overvaluation of securities (Commodity Credit Corp.).	
15 USC 714m(b)	Embezzlement, etc.; false entries; fraudulent issue of obligations of corporation (Commodity Credit Corp.).	
15 USC 714m(c)	Larceny, conversion of property (Commodity Credit Corp.).	

Title & Section Numbers	Caption of Section (Chapter Headings)	Relates to any persons(s) who...
15 USC 715e	Penalties for violation of chapter (Interstate Transportation of Petroleum Products).	
15 USC 717m	Investigations by Commission (Natural Gas).	without just cause, fail or refuse to attend and testify or to answer any lawful inquiry or to produce books, papers, correspondence, memoranda, and other records, if in his power to do so, in obedience to the subpena of the Commission.
15 USC 717t	General penalties (Natural Gas).	willfully and knowingly does or causes or suffers to be done any act, matter, or thing in this chapter prohibited or declared to be unlawful, or who willfully and knowingly omits or fails to do any act, matter, or thing in this chapter required to be done.
15 USC 797	Enforcement (Energy Supply and Environmental Coordination).	violates any provision of section 792 of this title or section 796 of this title or violates any rule, regulation, or order issued pursuant to any such provision.
15 USC 1004	Penalties (Miscellaneous - Commerce and Trade).	secures or attempts to secure the exemption from toll provided for in sections 1002 to 1004 of this title or an authorization referred to in section 1003 of this title, knowing that he is not entitled thereto.
15 USC 1007	Penalties (Miscellaneous - Commerce and Trade).	secures or attempts to secure the exemption from toll provided for in sections 1005 to 1007 of this title or an authorization referred to in section 1006 of this title, knowing that he is not entitled thereto.
15 USC 1172	Transportation of gambling devices as unlawful; exceptions; authority of Federal Trade Commission.	
15 USC 1173	Registration of manufacturers and dealers (Transportation of Gambling Devices).	

Title & Section Numbers	Caption of Section (Chapter Headings)	Relates to any persons(s) who...
15 USC 1174	Labeling and marking of shipping packages (Transportation of Gambling Devices).	[Requiring that all gambling devices, and all packages containing such, when shipped or transported, shall be plainly and clearly labeled or marked so that the name and address of the shipper and the consignee, and the nature of the article or the contents of the package may be readily ascertained on inspection of the outside of the article or package.]
15 USC 1175	Specific jurisdictions within which manufacturing, repairing, selling, possessing, etc., prohibited; exceptions (Gambling Devices).	[Making it unlawful to manufacture, recondition, repair, sell, transport, possess, or use any gambling device in the District of Columbia, in any possession of the U.S., within Indian country as defined in section 1151 of Title 18 or within the special maritime and territorial jurisdiction of the U.S. as defined in section 7 of Title 18, including on vessels documented under chapter 121 of Title 46 or documented under the laws of a foreign country.]
15 USC 1176	Penalties (Gambling Devices).	violates any provision of sections 1172, 1173, 1174, or 1175 of this title.
15 USC 1196	Penalties (Flammable Fabrics).	willfully violates section 1192 or 1197(b) of this title, or fails to comply with section 1202(c) of this title.
15 USC 1212	Violations; misdemeanor; penalties (Household Refrigerators).	
15 USC 1233	Violations and penalties (Disclosure of Automobile Information).	[Section pertains to failure to affix required label; failure to endorse required label; removal, alteration, or illegibility of required label.]
15 USC 1242	Introduction, manufacture for introduction, transportation or distribution in interstate commerce; penalty (Manufacture, Transportation, or Distribution of Switchblade Knives).	

Title & Section Numbers	Caption of Section (Chapter Headings)	Relates to any persons(s) who...
15 USC 1243	Manufacture, sale, or possession within specific jurisdictions; penalty (Manufacture, Transportation, or Distribution of Switchblade Knives).	
15 USC 1245	Ballistic knives (Manufacture, Transportation, or Distribution of Switchblade Knives).	possesses or uses a ballistic knife in the commission of a Federal crime of violence.
15 USC 1264	Penalties; exceptions (Hazardous Substances).	
15 USC 1611	Criminal liability for willful and knowing violation (Consumer Credit Cost Disclosure).	
15 USC 1644	Fraudulent use of credit cards; penalties.	
15 USC 1674	Restriction on discharge from employment by reason of garnishment (Consumer Credit Cost Disclosure).	
15 USC 1681q	Obtaining information under false pretenses (Credit Reporting Agencies).	obtains information on a consumer from a consumer reporting agency under false pretenses.
15 USC 1681r	Unauthorized disclosures by officers or employees (Credit Reporting Agencies).	
15 USC 1693n(a)	Criminal liability (Electronic Fund Transfers).	knowingly or willfully gives false or inaccurate information or fails to provide information which he is required to disclose by this subchapter or any regulation issued thereunder or otherwise fails to comply with any provision of this chapter.
15 USC 1717	Penalties for violations (Interstate Land Sales).	
15 USC 1825	Violations and penalties (Protection of Horses).	

Title & Section Numbers	Caption of Section (Chapter Headings)	Relates to any persons(s) who...
15 USC 2070	Criminal penalties (Consumer Product Safety).	knowingly and willfully violates section 2068 of this title after having received notice of noncompliance from the Commission.
15 USC 2613	Disclosure of data (Control of Toxic Substances).	
15 USC 2614	Prohibited acts (Control of Toxic Substances).	[Making it unlawful to fail or refuse to comply with any (a) rule promulgated or order issued under section 2603 of this title, (b) any requirements prescribed by section 2604 of this title, (c) any rule promulgated or order issued under section 2604 or 2605 of this title, or (d) any requirement of subchapter II of this chapter or any rule promulgated or order issued under subchapter II of this chapter.]
15 USC 2615	Penalties (Control of Toxic Substances).	
15 USC 2625	Administration (Control of Toxic Substances).	being an officer or employee who is subject to this subsection, violates this subsection.
15 USC 3414	Enforcement (Natural Gas Policy).	
15 USC 5408	Remedies and penalties (Fasteners).	knowingly certifies, marks, offers for sale, or sells a fastener in violation of this chapter or a regulation under this chapter.
15 USC 6309	Enforcement (Professional Boxing Safety).	being a manager, promoter, matchmaker, or licensee, knowingly violates, or coerces or causes any other person to violate, any provision of this chapter.
16 USC 3	Rules and regulations of national parks, reservations, and monuments; timber; leases.	violates any rules or regulations authorized by this section and sections 1, 2, and 4 of this title.
16 USC 9a	Government of parks, etc.; violation of regulations as misdemeanor.	

Title & Section Numbers	Caption of Section (Chapter Headings)	Relates to any persons(s) who...
16 USC 26	Regulations for hunting and fishing in park; punishment for violations; forfeitures (Yellowstone National Park).	
16 USC 45e	Violations of park regulations; penalty (Sequoia and Yosemite National Parks).	
16 USC 98	Protection of game and fish; forfeitures and punishments (Mount Rainier National Park).	
16 USC 114	Removal, disturbance, destruction, or molestation of ruins (Mesa Verde National Park).	
16 USC 117c	Hunting and fishing; general rules and regulations; protection of property; violation of statutes and rules; penalties (Mesa Verde National Park).	
16 USC 123	Settlement, residence, lumbering, or business within park punishable; admission of visitors (Crater Lake National Park).	
16 USC 127	Hunting and fishing; rules and regulations; punishment (Crater Lake National Park).	
16 USC 146	Offenses within park (Wind Cave National Park).	intrudes upon said park, or without permission, appropriates any object therein or commits unauthorized injury or waste in any form whatever upon the lands or other public property therein, or violates any of the rules and regulations prescribed hereunder.
16 USC 152	Additional land withdrawn; payment; management and control; regulations; sale of improvements; penalties; town lots (Cession of Indian Lands at Sulphur, Oklahoma).	
16 USC 170	Hunting and fishing; regulations; punishment (Glacier National Park).	

Title & Section Numbers	Caption of Section (Chapter Headings)	Relates to any persons(s) who...
16 USC 198c	Prohibited acts; rules and regulations; penalties for offenses (Rocky Mountain National Park).	
16 USC 204c	Hunting and fishing; general rules and regulations; protection of property; violation of statutes and rules; penalties (Lassen Volcanic National Park).	
16 USC 256b	Hunting and fishing; general rules and regulations; protection of property; violation of statutes or rules; penalties (Olympic National Park).	
16 USC 354	Offenses; punishment (Denali National Park).	
16 USC 371	Use of free bathhouses limited (Hot Springs National Park).	makes a false oath as to his financial condition in order to bathe at the free bathhouse.
16 USC 395c	Hunting and fishing; general rules and regulations; protection of property; violation of statutes and rules; penalties (Hawaii National Park).	
16 USC 403c-3	Criminal offenses concerning hunting, fishing, and property (Shenandoah National Park and Great Smoky Mountains National Park).	
16 USC 403h-3	Hunting, fishing, etc.; rules and regulations; protection of property; penalties for violating laws and rules (Shenandoah National Park and Great Smoky Mountains National Park).	
16 USC 404c-3	Criminal offenses concerning hunting, fishing, and property; prima facie evidence; rules and regulations (Mammoth Cave National Park).	

Title & Section Numbers	Caption of Section (Chapter Headings)	Relates to any persons(s) who...
16 USC 408k	Hunting and fishing; general rules and regulations; protection of property; violation of statutes or rules; penalties (Isle Royale National Park).	
16 USC 413	Offenses relating to structures and vegetation (National Military Parks).	willfully destroys, mutilates, defaces, injures, or removes any monument, statue, marker, guidepost, or other structure, or willfully destroys, cuts, breaks, injures, or removes any tree, shrub, or plant within the limits of any national military parks.
16 USC 414	Trespassing for hunting, or shooting (National Military Parks).	
16 USC 430v	Monuments and memorials; regulations; historical markers (National Military Parks).	
16 USC 433	American antiquities.	appropriates, excavates, injures, or destroys any historic or prehistoric ruin or monument, or any object of antiquity situated on lands owned or controlled by the government of the U.S. without permission of the Secretary of the Department of the government having jurisdiction over the land.
16 USC 460d	Construction and operation of public parks and recreational facilities in water resource development projects; lease of lands; preference for use; penalty; application of section 3401 of Title 18; citations and arrests with and without process; limitations; disposition of receipts (Public Parks and Recreational Facilities at Water Resource Development Projects).	
16 USC 460k-3	Charges and fees; permits; regulations; penalties; enforcement (National Conservation Recreational Areas).	
16 USC 460n-5	Regulation of area; violations and penalties (Lake Mead National Recreational Area).	

Title & Section Numbers	Caption of Section (Chapter Headings)	Relates to any persons(s) who...
16 USC 460xx-1	Management (San Pedro Riparian National Conservation Area).	violates any provision of this subchapter or any regulation promulgated by the Secretary to implement this subchapter.
16 USC 460ddd	Establishment (Gila Box Riparian National Conservation Area).	violates any regulation promulgated by the Secretary to implement the provisions of this subchapter.
16 USC 470ee	Prohibited acts and criminal penalties (Archaeological Resources Protection).	excavate, remove, damage, or otherwise alter or deface, or attempt to excavate, remove, damage, or otherwise alter or deface any archaeological resource located on public lands or Indian lands.
16 USC 551	Protection of national forests; rules and regulations.	
16 USC 606	Offense for unlawful cutting on mineral lands; punishment (Protection of Timber and Depredations).	
16 USC 666a	Penalties (Game, Fur-Bearing Animals, and Fish).	
16 USC 668(a)	Bald and golden eagles - Prohibited acts; criminal penalties.	takes, possesses, sells, purchases, barters, offers to sell, purchase or barter, transports, exports or imports any bald or golden eagle, alive or dead, or any part, nest, or egg thereof.
16 USC 668dd	National Wildlife Refuge System.	knowingly disturb, injure, cut, burn, remove, destroy, or possess any real or personal property of the United States, including natural growth, in any area of the System, or take or possess any fish, bird, mammal, or other wild vertebrate or invertebrate animals or part or nest thereof within any such area.
16 USC 670j	Enforcement provisions (Conservation on Public Lands).	hunts, traps, or fishes on any public land which is subject to a conservation and rehabilitation program implemented under this subchapter.

Title & Section Numbers	Caption of Section (Chapter Headings)	Relates to any persons(s) who...
16 USC 690g	Violation of laws and regulations; penalties (Game and Bird Preserves; Protection).	
16 USC 693a	Rules and regulations for administration of Ouachita National Forest; violations; penalties.	
16 USC 707(b)	Violations and penalties; forfeitures (Migratory Bird Treaty).	takes by any manner any migratory bird with intent to sell, offer to sell, barter or offer to barter such bird or sells, offers for sale, barters or offers to barter any migratory bird.
16 USC 730	Violations of law or regulations; punishment (Upper Mississippi River Wild Life and Fish Refuge).	
16 USC 742j-1(a)	Airborne hunting - Prohibition; penalty.	uses an aircraft to harass, shoot or attempt to shoot for the purpose of capturing or killing any bird, fish, or other animal.
16 USC 773e(a)(2)	Prohibited acts (Northern Pacific Halibut Act of 1982).	refuses to permit any enforcement officer to board a fishing vessel subject to such person's control for purposes of conducting any search or inspection in connection with the enforcement of the Convention, this subchapter or any regulation adopted under this subchapter.
16 USC 773g	Crimes and criminal penalties (Northern Pacific Halibut Act of 1982).	commits acts prohibited by section 773e(a)(2), (3), (4), or (6) of this title, or section 773e(b) of this title.
16 USC 825f	Investigations by Commission (Licensees and Public Utilities; Procedural and Administrative).	willfully fails or refuses to attend and testify or answer any lawful inquiry or to produce books, papers, correspondence, memoranda, contracts, agreements, or other records in obedience to the subpena of the Commission.
16 USC 825o	Penalties for violations; applicability of section (Licensees and Public Utilities; Procedural and Administrative).	willfully and knowingly does or causes or suffers to be done any act, matter, or thing in this chapter prohibited or declared to be unlawful.

Title & Section Numbers	Caption of Section (Chapter Headings)	Relates to any persons(s) who...
16 USC 831t(a)	Offenses; fines and punishment (Tennessee Valley Authority).	[Dealing with larceny, embezzlement and conversion.]
16 USC 831t(b)	Offenses; fines and punishment (Tennessee Valley Authority).	[Dealing with false entry, report or statement.]
16 USC 831t(c)	Offenses; fines and punishment (Tennessee Valley Authority).	[Dealing with conspiracy to defraud.]
16 USC 916c	Unlawful acts (Whaling Convention Act).	[Section pertains to whaling, transporting, or selling violations; records; reports; acts of commission or omission.]
16 USC 916f	Violations; fines and penalties (Whaling Convention Act).	
16 USC 973c(a)(8)	Prohibited acts (South Pacific Tuna Fishing).	refuses to permit any authorized officer or authorized party officer to board a fishing vessel for purposes of conducting a search or inspection in connection with the enforcement of the chapter or Treaty.
16 USC 973e	Criminal offenses (South Pacific Tuna Fishing).	commits any act prohibited by section 973c(a)(8), (10), (11), or (12) of this title.
16 USC 1174(a)	Penalties (North Pacific Fur Seals).	violates any provision of this chapter or of any permit or regulation issued thereunder.
16 USC 1338(a)	Criminal provisions - Violations; penalties; trial (Wild Horses and Burros).	removes or attempts to remove a wild free-roaming horse or burro from the public lands, converts a wild burro or horse to private use, maliciously causes the death or harassment of any wild horse or burro, possesses or permits to be processed into commercial products the remains of wild burro or horse, sells, directly or indirectly, a wild burro or horse maintained on private or leased land pursuant to section 1334 of this title, or willfully violates a regulation issued pursuant to this chapter.
16 USC 1375(b)	Penalties (Marine Mammal Protection).	violates any provision of this subchapter or of any permit or regulation issued thereunder.

Title & Section Numbers	Caption of Section (Chapter Headings)	Relates to any persons(s) who...
16 USC 1417(a)(5)	Prohibitions (Prohibition of Certain Tuna Harvesting Practices).	refuses to permit any duly authorized officer to board a vessel subject to that person's control for purposes of conducting any search or inspection in connection with enforcement of this subchapter.
16 USC 1540(b)	Criminal violations (Endangered Species).	violates any provision of this chapter, of any permit or certificate issued hereunder, or of any regulation issued in order to implement subsection (a)(1)(A), (B), (C), (D), (E), or (F), (a)(2)(A), (B), (C), or (D), (c), (d), (f), or (g) of section 1538 or violates any provision of any other regulation issued under this chapter.
16 USC 1857(1)(D)	Prohibited acts (Fishery Conservation).	refuses to permit any officer authorized to enforce the provisions of this chapter to board a fishing vessel subject to such person's control for purposes of conducting any search or inspection in connection with enforcement of this chapter or any regulation, permit, or agreement referred to in subparagraph (A) or (C).
16 USC 1857(1)(E)	Prohibited acts (Fishery Conservation).	forcibly assaults, resists, opposes, impedes, intimidates, or interferes with any such authorized officer in the conduct of any search or inspection described in paragraph (D).
16 USC 1857(1)(F)	Prohibited acts (Fishery Conservation).	resists a lawful arrest for any act prohibited by this section.
16 USC 1857(1)(H)	Prohibited acts (Fishery Conservation).	interferes with, delays, or prevents by any means, the apprehension or arrest of another person, knowing that such other person has committed any act prohibited by this section.
16 USC 1859	Criminal offenses (Fishery Conservation).	commits an act prohibited by section 1857(1)(D), (E), (F), (H), (I), or (L) of this title, or section 1857(2) of this title.

Title & Section Numbers	Caption of Section (Chapter Headings)	Relates to any persons(s) who...
16 USC 1912	Financial disclosure by officer or employee of Secretary (Mining Activity within National Park System Areas).	being an officer or employee who is subject to this section, knowingly violates this section or any regulation issued thereunder.
16 USC 2408	Criminal offenses (Antarctic Conservation).	
16 USC 2435(4)	Unlawful activities (Antarctic Marine Living Resources Convention).	refuses to permit any authorized officer or employee of the U.S. to board a vessel of the U.S. or a vessel subject to the jurisdiction of the U.S. for purposes of conducting any search or inspection in connection with the enforcement of the Convention, this chapter, or any regulations promulgated under this chapter.
16 USC 2435(5)	Unlawful activities (Antarctic Marine Living Resources Convention).	assaults, resists, opposes, impedes, intimidates, or interferes with any authorized officer or employee of the U.S. in the conduct of any search or inspection described in paragraph (4).
16 USC 2435(6)	Unlawful activities (Antarctic Marine Living Resources Convention).	resists a lawful arrest or detention for any act prohibited by this section.
16 USC 2435(7)	Unlawful activities (Antarctic Marine Living Resources Convention).	interferes with, delays, or prevents, by any means, the apprehension, arrest, or detention of another person, knowing that such other person has committed any act prohibited by this section.
16 USC 2438	Criminal offenses (Antarctic Marine Living Resources Convention).	commits any act prohibited by paragraph (4), (5), (6), or (7) of section 2435 of this title.
16 USC 3373	Penalties and sanctions (Control of Illegally Taken Fish and Wildlife).	

Title & Section Numbers	Caption of Section (Chapter Headings)	Relates to any persons(s) who...
16 USC 3606	Violations and penalties (North Atlantic Salmon Fishing).	conducts directed fishing for salmon in waters seaward of twelve miles from the baseline from which the breadths of territorial sea are measured in waters of the Atlantic Ocean north of 36 degrees latitude or violates any provision of the Convention or this chapter, or of any regulation promulgated under this chapter.
16 USC 3637(a)(2)	Prohibited acts and penalties (Pacific Salmon Fishing).	refuses to permit any officer authorized to enforce any provision of this chapter to board a fishing vessel subject to such person's control for purposes of conducting any search or inspection in connection with the enforcement of this chapter.
16 USC 3637(a)(3)	Prohibited acts and penalties (Pacific Salmon Fishing).	forcibly assaults, resists, opposes, impedes, intimidates, or interferes with any such authorized officer in the conduct of any search or inspection described in subparagraph (2).
16 USC 3637(a)(4)	Prohibited acts and penalties (Pacific Salmon Fishing).	resists a lawful arrest for any act prohibited by this section.
16 USC 3637(a)(5)	Prohibited acts and penalties (Pacific Salmon Fishing).	ships, transports, offers for sale, sells, purchases, imports, exports, or has custody, control, or possession of any fish taken or retained in violation of this chapter.
16 USC 3637(c)	Criminal penalty (Pacific Salmon Fishing).	commits an act that is unlawful under paragraph (2), (3), (4), or (6) of subsection (a) of this section.
16 USC 4223	Prohibited acts (African Elephant Conservation).	imports raw ivory from any country other than an ivory producing country or exports raw ivory from the U.S.
16 USC 4224	Penalties and enforcement (African Elephant Conservation).	violates section 4223 of this title.
16 USC 4910(a)	Prohibitions (Wild Exotic Bird Conservation).	imports any exotic bird in violation of any prohibitions under this title.

Title & Section Numbers	Caption of Section (Chapter Headings)	Relates to any persons(s) who...
16 USC 4910(a)(2)(A)	Criminal penalties (Wild Exotic Bird Conservation).	violates section 4910(a)(1) or (2) of this title or any permit issued under section 4911 of this title.
16 USC 5009(5)	Unlawful activities (North Pacific Anadromous Stocks Convention).	refuses to permit any enforcement officer to board a fishing vessel subject to such person's control for purposes of conducting any search or inspection in connection with the enforcement of the Convention or any regulation issued under this chapter.
16 USC 5009(6)	Unlawful activities (North Pacific Anadromous Stocks Convention).	forcibly assaults, resists, opposes, impedes, intimidates, or interferes with any enforcement officer in the conduct of any search or inspection described in paragraph (5).
16 USC 5009(7)	Unlawful activities (North Pacific Anadromous Stocks Convention).	resists a lawful arrest or detention for any act prohibited by this section.
16 USC 5009(8)	Unlawful activities (North Pacific Anadromous Stocks Convention).	interferes with, delays, or prevents, by any means, the apprehension, arrest, or detection of another person, knowing that such person has committed any act prohibited by this section.
16 USC 5010(b)	Penalties - Offenses (North Pacific Anadromous Stocks Convention).	commits any act prohibited by section 5009(5), (6), (7), or (8) of this title.
17 USC 506(a)	Criminal offenses (Copyrights).	infringes a copyright willfully and for purposes of commercial advantage or private financial gain.
18 USC 2	Principals (General Provisions).	commits an offense against the U.S. or aids, abets, counsels, commands, induces, or procures its commission or willfully causes an act to be done which if directly performed by him or another would be an offense against the U.S.

Title & Section Numbers	Caption of Section (Chapter Headings)	Relates to any persons(s) who...
18 USC 3	Accessory after the fact (General Provisions).	knowing that an offense against the U.S. has been committed, receives, relieves, comforts, or assists the offender in order to hinder or prevent his apprehension, trial, or punishment.
18 USC 4	Misprision of felony (General Provisions).	having knowledge of the actual commission of a felony cognizable by a court of the U.S., conceals and does not as soon as possible make known the same to some judge or other person in civil or military authority under the U.S.
18 USC 13	Laws of States adopted for areas within Federal jurisdiction (General Provisions).	within or upon any of the places existing, reserved or acquired as provided in section 7 of this title, is guilty of any act or omission, which would be punishable if committed or omitted within the jurisdiction of the State, Territory, Possession, or District in which such place is situated, by the laws thereof in force at the time.
18 USC 32(a)	Destruction of aircraft or aircraft facilities.	sets fire to, damages, destroys, disables, or wrecks any aircraft in the special aircraft jurisdiction of the U.S.
18 USC 32(b)	Destruction of aircraft or aircraft facilities.	performs an act of violence against any individual on board any civil aircraft registered in a country other than the U.S. while such aircraft is in flight, if such act is likely to endanger the safety of that aircraft.
18 USC 32(c)	Destruction of aircraft or aircraft facilities.	imparts or conveys any threat to do an act which would violate any of paragraphs (1) through (5) of subsection (a) or any of paragraphs (1) through (3) of subsection (b) of this section with an apparent determination and will to carry the threat into execution.
18 USC 33	Destruction of motor vehicles or motor vehicle facilities.	
18 USC 34	Penalty when death results (Aircraft and Motor Vehicles).	

Title & Section Numbers	Caption of Section (Chapter Headings)	Relates to any persons(s) who...
18 USC 35(b)	Imparting or conveying false information (Aircraft and Motor Vehicles).	imparts or conveys false information, knowing the information to be false, concerning an attempt or alleged attempt being made or to be made, to do any act which would be a crime prohibited by this chapter or chapter 97 or chapter 111 of this title.
18 USC 36	Drive-by shooting.	
18 USC 37	Violence at international airports.	
18 USC 41	Hunting, fishing, trapping; disturbance or injury on wildlife refuges.	
18 USC 42	Importation or shipment of injurious mammals, birds, fish, amphibian, and reptiles; permits, specimens for museums; regulations.	
18 USC 43	Animal enterprise terrorism.	intentionally causes physical disruption to the functioning of an animal enterprise by intentionally stealing, damaging, or causing the loss of, any property used by the animal enterprise.
18 USC 46	Transportation of water hyacinths.	knowingly delivers or receives for transportation, or transports, in interstate commerce, alligator grass, or water chestnut plants, or water hyacinth plants or the seeds or such grass or plants.
18 USC 47	Use of aircraft or motor vehicles to hunt certain wild horses or burros; pollution of watering holes.	uses an aircraft or a motor vehicle to hunt, for the purpose of capturing or killing, any wild unbranded horse, mare, colt, or burro running at large on any of the public land or ranges.
18 USC 81	Arson within special maritime and territorial jurisdiction.	
18 USC 111	Assaulting, resisting, or impeding certain officers or employees.	

Title & Section Numbers	Caption of Section (Chapter Headings)	Relates to any persons(s) who...
18 USC 112(a)	Protection of foreign officials, official guests, and internationally protected persons.	assaults, strikes, wounds, imprisons or offers violence to a foreign official, official guest, or internationally protected person or makes any other violent attack upon the person or liberty of such person.
18 USC 113(a)	Assaults within maritime and territorial jurisdiction.	
18 USC 113(a)(1)	Assaults within maritime and territorial jurisdiction.	[Section pertains to assault with intent to commit murder.]
18 USC 113(a)(2)	Assaults within maritime and territorial jurisdiction.	[Section pertains to assault with intent to commit any felony, except murder or a felony under chapter 109A.]
18 USC 113(a)(3)	Assaults within maritime and territorial jurisdiction.	[Section pertains to assault with a dangerous weapon, with intent to do bodily harm, and without just cause or excuse.]
18 USC 113(a)(5)	Assaults within maritime and territorial jurisdiction.	[Section pertains to simple assault.]
18 USC 113(a)(6)	Assaults within maritime and territorial jurisdiction.	[Section pertains to assault resulting in serious bodily injury.]
18 USC 113(a)(7)	Assaults within maritime and territorial jurisdiction.	[Section pertains to assault resulting in substantial bodily injury to an individual who has not attained the age of sixteen years.]
18 USC 113(b)	Assaults within maritime and territorial jurisdiction.	[Section pertains to definition of "substantial bodily injury" for purposes of above related section.]
18 USC 114	Maiming within maritime and territorial jurisdiction.	
18 USC 115(a)	Influencing, impeding, or retaliating against a Federal official by threatening or injuring a family member.	assaults, kidnaps, or murders, or attempts or conspires to kidnap or murder, a member of the immediate family of a U.S. official, a U.S. judge, a Federal law enforcement officer, or an official whose killing would be a crime under section 1114 of this title.

Title & Section Numbers	Caption of Section (Chapter Headings)	Relates to any persons(s) who...
18 USC 115(b)(1)	Influencing, impeding, or retaliating against a Federal official by threatening or injuring a family member.	[Deals with an assault in violation of this section.]
18 USC 115(b)(2)	Influencing, impeding, or retaliating against a Federal official by threatening or injuring a family member.	[Deals with a kidnap, attempt to kidnap, or conspiracy to kidnap in violation of this section.]
18 USC 115(b)(3)	Influencing, impeding, or retaliating against a Federal official by threatening or injuring a family member.	[Deals with a murder, attempt to murder, or conspiracy to murder in violation of this section.]
18 USC 115(b)(4)	Influencing, impeding, or retaliating against a Federal official by threatening or injuring a family member.	[Deals with a threat made in violation of this section.]
18 USC 116	Female genital mutilation.	knowingly circumcises, excises, or infibulates the whole or any part or the labia majora or labia minora or clitoris of another person who has not attained the age of 18 years.
18 USC 152	Concealment of assets; false oaths and claims; bribery (Bankruptcy).	
18 USC 153	Embezzlement against estate (Bankruptcy).	
18 USC 155	Fee agreements in cases under title 11 and receiverships (Bankruptcy).	
18 USC 156	Knowing disregard of bankruptcy law or rule (Bankruptcy).	being a bankruptcy petition preparer dismisses a bankruptcy case or related proceeding because of a knowing attempt in any manner to disregard the requirements of title 11, United States Code, or the Federal Rules or Bankruptcy Procedure.
18 USC 157	Bankruptcy fraud (Bankruptcy).	having devised or intending to devise a scheme or artifice to defraud and for the purpose of executing or concealing such a scheme or artifice or attempting to do so files a petition under title 11.

Title & Section Numbers	Caption of Section (Chapter Headings)	Relates to any persons(s) who...
18 USC 175	Prohibitions with respect to biological weapons.	knowingly develops, produces, stockpiles, transfers, acquires, retains, or possesses any biological agent, toxin, or delivery system for use as a weapon.
18 USC 201(b)(1)	Bribery of public officials and witnesses.	directly or indirectly, corruptly gives, offers or promises anything of value to any public official or person who has been selected to be a public official, or offers or promises any public official or any person who has been selected to be a public official to give anything of value to any other person or entity with intent to influence any official act.
18 USC 201(b)(2)	Bribery of public officials and witnesses.	directly or indirectly, corruptly demands, seeks, receives, accepts, or agrees to receive or accept anything of value personally or for any other person or entity in return for being influenced in their performance of any official act, to commit or aid in committing, or to collude in, or allow, any fraud, or make opportunity for the commission of any fraud, on the U.S., or for being induced to do or omit to do any act in violation of the official duty of such official or person and that person is a public official or person selected to be a public official.
18 USC 201(b)(3)	Bribery of public officials and witnesses.	corruptly gives anything of value with intent to influence the testimony under oath or affirmation of witness upon trial, hearing, or other proceeding.
18 USC 201(b)(4)	Bribery of public officials and witnesses.	seeks, receives, accepts, or agrees to receive or accept anything of value personally or for any other person or entity in return for being influenced in testimony under oath of affirmation as a witness upon any such trial, hearing, or other proceeding.

Title & Section Numbers	Caption of Section (Chapter Headings)	Relates to any persons(s) who...
18 USC 201(c)(1)	Bribery of public officials and witnesses.	gives, offers, or promises anything of value to any public official, former public official, or person selected to be a public official, for or because of any official act performed or to be performed by such public official, former public official, or person selected to be a public official.
18 USC 201(c)(2)	Bribery of public officials and witnesses.	gives, offers, or promises anything of value to any person, for or because of the testimony under oath or affirmation given or to be given by such person as a witness upon a trial, hearing, or other proceeding, before any court, any committee of either House or both Houses of Congress, or any agency, commission, or officer authorized by the laws of the U.S. to hear evidence or take testimony, or for or because of such person's absence therefrom.
18 USC 201(c)(3)	Bribery of public officials and witnesses.	demands, seeks, receives, accepts, or agrees to receive or accept anything of value personally for or because of the testimony under oath or affirmation given or to be given by such person as a witness upon any such trial, hearing, or other proceeding, or for or because of such person's absence therefrom.
18 USC 203	Compensation to members of Congress, officers, and others in matters affecting the government (Bribery, Graft, and Conflicts of Interest).	
18 USC 204	Practice in U.S. Claims Court or the U.S. Court of Appeals for the Federal Circuit by members of Congress (Bribery, Graft, and Conflicts of Interest).	
18 USC 205	Activities of officers and employees in claims against and other matters affecting the government (Bribery, Graft, and Conflicts of Interest).	

Title & Section Numbers	Caption of Section (Chapter Headings)	Relates to any persons(s) who...
18 USC 207	Restrictions on former officers, employees, and elected officials of the executive and legislative branches (Bribery, Graft, and Conflicts of Interest).	
18 USC 208	Acts affecting a personal financial interest (Bribery, Graft, and Conflicts of Interest).	
18 USC 209	Salary of government officials and employees payable only by the U.S. (Bribery, Graft, and Conflicts of Interest).	
18 USC 210	Offer to procure appointive public office (Bribery, Graft, and Conflicts of Interest).	
18 USC 211	Acceptance or solicitation to obtain appointive public office (Bribery, Graft, and Conflicts of Interest).	
18 USC 212	Offer of loan or gratuity to bank examiner (Bribery, Graft, and Conflicts of Interest).	
18 USC 213	Acceptance of loan or gratuity by bank examiner (Bribery, Graft, and Conflicts of Interest).	
18 USC 214	Offer for procurement of Federal Reserve bank loan and discount of commercial paper (Bribery, Graft, and Conflicts of Interest).	
18 USC 215	Receipt of commissions or gifts for procuring loans (Bribery, Graft, and Conflicts of Interest).	
18 USC 216	Penalties and injunctions (Bribery, Graft, and Conflicts of Interest).	
18 USC 217	Acceptance of consideration for adjustment of farm indebtedness (Bribery, Graft, and Conflicts of Interest).	

Title & Section Numbers	Caption of Section (Chapter Headings)	Relates to any persons(s) who...
18 USC 219	Officers and employees acting as agents of foreign principals (Bribery, Graft, and Conflicts of Interest).	
18 USC 224	Bribery in sporting contests (Bribery, Graft, and Conflicts of Interest).	
18 USC 225	Continuing financial crimes enterprise (Bribery, Graft, and Conflicts of Interest).	
18 USC 228	Failure to pay legal child support obligations.	willfully fails to pay past due support obligation with respect to a child who resides in another state.
18 USC 231	Civil disorders.	transports or manufactures for transportation in commerce any firearm, or explosive or incendiary device, knowing or having reason to know or intending that the same will be used unlawfully in furtherance of a civil disorder.
18 USC 241	Conspiracy against rights.	[Two or more persons conspire to injure, oppress, threaten, or intimidate any person in the free exercise or enjoyment of any right or privilege secured to him by the Constitution or laws of the U.S., or because of his having so exercised the same.]
18 USC 242	Deprivation of rights under color of law.	
18 USC 245(b)	Federally protected activities (Civil Rights).	whether or not acting under color of law, by force or threat of force willfully injures, intimidates, or interferes with, or attempts to injure, intimidate, or interfere with any person because he is or has been voting or because of his race, color, religion, or national origin.
18 USC 246	Deprivation of relief benefits (Civil Rights).	

Title & Section Numbers	Caption of Section (Chapter Headings)	Relates to any persons(s) who...
18 USC 247	Damage to religious property; obstruction of persons in the free exercise of religious beliefs.	
18 USC 248	Freedom of access to clinic entrances (Civil Rights).	by force or threat of force or by physical obstruction, intentionally injures, intimidates or interferes with or attempts to injure, intimidate or interfere with any person because that person is or has been obtaining or providing reproductive health services.
18 USC 285	Taking or using papers relating to claims (Claims and Services in Matters Affecting Government).	
18 USC 286	Conspiracy to defraud the government with respect to claims.	
18 USC 287	False, fictitious, or fraudulent claims (Claims and Services in Matters Affecting Government).	makes or presents to any person or officer in the civil, military, or naval service of the U.S. or to any department or agency thereof, any claim upon or against the U.S., or any department or agency thereof, knowing such claim to be false, fictitious, or fraudulent.
18 USC 288	False claims for postal losses.	
18 USC 289	False claims for pensions.	
18 USC 290	Discharge papers withheld by claim agent.	being a claim agent, attorney, or other person engaged in the collection of claims for pay, pension, or other allowances for any soldier, sailor or marine, retains, without the consent of the owner or owners thereof, the discharge papers of any such soldier, sailor, or marine, which may have been placed in his hands for the purpose of collecting said claims.
18 USC 292	Solicitation of employment and receipt of unapproved fees concerning Federal employees' compensation.	solicits employment for himself or another in respect to a case, claim or award for compensation under subchapter I of chapter 81 of title 5.

Title & Section Numbers	Caption of Section (Chapter Headings)	Relates to any persons(s) who...
18 USC 331	Mutilation, diminution, and falsification of coins.	fraudulently alters, defaces, mutilates, impairs, diminishes, falsifies, scales, or lightens any of the coins coined at the mints of the United States.
18 USC 332	Debasement of coins; alteration of official scales, or embezzlement of metals.	
18 USC 333	Mutilation of national bank obligations.	mutilates, cuts, defaces, disfigures, or perforates, or unites or cements together, or does any other thing to any bank bill, draft, note, or other evidence of debt, with intent to render such bank bill, draft, note or other evidence of debt unfit to be reissued.
18 USC 334	Issuance of Federal Reserve or national bank notes.	being a Federal Reserve Agent, issues or puts in circulation any Federal Reserve notes, without complying with or in violation of the provisions of law regulating the issuance and circulation of such Federal Reserve notes.
18 USC 335	Circulation of obligations of expired corporations.	
18 USC 336	Issuance of circulating obligations of less than $1.	
18 USC 337	Coins as security for loans.	lends or borrows money or credit upon the security of such coins of the United States as the Secretary of the Treasury may from time to time designate by proclamation, during any period designated in such proclamation.
18 USC 342	Operation of a common carrier under the influence of alcohol or drugs.	
18 USC 351(a)	Congressional, Cabinet, and Supreme Court assassination, kidnapping, and assault; penalties.	kills any individual who is a member of Congress or a member of Congress-elect, member of the executive branch, etc.

Title & Section Numbers	Caption of Section (Chapter Headings)	Relates to any persons(s) who...
18 USC 351(b)	Congressional, Cabinet, and Supreme Court assassination, kidnapping, and assault; penalties.	kidnaps any individual designated in subsection (a) above.
18 USC 351(c)	Congressional, Cabinet, and Supreme Court assassination, kidnapping, and assault; penalties.	attempts to kill or kidnap any individual designated in subsection (a) above.
18 USC 351(d)	Congressional, Cabinet, and Supreme Court assassination, kidnapping, and assault; penalties.	[Two or more persons conspire to kill or kidnap any individual designated in subsection (a) of this section and one or more of such persons do any act to effect the object of the conspiracy.]
18 USC 351(e)	Congressional, Cabinet, and Supreme Court assassination, kidnapping, and assault; penalties.	assaults any person designated in subsection (a) above.
18 USC 371	Conspiracy to commit offense or to defraud U.S.	
18 USC 372	Conspiracy to impede or injure officer.	
18 USC 373	Solicitation to commit a crime of violence.	
18 USC 401	Power of court (Contempt).	[Provides a court of the U.S. shall have power to punish by fine or imprisonment, at its discretion, contempt of its authority.]
18 USC 402	Contempts constituting crimes (Contempt).	[Section pertains to a person, corporation, or association willfully disobeying any lawful writ, process, decree, order, rule, or command of any district court of the United States or any court of the District of Columbia, by doing any act or thing therein, or thereby forbidden, if the act or thing so done be of such character as to constitute also a criminal offense.]
18 USC 403	Protection of the privacy of child victims and child witnesses.	[Deals with a knowing or intentional violation of privacy protection accorded by section 3509 of this title.]

Title & Section Numbers	Caption of Section (Chapter Headings)	Relates to any persons(s) who...
18 USC 435	Contracts in excess of specific appropriation (Contracts).	being an officer or employee of the United States, knowingly contracts for the erection, repair, or furnishing of any public building to pay for a larger amount than the specific sum appropriated for such purpose.
18 USC 436	Convict labor contracts.	being an officer, agent, or employee of the United States, contracts with any person or corporation to hire out the labor of any prisoners confined for violation of any laws of the United States.
18 USC 438	Indian contracts for services generally.	receives money contrary to sections 81 and 82 of title 25.
18 USC 439	Indian enrollment contracts.	collects or receives any moneys from any applicants for enrollment as citizens in the Five Civilized Tribes.
18 USC 440	Mail contracts.	being a person employed in the Postal Service, becomes interested in any contract for carrying the mail or acts as agent, with or without compensation, for any contractor or person offering to become a contractor in any business before the Postal Service.
18 USC 441	Postal supply contracts.	[Section relates to no contract for furnishing supplies to the Postal Service shall be made with any person who has entered, or proposed to enter, into any combination to prevent the making of any bid for furnishing such supplies, or to fix a price or prices therefore.]

Title & Section Numbers	Caption of Section (Chapter Headings)	Relates to any persons(s) who...
18 USC 442	Printing contracts.	[Provides neither the Public Printer, superintendent of printing or binding, nor any of their assistants shall during their continuance in office, have any interest in the publication of any newspaper or periodical, or in any printing, binding, engraving, or lithographing of any kind, or in any contract for furnishing paper or other material connected with the public printing, binding, lithographing, or engraving.]
18 USC 443	War contracts.	willfully secrets, mutilates, obliterates, or destroys any records of a war contractor relating to the negotiation, award, performance, payment, interim financing, cancellation or other termination, or settlement of a war contract of $25,000 or more.
18 USC 470	Counterfeit acts committed outside the U.S.	
18 USC 471	Obligations or securities of the U.S. (Counterfeiting and Forgery).	
18 USC 472	Uttering counterfeit obligations or securities.	
18 USC 473	Dealing in counterfeit obligations or securities.	buys, sells, exchanges, transfers, receives, or delivers any false, forged, counterfeited, or altered obligation or other security of the U.S. with intent that same be passed, published, or used as true and genuine.
18 USC 474	Plates or stones for counterfeiting obligations and securities.	
18 USC 476	Taking impressions of tools used for obligations or securities.	
18 USC 477	Possessing or selling impressions of tools used for obligations or securities.	
18 USC 478	Foreign obligations or securities.	

Title & Section Numbers	Caption of Section (Chapter Headings)	Relates to any persons(s) who...
18 USC 479	Uttering counterfeit foreign obligations or securities.	
18 USC 480	Possessing counterfeit foreign obligations or securities.	
18 USC 481	Plates or stones for counterfeiting foreign obligations or securities.	
18 USC 482	Foreign bank notes (Counterfeiting and Forgery).	falsely makes, alters, forges, or counterfeits any banknote or bill issued by a bank or corporation of any foreign country to circulate as money.
18 USC 483	Uttering counterfeit foreign bank notes.	
18 USC 484	Connecting parts of different notes (Counterfeiting and Forgery).	connects together different parts of two or more notes, bills, or other genuine instruments issued under the authority of the U.S., or by any foreign government, or corporation, as to produce one instrument.
18 USC 485	Coins or bars (Counterfeiting and Forgery).	falsely makes, forges, or counterfeits any coin or bar in resemblance or similitude of any coin of a denomination higher than 5 cents or any gold or silver bar coined or stamped at any mint or assay office, or in resemblance or similitude of any foreign gold or silver coin current in the U.S.
18 USC 486	Uttering coins of gold, silver, or other material.	
18 USC 487	Making or possessing counterfeit dies for coins.	
18 USC 488	Making or possessing counterfeit dies for foreign coins.	
18 USC 490	Minor coins (Counterfeiting and Forgery).	falsely makes, forges, or counterfeits any coin in the resemblance or similitude of any of the one-cent and 5-cent coins minted in the U.S.

Title & Section Numbers	Caption of Section (Chapter Headings)	Relates to any persons(s) who...
18 USC 491	Tokens or paper used as money (Counterfeiting and Forgery).	
18 USC 492	Forfeiture of counterfeit paraphernalia (Counterfeiting and Forgery).	
18 USC 493	Bonds and obligations of certain lending agencies (Counterfeiting and Forgery).	
18 USC 494	Contractors' bonds, bids, and public records (Counterfeiting and Forgery).	falsely makes, alters, forges, or counterfeits any bond, bid, proposal, contract, guarantee, security, official bond, public record, affidavit, or other writing for the purpose of defrauding the U.S.
18 USC 495	Contracts, deeds, and powers of attorney (Counterfeiting and Forgery).	falsely makes, alters, forges, or counterfeits any deed, power of attorney, order, certificate, receipt, contract or other writing, for the purpose of obtaining or receiving or of enabling any other person to obtain or receive from the U.S. or any officers or agents thereof, any sum of money.
18 USC 496	Customs matter (Counterfeiting and Forgery).	falsely alters any writing made or required to be made in connection with the entry or withdrawal of imports or collection of customs duties, or uses same knowing them to be falsely altered.
18 USC 497	Letters patent (Counterfeiting and Forgery).	falsely forges, counterfeits, or alters any letters patent granted or purporting to have been granted by the President of the U.S.
18 USC 498	Military or naval discharge certificates (Counterfeiting and Forgery).	
18 USC 499	Military, naval or official passes (Counterfeiting and Forgery).	
18 USC 500	Money orders (Counterfeiting and Forgery).	

Title & Section Numbers	Caption of Section (Chapter Headings)	Relates to any persons(s) who...
18 USC 501	Postage stamps, postage meter stamps, and postal cards (Counterfeiting and Forgery).	
18 USC 502	Postage and revenue stamps of foreign governments (Counterfeiting and Forgery).	
18 USC 503	Postmarking stamps (Counterfeiting and Forgery).	forges or counterfeits any postmarking stamp or impression thereof with intent to make it appear that such impression is a genuine postmark.
18 USC 505	Seals of courts; signatures of judges, or court officers (Counterfeiting and Forgery).	
18 USC 506	Seals of departments or agencies (Counterfeiting and Forgery).	
18 USC 507	Ship's papers (Counterfeiting and Forgery).	falsely makes, forges, counterfeits, or alters any instrument in limitation of or purporting to be, an abstract or official copy or certificate of the recording, registry, or enrollment of any vessel, in the office of any collector of the customs, or a license to any vessel for carrying of the coasting trade or fisheries of the U.S.
18 USC 508	Transportation requests of government (Counterfeiting and Forgery).	
18 USC 509	Possessing and making plates or stones for government transportation requests (Counterfeiting and Forgery).	controls, holds, or possesses any plate, stone, or other thing, of any art thereof, from which has been printed or may be printed in any form or request for government transportation, or uses such plate, stone or other thing, or knowingly permits or suffers the same to be used in making any such form or request or any part of such form or request.
18 USC 510	Forging endorsements on Treasury checks or bonds or securities of the U.S. (Counterfeiting and Forgery).	

Title & Section Numbers	Caption of Section (Chapter Headings)	Relates to any persons(s) who...
18 USC 511	Altering or removing motor vehicle identification numbers (Counterfeiting and Forgery).	
18 USC 513	Securities of the states and private entities (Counterfeiting and Forgery).	
18 USC 541	Entry of goods falsely classified (Customs).	
18 USC 542	Entry of goods by means of false statements.	
18 USC 543	Entry of goods for less than legal duty.	
18 USC 544	Relanding of goods.	[Section states that if any merchandise entered or withdrawn for exportation without payment of the duties thereon, or with intent to obtain a drawback of the duties paid, or of any other allowances given by law on the exportation thereof, is relanded at any place in the U.S. without entry having been made, such merchandise shall be considered as having been imported into the U.S. contrary to law.]
18 USC 545	Smuggling goods into the U.S.	
18 USC 546	Smuggling goods into foreign countries.	
18 USC 547	Depositing goods in buildings on boundaries.	receives or deposits any merchandise in any building upon the boundary line between the U.S. and any foreign country or carries any merchandise through the same.
18 USC 548	Removing or repacking goods in warehouse.	
18 USC 549	Removing goods from customs custody; breaking seals.	
18 USC 550	False claim for refund of duties.	

Title & Section Numbers	Caption of Section (Chapter Headings)	Relates to any persons(s) who...
18 USC 551	Concealing or destroying invoices or other papers.	
18 USC 552	Officers aiding importation of obscene or treasonous books and articles.	
18 USC 553(a)(1)	Importation or exportation of stolen motor vehicles, off-highway mobile equipment, vessels or aircraft.	imports, exports, or attempts to import or export any motor vehicle, off-highway mobile equipment, vessel, aircraft, or part of any motor vehicle, off-highway mobile equipment, vessel or aircraft, knowing same to have been stolen.
18 USC 553(a)(2)	Importation or exportation of stolen motor vehicles, off-highway mobile equipment, vessels or aircraft.	imports, exports, or attempts to import or export any motor vehicle, etc., knowing that the identification number of such motor vehicle, equipment, or part has been removed, obliterated, tampered with, or altered.
18 USC 592	Troops at polls (Elections and Political Activities).	as an officer of the Army or Navy, or other person in the civil, military, or naval service of the U.S., orders, brings, keeps, or has under his authority or control any troops or armed men at any place where a general or special election is held, unless such force be necessary to repel armed enemies of the U.S.
18 USC 593	Interference by armed forces (Elections and Political Activities).	
18 USC 594	Intimidation of voters.	
18 USC 595	Interference by administrative employees of Federal, State, or Territorial Governments.	uses official authority for the purpose of interfering with, or affecting, the nomination or election of any candidate for the office of President, Vice President, Presidential elector, Member of the Senate, Member of the House of Representatives, Delegate from the District of Columbia, or Resident Commissioner.

Title & Section Numbers	Caption of Section (Chapter Headings)	Relates to any persons(s) who...
18 USC 596	Polling armed forces.	within or without the Armed Forces of the United States, polls any member of the such forces with reference to his choice of or his vote for any candidate.
18 USC 597	Expenditures to influence voting.	
18 USC 598	Coercion by means of relief appropriations.	
18 USC 599	Promise of appointment by candidate.	
18 USC 600	Promise of employment or other benefit for political activity.	
18 USC 601	Deprivation of employment or other benefit for political contribution.	
18 USC 602	Solicitation of political contributions.	
18 USC 603	Making political contributions.	being an officer or employee of the United States makes any contribution within the meaning of section 301(8) of the Federal Election Campaign Act of 1971, if the person receiving such contribution is the employer or employing authority of the person making the contributions.
18 USC 604	Solicitation from persons on relief.	
18 USC 605	Disclosure of names of persons on relief.	
18 USC 606	Intimidation to secure political contributions.	

Title & Section Numbers	Caption of Section (Chapter Headings)	Relates to any persons(s) who...
18 USC 607	Place of solicitation.	solicit or receive any contribution within the meaning of section 301(8) of the Federal Election Campaign Act of 1971 in any room or building occupied in the discharge of official duties by any person mentioned in section 603.
18 USC 608	Absent uniformed services voters and overseas voters.	knowingly deprives or attempts to deprive any person of a right under the Uniformed and Overseas Citizens Absentee Voting Act.
18 USC 609	Use of military authority to influence vote of member of the Armed Forces.	
18 USC 610	Coercion of political activity.	intimidate, threaten, command, or coerce, or attempt to intimidate, threaten, command, or coerce, any employee of the Federal Government to engage in, or not to engage in, any political activity.
18 USC 611	Voting by aliens.	
18 USC 641	Public money, property or records (Embezzlement and Theft).	embezzles, steals, purloins, or knowingly converts to his use or the use of another, or without authority, sells, conveys, or disposes of any record, voucher, money or thing of value of the U.S. or any department or agency thereof.
18 USC 642	Tools and materials for counterfeiting purposes (Embezzlement and Theft).	
18 USC 643	Accounting generally for public money (Embezzlement and Theft).	being an officer, employee or agent of the U.S. or any department or agency thereof, having received public money which he is not authorized to retain as salary, pay, or emolument, fails to render his accounts for the same as provided by law.

Title & Section Numbers	Caption of Section (Chapter Headings)	Relates to any persons(s) who...
18 USC 644	Banker receiving unauthorized deposit of public money (Embezzlement and Theft).	
18 USC 645	Court officers generally (Embezzlement and Theft).	being a U.S. marshal, clerk, receiver, referee, trustee, or other officer of a U.S. court, or any deputy, assistant, or employee of any such officer, retains or converts to his own use or to the use of another or after demand by the party entitled thereto, unlawfully retains any money coming into his hands by virtue of his official relation, position, or employment.
18 USC 646	Court officers depositing registry moneys (Embezzlement and Theft).	
18 USC 647	Receiving loan from court officer (Embezzlement and Theft).	knowingly receives, from a clerk or other officer of a court of the U.S., as a deposit, loan, or otherwise, any money belonging in the registry of such court.
18 USC 648	Custodians, generally, misusing public funds (Embezzlement and Theft).	
18 USC 649	Custodians failing to deposit moneys; persons affected (Embezzlement and Theft).	
18 USC 650	Depositaries failing to safeguard deposits (Embezzlement and Theft).	
18 USC 651	Disbursing officer falsely certifying full payment (Embezzlement and Theft).	
18 USC 652	Disbursing officer paying lesser in lieu of lawful amount (Embezzlement and Theft).	
18 USC 653	Disbursing officer misusing public funds (Embezzlement and Theft).	

Title & Section Numbers	Caption of Section (Chapter Headings)	Relates to any persons(s) who...
18 USC 654	Officer or employee of U.S. converting property of another (Embezzlement and Theft).	
18 USC 655	Theft by bank examiner.	
18 USC 656	Theft, embezzlement, or misapplication by bank officer or employee.	
18 USC 657	Lending, credit and insurance institutions (Embezzlement and Theft).	being an officer, agent or employee of or connected in any capacity with the Federal Deposit Insurance Corporation, etc., embezzles, abstracts, purloins, or willfully misapplies any moneys, funds, credits, securities, or other things of value belonging to such institution.
18 USC 658	Property mortgaged or pledged to farm credit agencies (Embezzlement and Theft).	conceals, removes, disposes of, or converts to his own use or to that of another, any property mortgaged or pledged to, or held by the Farm Credit Administration, any Federal intermediate credit bank, or the Federal Crop Insurance Corporation, etc.
18 USC 659	Interstate or foreign shipments by carrier; State prosecutions (Embezzlement and Theft).	
18 USC 660	Carrier's funds derived from commerce; State prosecutions (Embezzlement and Theft).	
18 USC 661	Within special maritime and territorial jurisdiction (Embezzlement and Theft).	
18 USC 662	Receiving stolen property, within special maritime and territorial jurisdiction.	

Title & Section Numbers	Caption of Section (Chapter Headings)	Relates to any persons(s) who...
18 USC 663	Solicitation or use of gifts (Embezzlement and Theft).	solicits any gift of money or other property, and represents that such gift is being solicited for the use of the U.S. with the intention of embezzling, stealing, or purloining such gift, or converting the same to another use or purpose.
18 USC 664	Theft or embezzlement from employee benefit plan.	
18 USC 665(a)	Theft or embezzlement from employment and training funds; improper inducement; obstruction of investigations.	being an officer, director, agent or employee of or connected in any capacity with any agency or organization receiving financial assistance or any funds under the Comprehensive Employment and Training Act or the Job Training Partnership Act, knowingly enrolls an ineligible participant, or embezzles, willfully misapplies, or steals any of the moneys, funds, assets, or property which are the subject of a financial assistance agreement or contract pursuant to such Act.
18 USC 665(b)	Theft or embezzlement from employment and training funds; improper inducement; obstruction of investigations.	by threat or procuring dismissal of any person from employment or of refusal to employ or refusal to renew a contract of employment in connection with a financial assistance agreement or contract under Comprehensive Employment and Training Act induces any person to give up any money or thing of value to any person.
18 USC 665(c)	Theft or embezzlement from employment and training funds; improper inducement; obstruction of investigations.	willfully obstructs or impedes or endeavors to obstruct or impede an investigation or inquiry under the Comprehensive Employment and Training Act or the Job Training Partnership Act.
18 USC 666(a)(1)(A)	Theft or bribery concerning programs receiving Federal funds.	as an agent of an organization, or of a State, local or Indian tribal government, embezzles, steals, obtains by fraud, or otherwise without authority knowingly converts to the use of a person other than the rightful owner or intentionally misapplies property.

Title & Section Numbers	Caption of Section (Chapter Headings)	Relates to any persons(s) who...
18 USC 666(a)(1)(B)	Theft or bribery concerning programs receiving Federal funds.	as an agent of an organization, or of a State, local or Indian tribal government, corruptly solicits or demands for the benefit of any person, or accepts or agrees to accept, anything of value from any person, intending to be influenced or rewarded in connection with any business, transaction, or series of transactions of such organization, government, or agency involving anything of a specified value.
18 USC 666(a)(2)	Theft or bribery concerning programs receiving Federal funds.	corruptly gives, offers, or agrees to give anything of value to any person, with intent to influence or reward an agent of an organization or of a State, local, or Indian tribal government, or any agency thereof, in connection with any business, transaction, or series of transactions of such organization, government, or agency involving anything of a specified value.
18 USC 667	Theft of livestock.	
18 USC 668	Theft of major artwork.	
18 USC 669	Theft or embezzlement in connection with health care.	
18 USC 700	Desecration of the flag of the United States; penalties.	
18 USC 701	Official badges, identification cards, other insignia.	manufactures, sells or possesses any badge, identification card, or other insignia, of the design prescribed by the head of any department or agency of the United States for use by any officer or employee thereof.
18 USC 702	Uniform of armed forces and Public Health Service.	in any place within the jurisdiction of the United States, without authority, wears the uniform or a distinctive part thereof of the uniform of any of the armed forces of the United States or Public Health Service.

Title & Section Numbers	Caption of Section (Chapter Headings)	Relates to any persons(s) who...
18 USC 703	Uniform of friendly nation.	within the jurisdiction of the United States, with intent to deceive or mislead, wears any naval, military, police or other official uniform, decoration, or regalia of any foreign state, nation, or government with which the United States is at peace.
18 USC 704	Military medals or decorations.	knowingly wears, manufactures, or sells any decoration or medal authorized by Congress for the armed forces of the Unites States.
18 USC 705	Badge or medal of veterans' organizations.	
18 USC 706	Red Cross.	wears or displays the sign of the Red Cross or any insignia colored in imitation thereof for the fraudulent purpose of inducing the belief that he is a member of or an agent for the American National Red Cross.
18 USC 707	4-H club emblem fraudulently used.	
18 USC 708	Swiss Confederation coat of arms.	willfully uses as a trade mark, commercial label, or portion thereof, or as an advertisement or insignia for any business or organization or for any trade or commercial purpose, the coat of arms of the Swiss Confederation.
18 USC 709	False advertising or misuse of names to indicate Federal agency.	
18 USC 710	Cremation urns for military use.	knowingly uses, manufactures, or sells any cremation urn of a design approved by the Secretary of Defense for use to retain the cremated remains of deceased members of the armed forces.
18 USC 711	"Smokey Bear" character or name.	knowingly and for profit manufactures, reproduces, or uses the character "Smokey Bear".

Title & Section Numbers	Caption of Section (Chapter Headings)	Relates to any persons(s) who...
18 USC 711a	“Woodsy Owl” character, name, or slogan.	knowingly and for profit manufactures, reproduces, or uses the character “Woodsy Owl”, the name “Woodsy Owl”, or the associated slogan, “Give a Hoot, Don’t Pollute”.
18 USC 712	Misuse of names, words, emblems, or insignia.	
18 USC 713	Use of likeness of the great seal of the United States, the seals of the President and Vice President, and the seal of the United States Senate.	
18 USC 715	“The Golden Eagle Insignia”.	knowingly manufactures, reproduces, or uses the “The Golden Eagle Insignia”, or any facsimile thereof, in such a manner as is likely to cause confusion, or to cause mistake, or to deceive.
18 USC 751	Prisoners in custody or institution or officer (Escape and Rescue).	
18 USC 752	Instigating or assisting escape.	
18 USC 753	Rescue to prevent execution.	
18 USC 755	Officer permitting escape.	
18 USC 756	Internee of belligerent nation (Escape and Rescue).	aids or entices any person belonging to the armed forces of a belligerent nation or faction who is interned in the U.S. in accordance with the law of nations, to escape or attempt to escape from the jurisdiction of the U.S. or from the limits of internment prescribed.
18 USC 757	Prisoners of war or enemy aliens (Escape and Rescue).	procures the escape of any prisoner of war held by the U.S. or any of its allies.

Title & Section Numbers	Caption of Section (Chapter Headings)	Relates to any persons(s) who...
18 USC 758	High speed flight from immigration checkpoint.	flees or evades a checkpoint operated by the Immigration and Naturalization Service, or any other Federal law enforcement agency, in a motor vehicle and flees Federal, State, or local law enforcement agents in excess of the legal speed limit.
18 USC 792	Harboring or concealing persons.	harbors or conceals any person who he knows, or has reasonable grounds to believe or suspect, has committed, or is about to commit, an offense under sections 793 or 794 of this title.
18 USC 793(a)	Gathering, transmitting, or losing defense information (Espionage and Censorship).	for the purpose of obtaining information respecting the national defense with intent or reason to believe that the information is to be used to the injury of the U.S., goes upon, enters, flies over, or otherwise obtains information concerning any vessel or property under the control of the U.S.
18 USC 793(b)	Gathering, transmitting, or losing defense information (Espionage and Censorship).	for the purpose aforesaid, copies, takes, makes, or attempts to copy, take, make or obtain any sketch, photograph, photographic negative, blueprint, map, model, instrument, appliance, document, writing, or note of anything connected with the national defense.
18 USC 793(c)	Gathering, transmitting, or losing defense information (Espionage and Censorship).	receives, or attempts to receive any document, writing, code book, signal book, sketch, photograph, photographic negative, blueprint, plan, map, model, instrument, appliance, or note for aforesaid purpose.
18 USC 793(d)	Gathering, transmitting, or losing defense information (Espionage and Censorship).	lawfully having possession of, access to, or control over any document, writing, code book, etc., having information relating to the national defense, willfully communicates, delivers, transmits or causes to be communicated, delivered, or transmitted, or attempts to communicate, deliver, or transmit the same to any person not entitled to receive it.

Title & Section Numbers	Caption of Section (Chapter Headings)	Relates to any persons(s) who...
18 USC 793(e)	Gathering, transmitting, or losing defense information (Espionage and Censorship).	having unauthorized possession of, access to, or control over any document, writing, code book, etc., having information relating to the national defense, willfully communicates, delivers, transmits or causes to be communicated, delivered, or transmitted, or attempts to communicate, deliver, or transmit the same to any person not entitled to receive it.
18 USC 793(f)	Gathering, transmitting, or losing defense information (Espionage and Censorship).	being entrusted with or having lawful possession or control of any document, etc., having information relating to the national defense, through negligence, permits the same to be removed from its proper place of custody or delivered to anyone in violation of his trust, or having knowledge that the same has been illegally removed from its proper place of custody or delivered to anyone in violation of that person's trust.
18 USC 793(g)	Gathering, transmitting, or losing defense information (Espionage and Censorship).	[Two or more persons conspire to violate any of the foregoing provisions of this section.]
18 USC 794	Gathering or delivering defense information to aid foreign government (Espionage and Censorship).	
18 USC 795	Photographing and sketching defense installations (Espionage and Censorship).	
18 USC 796	Use of aircraft for photographing defense installations (Espionage and Censorship).	
18 USC 797	Publication and sale of photographs of defense installations (Espionage and Censorship).	
18 USC 798	Disclosure of classified information (Espionage and Censorship).	

Title & Section Numbers	Caption of Section (Chapter Headings)	Relates to any persons(s) who...
18 USC 799	Violation of regulations of National Aeronautics and Space Administration (Espionage and Censorship).	violate, attempt to violate, or conspire to violate any regulation or order promulgated by the Administrator of the National Aeronautics and Space Administration for the protection or security of any laboratory, station, base or other facility, or any aircraft, missile, spacecraft, or equipment in the custody of the Administration.
18 USC 831	Prohibited transactions involving nuclear materials.	
18 USC 836	Transportation of fireworks into State prohibiting sale or use.	
18 USC 842(a)	Unlawful acts (Importation, Manufacture, Distribution and Storage of Explosive Materials).	engages in the business of importing, manufacturing, or dealing in explosive materials without a license issued under this chapter.
18 USC 842(b)	Unlawful acts (Importation, Manufacture, Distribution and Storage of Explosive Materials).	as a licensee knowingly distributes explosive material to any person except a licensee, a permittee, or a resident of the State where distribution is made and in which the licensee is licensed to do business or a State contiguous thereto if permitted by law of the State of the purchaser's residence.
18 USC 842(c)	Unlawful acts (Importation, Manufacture, Distribution and Storage of Explosive Materials).	distributes explosive materials to any person who the licensee has reason to believe intends to transport such explosive materials into a State where the purchase, possession, or use of explosive materials is prohibited or which does not permit its residents to transport or ship explosive materials into it or to receive explosive materials in it.

Title & Section Numbers	Caption of Section (Chapter Headings)	Relates to any persons(s) who...
18 USC 842(d)	Unlawful acts (Importation, Manufacture, Distribution and Storage of Explosive Materials).	knowingly distributes explosive materials to any individual who is under twenty-one years of age, has been convicted in any court of a crime punishable by imprisonment for a term exceeding one year, is under indictment for a crime punishable by imprisonment for a term exceeding one year, is a fugitive from justice, is an unlawful user of or addicted to any controlled substance, or has been adjudicated a mental defective.
18 USC 842(e)	Unlawful acts (Importation, Manufacture, Distribution and Storage of Explosive Materials).	knowingly distributes any explosive materials to any person in any State where the purchase, possession, or use by such person of such explosive materials would be in violation of any State law or any published ordinance applicable at the place of distribution.
18 USC 842(f)	Unlawful acts (Importation, Manufacture, Distribution and Storage of Explosive Materials).	willfully manufactures, imports, purchases, distributes, or receives explosive materials without making such records as the Secretary may by regulation require.`
18 USC 842(g)	Unlawful acts (Importation, Manufacture, Distribution and Storage of Explosive Materials).	makes any false entry in any record which licensee is required to keep pursuant to this section.
18 USC 842(h)	Unlawful acts (Importation, Manufacture, Distribution and Storage of Explosive Materials).	receives, possesses, transports, ships, conceals, stores, barters, sells, disposes of, or pledges or accepts as security for a loan, any stolen explosive materials which have been shipped or transported in interstate or foreign commerce knowing or having reasonable cause to believe that the explosive materials were stolen.
18 USC 842(j)	Unlawful acts (Importation, Manufacture, Distribution and Storage of Explosive Materials).	stores any explosive materials in a manner not in conformity with regulations promulgated by the Secretary.

Title & Section Numbers	Caption of Section (Chapter Headings)	Relates to any persons(s) who...
18 USC 842(k)	Unlawful acts (Importation, Manufacture, Distribution and Storage of Explosive Materials).	having knowledge of the theft or loss of any explosive materials from his stock, fails to report such theft or loss within twenty-four hours of discovery thereof to the Secretary and to appropriate local authorities.
18 USC 844(d)	Penalties (Importation, Manufacture, Distribution and Storage of Explosive Materials).	transports and receives, or attempts to transport and receive in interstate or foreign commerce any explosive with knowledge that it will be used to kill, injure, or intimidate any individual or unlawfully damage or destroy any building, vehicle, or real property.
18 USC 844(e)	Penalties (Importation, Manufacture, Distribution and Storage of Explosive Materials).	through the use of mail, telephone, telegraph, or other instrument of commerce, willfully makes a threat, or maliciously conveys false information knowing the same to be false, concerning an attempt or alleged attempt being made to kill, injure or intimidate any individual.
18 USC 844(f)	Penalties (Importation, Manufacture, Distribution and Storage of Explosive Materials).	maliciously damages or destroys, or attempts to damage or destroy, by means of fire or an explosive, any building, vehicle, or other personal or real property in whole or in part owned or possessed by, or leased to the U.S.
18 USC 844(h)	Penalties (Importation, Manufacture, Distribution and Storage of Explosive Materials).	uses fire or an explosive to commit any felony which may be prosecuted in a court of the U.S.
18 USC 844(i)	Penalties (Importation, Manufacture, Distribution and Storage of Explosive Materials).	maliciously damages or destroys, or attempts to damage or destroy, by means of fire or an explosive, any building, vehicle, or other real or personal property used in interstate or foreign commerce or in any activity affecting interstate or foreign commerce.
18 USC 844(m)	Penalties (Importation, Manufacture, Distribution and Storage of Explosive Materials).	conspires to commit an offense under subsection (h).

Title & Section Numbers	Caption of Section (Chapter Headings)	Relates to any persons(s) who...
18 USC 871	Threats against President and successors to the Presidency.	
18 USC 872	Extortion by officers or employees of the U.S.	
18 USC 873	Blackmail.	
18 USC 874	Kickbacks from public works employees.	
18 USC 875(a)	Interstate communications (Extortion and Threats).	transmits in interstate or foreign commerce any communication containing any demand or request for ransom or reward for the release of any kidnapped person.
18 USC 875(b)	Interstate communications (Extortion and Threats).	with intent to extort from any person, firm, association, or corporation, any money or other thing of value, transmits in interstate or foreign commerce any communication containing any threat to kidnap any person or any threat to injure the person of another.
18 USC 875(c)	Interstate communications (Extortion and Threats).	transmits in interstate or foreign commerce any communication containing any threat to kidnap any person or any threat to injure the person of another.
18 USC 875(d)	Interstate communications (Extortion and Threats).	with intent to extort from any person, any money or other thing of value, transmits in interstate or foreign commerce any communication containing any threat to injure the property or reputation of the addressee or of another or the reputation of a deceased person or any threat to accuse the addressee or any other person of a crime.
18 USC 876	Mailing threatening communications.	
18 USC 877	Mailing threatening communications from foreign country.	

Title & Section Numbers	Caption of Section (Chapter Headings)	Relates to any persons(s) who...
18 USC 878(a)	Threats and extortion against foreign officials, official guests, or internationally protected persons.	knowingly and willfully threatens to violate section 112, 1116, or 1201 by killing, kidnapping, or assaulting a foreign official, official guest, or internationally protected person.
18 USC 878(b)	Threats and extortion against foreign officials, official guests, or internationally protected persons.	in connection with any violation of subsection (a) or actual violation of section 112, 1116, or 1201 makes any extortionate demand.
18 USC 879	Threats against former Presidents and certain other persons protected by the Secret Service.	
18 USC 880	Receiving the proceeds of extortion.	
18 USC 892	Making extortionate extensions of credit.	
18 USC 893	Financing extortionate extensions of credit.	
18 USC 894	Collection of extensions of credit by extortionate means.	
18 USC 911	Citizen of the U.S. (False Personation).	falsely and willfully represents himself to be a citizen of the U.S.
18 USC 912	Officer or employee of the U.S. (False Personation).	falsely assumes or pretends to be an officer or employee acting under the authority of the U.S., or any department, agency or officer thereof.
18 USC 913	Impersonator making arrest or search (False Personation).	
18 USC 914	Creditors of the U.S. (False Personation).	falsely personates any true and lawful holder of any share or sum in the public stocks or debt of the U.S.
18 USC 915	Foreign diplomats, consuls, or officers (False Personation).	falsely assumes or pretends to be a diplomatic, consular or other official of a foreign government duly accredited as such to the U.S.

Title & Section Numbers	Caption of Section (Chapter Headings)	Relates to any persons(s) who...
18 USC 916	4-H Club members or agents (False Personation).	falsely and with intent to defraud, holds himself out as or represents or pretends himself to be a member of, associated with, or an agent or representative for the 4-H clubs.
18 USC 917	Red Cross members or agents (False Personation).	falsely or fraudulently holds himself out as or represents or pretends to be a member of or an agent for the American National Red Cross for the purpose of soliciting, collecting, or receiving money or material.
18 USC 922(a)-(w)	Unlawful acts (Firearms).	[Making it unlawful for... any person, except a licensed importer, to import, manufacture, or deal in firearms or ammunition; for any licensed importer to sell or deliver any firearm or ammunition to any individual who the licensee knows or has reasonable cause to believe is less than eighteen years of age; any person to sell or otherwise dispose of any firearm or ammunition to any person knowing or having reasonable cause to believe that such person has been convicted of a crime punishable by imprisonment for a term exceeding one year, is a fugitive from justice, is addicted to any controlled substance, or has been committed to a mental institution; any person to transport or ship in interstate or foreign commerce any stolen firearm or ammunition, knowing or having reasonable cause to believe that such was stolen; any person to knowingly possess a firearm that has moved in interstate commerce at a place the individual knows is a school zone.]
18 USC 922(x)(1)	Unlawful acts (Firearms).	sells, delivers, or otherwise transfers a handgun or ammunition to a person who the transferor knows or has cause to believe is a juvenile.
18 USC 923	Licensing (Firearms).	[No person shall engage in the business of importing, manufacturing, or dealing in firearms, or importing or manufacturing ammunition, until he has filed an application for and received a license to do so.]

Title & Section Numbers	Caption of Section (Chapter Headings)	Relates to any persons(s) who...
18 USC 924(a)	Penalties (Firearms).	makes any false statement or representation with respect to the information required by this chapter.
18 USC 924(b)	Penalties (Firearms).	ships, transports, or receives a firearm or ammunition in interstate or foreign commerce.
18 USC 924(c)	Penalties (Firearms).	uses or carries a firearm in relation to any crime of violence or drug trafficking crime.
18 USC 924(e)	Penalties (Firearms).	violates section 922(g) of this title and has three pervious convictions by any court referred to in section 922(g)(1) of this title.
18 USC 924(f)	Penalties (Firearms).	violates section 922(p) of this title.
18 USC 924(g)	Penalties (Firearms).	engages in criminal conduct which constitutes an offense listed in section 1961(1).
18 USC 924(h)	Penalties (Firearms).	transfers a firearm knowing that such firearm will be used to commit a crime of violence or drug trafficking crime.
18 USC 924(i)	Penalties (Firearms).	knowingly violates section 922(u) of this title.
18 USC 924(j)	Penalties (Firearms).	in the course of violating subsection (c), causes the death of a person through the use of a firearm.
18 USC 929(a)	Use of restricted ammunition.	during, and in relation to, the commission of a crime of violence or drug trafficking crime uses or carries a firearm and is in possession of armor piercing ammunition.
18 USC 930	Possession of firearms and dangerous weapons in Federal facilities.	

Title & Section Numbers	Caption of Section (Chapter Headings)	Relates to any persons(s) who...
18 USC 951	Agents of foreign governments (Foreign Relations).	acts in the United States as an agent of a foreign government without prior notification to the Attorney General.
18 USC 952	Diplomatic codes and correspondence (Foreign Relations).	by virtue of his employment by the United States, obtains from another or has or has had custody of or access to, any official diplomatic code or any matter prepared in any such code, or which purports to have been prepared in any such code willfully publishes or furnishes to another any such code or matter.
18 USC 953	Private correspondence with foreign governments (Foreign Relations).	directly or indirectly commences or carries on any correspondence or intercourse with any foreign government or any officer or agent thereof, with intent to influence the measures or conduct of any foreign government or of any officer or agent thereof, in relation to any disputes or controversies with the United States.
18 USC 954	False statements influencing foreign government (Foreign Relations).	willfully and knowingly makes any untrue statement under oath before any person authorized and empowered to administer oaths, which the affiant has knowledge or reason to believe will, or may be used to influence the measures or conduct of any foreign government, to the injury of the United States.
18 USC 955	Financial transactions with foreign governments (Foreign Relations).	
18 USC 956	Conspiracy to kill, kidnap, maim, or injure persons or damage property in a foreign country (Foreign Relations).	
18 USC 957	Possession of property in aid of foreign government (Foreign Relations).	knowingly and willfully controls or possesses any property or papers used or designed or intended for use in violating any penal statute, or any of the rights or obligations of the United States under any treaty or the law of nations.

Title & Section Numbers	Caption of Section (Chapter Headings)	Relates to any persons(s) who...
18 USC 958	Commission to serve against friendly nation (Foreign Relations).	accepts and exercises a commission to serve a foreign prince, state, colony, district, or people, in war, against any prince, state, colony, district or people, with whom the United States is at peace.
18 USC 959	Enlistment in foreign service (Foreign Relations).	enlists himself or to go beyond the jurisdiction of the United States with intent to be enlisted or entered in the service of any foreign prince, state, colony, district, or people as a soldier or as a marine or seaman on board any vessel of war.
18 USC 960	Expedition against friendly nation (Foreign Relations).	knowingly begins or sets on foot or provides or prepares a means for or furnishes the money for, any naval or military expedition or enterprise to be carried on from thence against the territory or dominion of any foreign prince or state, or colony or district with whom the United States is at peace.
18 USC 961	Strengthening armed vessel of foreign nation (Foreign Relations).	increases or augments the force of any ship of war, cruiser, or other armed vessel which, at the time of her arrival within the United States, was a ship of war, or cruiser, or vessel in the service of any foreign prince, state, colony, district, or people at war with anyone whom the United States is at peace, by adding to the number of the guns of such vessel, or by adding thereto any equipment solely applicable to war.
18 USC 962	Arming vessel against friendly nation (Foreign Relations).	
18 USC 963	Detention of armed vessel (Foreign Relations).	takes, or attempts to take, or authorizes the taking of any such detained vessel, out of port of the United States.
18 USC 964	Delivering armed vessel to belligerent nation (Foreign Relations).	

Title & Section Numbers	Caption of Section (Chapter Headings)	Relates to any persons(s) who...
18 USC 965	Verified statements as prerequisite to vessel's departure (Foreign Relations).	takes, or attempts to take, or authorizes the taking of any such vessel, out of port or from the United States without a verified statement.
18 USC 966	Departure of vessel forbidden for false statements (Foreign Relations).	
18 USC 967	Departure of vessel forbidden in aid of neutrality (Foreign Relations).	
18 USC 970(a)	Protection of property occupied by foreign governments.	injures, damages, or destroys any property, real or personal, located in the U.S. and belonging to or utilized or occupied by any foreign government or international organization.
18 USC 1001	Statements or entries generally (Fraud and False Statements).	knowingly and willfully falsifies, conceals, or covers up by any trick, scheme, or device a material fact, or makes any false statement or representation or makes or uses any false writing or document knowing the same to contain any false, fictitious, or fraudulent statement or entry.
18 USC 1002	Possession of false papers to defraud the U.S.	
18 USC 1003	Demands against the U.S. (Fraud and False Statements).	knowingly and fraudulently demands or endeavors to obtain any share or sum in the public stocks of the U.S.
18 USC 1004	Certification of checks (Fraud and False Statements).	as an officer, director, agent, or employee of any Federal Reserve bank, receives any fictitious obligation, directly or collaterally, in order to evade any of the provisions of law relating to certification of checks.

Title & Section Numbers	Caption of Section (Chapter Headings)	Relates to any persons(s) who...
18 USC 1005	Bank entries, reports and transactions (Fraud and False Statements).	as an officer, director, agent or employee of any Federal Reserve bank, puts in circulation any notes of such bank, agency, or organization or company without authority from the directors of such.
18 USC 1006	Federal credit institutions entries, reports, and transactions (Fraud and False Statements).	
18 USC 1007	Federal Deposit Insurance Corporation transactions (Fraud and False Statements).	for the purpose of influencing in any way the action of the Federal Deposit Insurance Corporation, makes or invites reliance on a false, forged, or counterfeit statement, document, or thing.
18 USC 1010	Department of Housing and Urban Development and Federal Housing Administration transactions (Fraud and False Statements).	
18 USC 1011	Federal land bank mortgage transactions (Fraud and False Statements).	
18 USC 1012	Department of Housing and Urban Development transactions (Fraud and False Statements).	
18 USC 1013	Farm loan bonds and credit bank debentures (Fraud and False Statements).	
18 USC 1014	Loan and credit applications generally; renewals and discounts; crop insurance (Fraud and False Statements).	
18 USC 1015	Naturalization, citizenship or alien registry (Fraud and False Statements).	
18 USC 1016	Acknowledgment of appearance or oath (Fraud and False Statements).	as an officer authorized to administer oaths or to take and certify acknowledgments, knowingly makes any false acknowledgment, certificate, or statement concerning the appearance before him.

Title & Section Numbers	Caption of Section (Chapter Headings)	Relates to any persons(s) who...
18 USC 1017	Government seals wrongfully used and instruments wrongfully sealed (Fraud and False Statements).	
18 USC 1018	Official certificates or writings (Fraud and False Statements).	as a public officer or other person authorized by any law of the U.S. to make or give a certificate or other writing, knowingly makes and delivers as true such certificate or writing, containing any statement which he knows to be false, in a case where the punishment thereof is not elsewhere expressly provided by law.
18 USC 1019	Certificates by consular officers (Fraud and False Statements).	being consul, vice consul, or other person employed in the consular service of the U.S. knowingly certifies falsely to any invoice or other paper to which his certificate is authorized or required by law.
18 USC 1020	Highway projects (Fraud and False Statements).	as an officer, agent or employee of the U.S. makes a false statement, false representation, or false report as to the character, quality, quantity, or cost of the material used or to be used, or the quantity or quality of the work performed, or the cost thereof in connection with the submission of plans, maps, specifications, contracts, or costs of construction of any highway or related project submitted for approval to the Secretary of Transportation.
18 USC 1021	Title records (Fraud and False Statements).	
18 USC 1022	Delivery of certificate, voucher, receipt for military or naval property (Fraud and False Statements).	being authorized to deliver any certificate, voucher, receipt, or other paper certifying the receipt of arms, ammunition, provisions, clothing, or other property, used or to be used in the military service, delivers same to any other person without full knowledge of the truth of the facts stated therein and with intent to defraud the U.S.
18 USC 1023	Insufficient delivery of money or property for military or naval service (Fraud and False Statements).	

Title & Section Numbers	Caption of Section (Chapter Headings)	Relates to any persons(s) who...
18 USC 1024	Purchase or receipt of military, naval, or veteran's facilities property (Fraud and False Statements).	
18 USC 1025	False pretenses on high seas and other waters (Fraud and False Statements).	
18 USC 1026	Compromise, adjustment, or cancellation of farm indebtedness (Fraud and False Statements).	
18 USC 1027	False statements and concealment of facts in relation to documents required by the Employee Retirement Income Security Act of 1974 (Fraud and False Statements).	
18 USC 1028	Fraud and related activity in connection with identification documents (Fraud and False Statements).	
18 USC 1029	Fraud and related activity in connection with access devices (Fraud and False Statements).	
18 USC 1030(a)(1)	Fraud and related activity in connection with computer (Fraud and False Statements).	accesses a computer without authorization or exceeds authorized access and obtains information that has been determined by the U.S. government pursuant to an Executive order or statute to require protection against unauthorized disclosure for reasons of national defense or foreign relations.
18 USC 1030(a)(2)	Fraud and related activity in connection with computer (Fraud and False Statements).	accesses a computer without authorization and obtains information contained in a financial record of a financial institution, or of a card issuer as defined in section 1602(n) of title 15.
18 USC 1030(a)(3)	Fraud and related activity in connection with computer (Fraud and False Statements).	accesses a computer of a department or agency of the U.S. and such conduct adversely affects the use of the Government's operation of such computer.

Title & Section Numbers	Caption of Section (Chapter Headings)	Relates to any persons(s) who...
18 USC 1030(a)(4)	Fraud and related activity in connection with computer (Fraud and False Statements).	accesses a protected computer without authorization with intent to defraud.
18 USC 1030(a)(5)	Fraud and related activity in connection with computer (Fraud and False Statements).	causes the transmission of a program, information, code, or command and as a result of such conduct, intentionally causes damage without authorization to a protected computer.
18 USC 1030(a)(6)	Fraud and related activity in connection with computer (Fraud and False Statements).	with intent to defraud traffics (as defined in section 1029) in any password or similar information through which a computer may be accessed without authorization.
18 USC 1030(b)	Fraud and related activity in connection with computer (Fraud and False Statements).	attempts to commit an offense under subsection (a) of this section.
18 USC 1031	Major fraud against the U.S. (Fraud and False Statements).	
18 USC 1032	Concealment of assets from conservator, receiver, or liquidating agent of financial institution (Fraud and False Statements).	
18 USC 1033	Crimes by or affecting person engaged in the business of insurance whose activities affect interstate commerce (Fraud and False Statements).	
18 USC 1035	False statements relating to health care matters.	in any matter involving a health care benefit program, knowingly and willfully falsifies, conceals, or covers up by any trick, scheme, or device a material fact.
18 USC 1071	Concealing person from arrest.	conceals any person for whose arrest a warrant or process has been issued under provisions of any law of the United States.
18 USC 1072	Concealing escaped prisoner.	conceals any prisoner after escape from custody of the Attorney General or from a Federal penal or correctional institution.

Title & Section Numbers	Caption of Section (Chapter Headings)	Relates to any persons(s) who...
18 USC 1073	Flight to avoid prosecution or giving testimony.	moves or travels in interstate commerce with intent to avoid prosecution, or custody or confinement after conviction, for a crime punishable by death or which is a felony.
18 USC 1074	Flight to avoid prosecution for damaging or destroying any building or other real or personal property.	moves or travels in interstate commerce with intent to avoid prosecution for willfully attempting to or damaging any building or personal property.
18 USC 1082	Gambling ships.	sets up, owns, or holds any interest in any gambling ship if such gambling ship is on the high seas or is an American vessel.
18 USC 1084	Transmission of wagering information; penalties.	
18 USC 1091	Genocide.	with intent to destroy, in whole or in substantial part, a national, ethnic, racial or religious group, kills, or causes serious bodily injury to members of that group.
18 USC 1111(a)	Murder.	unlawfully kills a human being with malice aforethought.
18 USC 1112	Manslaughter.	
18 USC 1113	Attempt to commit murder or manslaughter.	
18 USC 1114	Protection of the officers and employees of the U.S. (Homicide).	kills or attempts to kill any officer or employee of the U.S.
18 USC 1115	Misconduct or neglect of ship officers (Homicide).	
18 USC 1116	Murder or manslaughter of foreign officials, official guests, or internationally protected persons.	
18 USC 1117	Conspiracy to murder.	[Two or more persons conspire to violate section 1111, 1114, 1116, or 1119 of this title and one or more of such persons do any overt act to effect the object of the conspiracy.]

Title & Section Numbers	Caption of Section (Chapter Headings)	Relates to any persons(s) who...
18 USC 1118	Murder by a federal prisoner.	
18 USC 1119	Foreign murder of U.S. nationals.	
18 USC 1120	Murder by escaped prisoners.	being a person having escaped from a Federal correctional institution where the person was confined under a sentence for a term of life imprisonment, kills another.
18 USC 1121	Killing persons aiding Federal investigations or State correctional officers.	
18 USC 1122	Protection against the human immunodeficiency virus.	knowingly donates or sells blood, semen, tissues, organs, or other bodily fluids for use by another, after testing positive for HIV.
18 USC 1153	Offenses committed within Indian country.	
18 USC 1154	Intoxicants dispensed in Indian country.	
18 USC 1155	Intoxicants dispensed on school site (Indians).	manufactures, sells, gives away or in any manner furnishes to anyone intoxicating drinks of any kind on any tract of land in the former Indian country upon which is located any Indian school.
18 USC 1156	Intoxicants possessed unlawfully (Indians).	possesses intoxicating liquors in the Indian country or where the introduction is prohibited by treaty or an Act of Congress.
18 USC 1158	Counterfeiting Indian Arts and Crafts Board trade-mark.	
18 USC 1159	Misrepresentation of Indian produced goods and products.	
18 USC 1163	Embezzlement and theft from Indian tribal organizations.	

Title & Section Numbers	Caption of Section (Chapter Headings)	Relates to any persons(s) who...
18 USC 1164	Destroying boundary and warning signs (Indians).	willfully destroys, defaces, or removes any sign erected by an Indian tribe to indicate the boundary of an Indian reservation or any Indian country.
18 USC 1165	Hunting, trapping, or fishing on Indian land.	
18 USC 1167	Theft from gaming establishments on Indian lands.	
18 USC 1168	Theft by officers or employees of gaming establishments on Indian lands.	
18 USC 1169	Reporting of child abuse (Indians).	
18 USC 1170	Illegal trafficking in Native American human remains and cultural items.	
18 USC 1201(a)	Kidnapping.	seizes, confines, inveigles, decoys, kidnaps, abducts, or carries away and holds for ransom or reward or otherwise any person, except in the case of a minor by the parent thereof.
18 USC 1201(c)	Kidnapping.	[Two or more persons conspire to violate this section, and one or more of such persons do any overt act to effect the object of the conspiracy.]
18 USC 1201(d)	Kidnapping.	attempts to violate subsection (a).
18 USC 1202	Ransom money.	
18 USC 1203	Hostage taking (Kidnapping).	
18 USC 1204	International parental kidnapping.	
18 USC 1231	Transportation of strikebreakers (Labor).	

Title & Section Numbers	Caption of Section (Chapter Headings)	Relates to any persons(s) who...
18 USC 1262	Transportation into State prohibiting sale (Liquor Traffic).	imports, brings, or transports any intoxicating liquor into any State, Territory, District, or Possession in which all sales are prohibited.
18 USC 1263	Marks and labels on packages (Liquor Traffic).	knowingly ships into any place within the United States any package containing liquor unless such shipment is accompanied by copy of a bill of lading showing the nature of the contents and quantity contained therein.
18 USC 1264	Delivery to consignee (Liquor Traffic).	knowingly delivers to any person other than the person to whom it has been consigned, any liquor fit for use for beverage purposes which has been shipped into any place within the United States.
18 USC 1265	C.O.D. shipments prohibited (Liquor Traffic).	
18 USC 1301	Importing or transporting lottery tickets.	
18 USC 1302	Mailing lottery tickets or related matter.	
18 USC 1303	Postmaster or employee as lottery agent.	
18 USC 1304	Broadcasting lottery information.	broadcasts by means of any radio or television station for which a license is required any advertisement of or information concerning any lottery.
18 USC 1306	Participation by financial institutions (Lotteries).	knowingly violates section 5136A of the Revised Statutes of the U.S., section 9A of the Federal Reserve Act, or section 20 of the Federal Deposit Insurance Act.
18 USC 1341	Frauds and swindles (Mail Fraud).	
18 USC 1342	Fictitious name or address (Mail Fraud).	

Title & Section Numbers	Caption of Section (Chapter Headings)	Relates to any persons(s) who...
18 USC 1343	Fraud by wire, radio or television.	
18 USC 1344	Bank fraud.	
18 USC 1347	Health care fraud.	
18 USC 1361	Government property or contracts (Malicious Mischief).	injures or commits any depredation against any property of the U.S. or any property which has been or is being manufactured or constructed for the U.S.
18 USC 1362	Communication lines, stations, or systems (Malicious Mischief).	willfully or maliciously injures or destroys or attempts willfully or maliciously to injure or destroy any of the works, property, or material of any radio, telegraph, telephone or cable, line, station, or system, or other means of communication, operated or controlled by the U.S.
18 USC 1363	Buildings or property within special maritime and territorial jurisdiction (Malicious Mischief).	destroys or injures or attempts to destroy or injure any structure, conveyance, or other real or personal property.
18 USC 1364	Interference with foreign commerce by violence (Malicious Mischief).	
18 USC 1365(a)	Tampering with consumer products (Malicious Mischief).	tampers with any consumer product that affects interstate or foreign commerce, or the labeling of, or container for, any such product, or attempts to do so.
18 USC 1365(b)	Tampering with consumer products (Malicious Mischief).	with intent to cause serious injury to the business of any person, taints any consumer product or renders materially false or misleading the labeling of, or container for, a consumer product, if such product affects interstate or foreign commerce.

Title & Section Numbers	Caption of Section (Chapter Headings)	Relates to any persons(s) who...
18 USC 1365(c)	Tampering with consumer products (Malicious Mischief).	communicates false information that a consumer product has been tainted, if such product or the results of such communication affect interstate or foreign commerce, and if such tainting, had it occurred, would create a risk of death or bodily injury to another person.
18 USC 1365(d)	Tampering with consumer products (Malicious Mischief).	threatens, under circumstances in which the threat may reasonably be expected to be believed conduct that if it occurred would violate subsection (a) of this section.
18 USC 1365(e)	Tampering with consumer products (Malicious Mischief).	[A conspiracy of two or more persons to commit an offense under subsection (a) of this section.]
18 USC 1366	Destruction of an energy facility.	
18 USC 1367	Interference with the operation of a satellite.	
18 USC 1381	Enticing desertion and harboring deserters (Military and Navy).	
18 USC 1382	Entering military, naval, or Coast Guard property.	goes upon any military, naval, or Coast Guard reservation, post, fort, arsenal, yard, station, or installation, for any purpose prohibited by law.
18 USC 1384	Prostitution near military and naval establishments.	
18 USC 1385	Use of Army and Air Force as posse comitatus.	willfully uses any part of the Army or the Air Force as a posse comitatus or otherwise to execute the laws.
18 USC 1386	Keys and keyways used in security applications by the Department of Defense.	steals, purloins, embezzles, or obtains by false pretense any lock or key to any lock, knowing that such lock or key has been adopted by any part of the Department of Defense for use in protecting conventional arms, ammunition or explosives.

Title & Section Numbers	Caption of Section (Chapter Headings)	Relates to any persons(s) who...
18 USC 1421	Accounts of court officers (Nationality and Citizenship).	being a clerk or assistant clerk of a court charged by law with a duty to render true accounts of moneys received in any proceeding relating to citizenship, naturalization, or registration of aliens or to pay over any balance of such moneys due to the United States, willfully neglects to do so.
18 USC 1422	Fees in naturalization proceedings.	knowingly demands, charges, solicits, collects, or receives any additional fees or moneys in proceedings relating to naturalization or citizenship beyond the fees or moneys authorized by law.
18 USC 1423	Misuse of evidence of citizenship or naturalization.	
18 USC 1424	Personation or misuse of papers in naturalization proceedings.	
18 USC 1425	Procurement of citizenship or naturalization unlawfully.	
18 USC 1426	Reproduction of naturalization or citizenship papers.	
18 USC 1427	Sale of naturalization or citizenship papers.	
18 USC 1428	Surrender of canceled naturalization certificate.	fails to surrender canceled certificate of citizenship within sixty days of cancellation.
18 USC 1429	Penalties for neglect or refusal to answer subpena.	
18 USC 1460	Possession with intent to sell, and sale, of obscene matter on Federal property.	
18 USC 1461	Mailing obscene or crime-inciting matter.	
18 USC 1462	Importation or transportation of obscene matter.	
18 USC 1463	Mailing indecent matter on wrappers or envelopes.	

Title & Section Numbers	Caption of Section (Chapter Headings)	Relates to any persons(s) who...
18 USC 1464	Broadcasting obscene language.	
18 USC 1465	Transportation of obscene matters for sale or distribution.	
18 USC 1466	Engaging in the business of selling or transferring obscene matter.	
18 USC 1468	Distributing obscene material by cable or subscription television.	
18 USC 1501	Assault on process server (Obstruction of Justice).	
18 USC 1502	Resistance to extradition agent (Obstruction of Justice).	
18 USC 1503	Influencing or injuring officer or juror generally (Obstruction of Justice).	
18 USC 1504	Influencing juror by writing (Obstruction of Justice).	
18 USC 1505	Obstruction of proceedings before departments, agencies and committees (Obstruction of Justice).	
18 USC 1506	Theft or alteration of record or process; false bail (Obstruction of Justice).	
18 USC 1507	Picketing or parading (Obstruction of Justice).	with the intent of interfering with, obstructing, or impeding the administration of justice, or influencing any judge, juror, witness, or court officer in the discharge of his duty, pickets or parades in or near a building housing a court of the U.S., or in or near a building or residence occupied or used by such judge, juror, witness, or court officer.
18 USC 1508	Recording, listening to, or observing proceedings of grand or petit juries (Obstruction of Justice).	

Title & Section Numbers	Caption of Section (Chapter Headings)	Relates to any persons(s) who...
18 USC 1509	Obstruction of court orders.	
18 USC 1510	Obstruction of criminal investigations.	
18 USC 1511	Obstruction of state or local law enforcement.	
18 USC 1512(a)	Tampering with a witness, victim, or an informant.	kills or attempts to kill another person to prevent the attendance or testimony of any person in an official proceeding.
18 USC 1512(b)	Tampering with a witness, victim, or an informant.	uses intimidation or physical force, threatens, or corruptly persuades another person, or attempts to do so, or engages in misleading conduct toward another person with intent to influence, delay, or prevent testimony of any person in an official proceeding.
18 USC 1512(c)	Tampering with a witness, victim, or an informant.	intentionally harasses another person and thereby hinders, delays, prevents, or dissuades any person from attending or testifying in an official proceeding.
18 USC 1513	Retaliating against a victim, witness, or an informant.	
18 USC 1516	Obstruction of federal audit.	
18 USC 1517	Obstructing examination of financial institution.	
18 USC 1518	Obstruction of criminal investigations of health care offenses (Obstruction of Justice).	
18 USC 1541	Issuance without authority (Passports and Visas).	
18 USC 1542	False statement in application and use of passport.	
18 USC 1543	Forgery or false use of passport.	

Title & Section Numbers	Caption of Section (Chapter Headings)	Relates to any persons(s) who...
18 USC 1544	Misuse of passport.	
18 USC 1545	Safe conduct violation (Passports and Visas).	violates any safe conduct or passport duly obtained and issued under authority of the United States.
18 USC 1546	Fraud and misuse of visas, permits, and other documents.	
18 USC 1581	Peonage, obstructing enforcement.	
18 USC 1582	Vessels for slave trade.	
18 USC 1583	Enticement into slavery.	
18 USC 1584	Sale into involuntary servitude.	
18 USC 1585	Seizure, detention, transportation or sale of slaves.	
18 USC 1586	Service on vessel in slave trade.	
18 USC 1587	Possession of slaves aboard vessel.	
18 USC 1588	Transportation of slaves from U.S.	
18 USC 1621	Perjury generally.	after taking an oath before a competent tribunal, officer, or person in any case in which a law of the United States authorizes an oath to be administered, subscribes any material matter which he does not believe to be true.
18 USC 1622	Subornation of perjury.	procures another to commit any perjury.
18 USC 1623	False declarations before grand jury or court.	

Title & Section Numbers	Caption of Section (Chapter Headings)	Relates to any persons(s) who...
18 USC 1654	Arming or serving on privateers.	fits out and arms, or attempts to fit out and arm or is concerned in furnishing, fitting out, or arming any private vessel of war or privateer, with intent that such vessel shall be employed to cruise or commit hostilities upon the citizens of the United States.
18 USC 1656	Conversion of surrender of vessel.	
18 USC 1657	Corruption of seamen and confederating with pirates.	
18 USC 1658	Plunder of distressed vessel.	
18 USC 1659	Attack to plunder vessel.	
18 USC 1693	Carriage of mail generally.	being concerned in carrying out the mail, collects, receives, or carries any letter or packet, contrary to law.
18 USC 1695	Carriage of matter out of mail on vessels.	carries any letter or packet on board any vessel which carries the mail, otherwise than in such mail.
18 USC 1696	Private express for letters and packets.	transmits by private express or other unlawful means, or delivers to any agent thereof, or deposits at any appointed place, for the purpose of being so transmitted any letter or packet.
18 USC 1700	Desertion of mails (Postal Service).	having taken charge of any mail, voluntarily quits or deserts the same before he has delivered it into the post office at the termination of the route.
18 USC 1701	Obstruction of mails generally.	knowingly and willfully obstructs or retards the passage of the mail, or any carrier or conveyance carrying the mail.

Title & Section Numbers	Caption of Section (Chapter Headings)	Relates to any persons(s) who...
18 USC 1702	Obstruction of correspondence (Postal Service).	takes any letter, postal card, or package out of any post office or any authorized depository for mail matter, or from any letter or mail carrier, or which has been in any post office or authorized depository, or in the custody of any letter or mail carrier, before it has been delivered to whom it was directed.
18 USC 1703	Delay or destruction of mail or newspapers (Postal Service).	
18 USC 1704	Keys or locks stolen or reproduced (Postal Service).	
18 USC 1705	Destruction of letter boxes or mail (Postal Service).	
18 USC 1706	Injury to mail bags (Postal Service).	
18 USC 1707	Theft of property used by Postal Service.	
18 USC 1708	Theft or receipt of stolen mail matter generally.	
18 USC 1709	Theft of mail matter by officer or employee.	
18 USC 1710	Theft of newspapers (Postal Service).	being a Postal Service officer or employee takes or steals any newspaper or package of newspapers from any post office.
18 USC 1711	Misappropriation of postal funds.	
18 USC 1712	Falsification of postal returns to increase compensation.	
18 USC 1715	Firearms as nonmailable; regulations (Postal Service).	

Title & Section Numbers	Caption of Section (Chapter Headings)	Relates to any persons(s) who...
18 USC 1716	Injurious articles as nonmailable (Postal Service).	[Section pertains to all kinds of poison, and all articles and compositions containing poison, and all poisonous animals, insects, reptiles, and all explosives, etc., or material which may kill or injure another, or injure the mails or other property, are nonmailable and should not be conveyed in mails or delivered from any post office or station thereof.]
18 USC 1716A	Nonmailable locksmithing devices and motor vehicle master keys (Postal Service).	
18 USC 1716B	Nonmailable plants (Postal Service).	
18 USC 1716C	False agricultural certifications (Postal Service).	
18 USC 1716D	Nonmailable injurious animals, plant pests, plants, and illegally taken fish, wildlife, and plants (Postal Service).	
18 USC 1717	Letters and writings as nonmailable (Postal Service).	uses or attempts to use the mails or Postal Service for the transmission of any matter declared by this section to be unmailable.
18 USC 1720	Canceled stamps and envelopes (Postal Service).	uses or attempts to use in payment of postage, any canceled postage stamp.
18 USC 1721	Sale or pledge of stamps (Postal Service).	being a Postal Service officer or employee, knowingly and willfully, uses or disposes of postage stamps, stamped envelopes, or postal cards entrusted to his care or custody in the payment of debts, or sells or disposes of postage stamps or postal cards for any larger or less sum than the values indicated on their faces.
18 USC 1726	Postage collected unlawfully.	
18 USC 1728	Weight of mail increased fraudulently (Postal Service).	

Title & Section Numbers	Caption of Section (Chapter Headings)	Relates to any persons(s) who...
18 USC 1730	Uniform of carriers (Postal Service).	not being connected with the letter-carrier branch of the Postal Service, wears the uniform or badge which may be prescribed by the Postal Service to be worn by letter carriers.
18 USC 1731	Vehicles falsely labeled as carriers (Postal Service).	
18 USC 1732	Approval of bond or sureties by postmaster.	being a postmaster, affixes his signature to the approval of any bond of a bidder before the said bond or contract is signed by the bidder or contractor and his sureties.
18 USC 1733	Mailing periodical publications without prepayment of postage.	
18 USC 1735	Sexually oriented advertisements (Postal Service).	uses the mails for mailing or delivery of any sexually oriented advertisements in violation of section 3010 of title 39.
18 USC 1737	Manufacturer of sexually related mail matter (Postal Service).	
18 USC 1738	Mailing private identification documents without a disclaimer (Postal Service).	
18 USC 1751(a)	Presidential and Presidential staff assassination, kidnapping, and assault; penalties.	kills said individual.
18 USC 1751(b)	Presidential and Presidential staff assassination, kidnapping, and assault; penalties.	kidnaps said individual.
18 USC 1751(c)	Presidential and Presidential staff assassination, kidnapping, and assault; penalties.	attempts to kill or kidnap said individual.
18 USC 1751(d)	Presidential and Presidential staff assassination, kidnapping, and assault; penalties.	[Two or more persons conspire to kill or kidnap any individual designated in subsection (a).]

Title & Section Numbers	Caption of Section (Chapter Headings)	Relates to any persons(s) who...
18 USC 1751(e)	Presidential and Presidential staff assassination, kidnapping, and assault; penalties.	assaults any person designated in subsection (a)(1).
18 USC 1752	Temporary residences and offices of the President and others.	willfully and knowingly enters or remains in any building or grounds designated by the Secretary of the Treasury as temporary residences of the President or other person protected by the Secret Service.
18 USC 1761	Transportation or importation (Prison-Made Goods).	knowingly transports in interstate commerce or from any foreign country into the United States any goods, wares, or merchandise manufactured, produced, or mined, wholly or in part by convicts or prisoners.
18 USC 1791	Providing or possessing contraband in prison (Prisons).	
18 USC 1792	Mutiny and riot prohibited (Prisons).	
18 USC 1793	Trespass on Bureau of Prisons reservations and land.	
18 USC 1821	Transportation of dentures (Professions and Occupations).	transports by mail or otherwise to or within the District of Columbia any set of artificial teeth or prosthetic dental appliance, constructed from any cast or impression made by any person other than a person licensed to practice dentistry.
18 USC 1831	Economic espionage (Protection of Trade Secrets).	intending or knowing that the offense will benefit any foreign government, steals, or without authorization appropriates, takes, carriers away, or conceals, or by fraud, artifice, or deception obtains a trade secret.
18 USC 1832	Theft of trade secrets.	

Title & Section Numbers	Caption of Section (Chapter Headings)	Relates to any persons(s) who...
18 USC 1851	Coal depredations (Public Lands).	mines or removes coal of any character from beds or deposits in lands of, or reserved to the U.S., with intent wrongfully to appropriate, sell, or dispose of same.
18 USC 1852	Timber removed or transported (Public Lands).	cuts, or wantonly destroys, any timber growing on the public lands of the U.S.
18 USC 1853	Trees cut or injured (Public Lands).	
18 USC 1854	Trees boxed for pitch or turpentine (Public Lands).	cuts, chips, chops, or boxes any tree upon any lands belonging to the U.S. for the purpose of obtaining from such tree any pitch, turpentine, or other substance.
18 USC 1855	Timber set afire (Public Lands).	
18 USC 1856	Fires left unattended and unextinguished (Public Lands).	
18 USC 1857	Fences destroyed; livestock entering (Public Lands).	breaks, opens, or destroys any gate, fence, hedge, or wall inclosing any lands of the U.S. reserved or purchased for any public use.
18 USC 1858	Survey marks destroyed or removed (Public Lands).	
18 USC 1859	Surveys interrupted (Public Lands).	by threats or force, interrupts, hinders, or prevents the surveying of the public lands by the person authorized to survey the same.
18 USC 1860	Bids at land sales (Public Lands).	bargains, contracts, or agrees, or attempts to bargain, contract, or agree with another that such other shall not bid upon or purchase any parcel of lands of the U.S. offered at public sale.
18 USC 1861	Deception of prospective purchasers (Public Lands).	
18 USC 1863	Trespass on national forest lands (Public Lands).	

Title & Section Numbers	Caption of Section (Chapter Headings)	Relates to any persons(s) who...
18 USC 1864	Hazardous or injurious devices on Federal lands (Public Lands).	
18 USC 1901	Collecting or disbursing officer trading in public property (Public Officers and Employees).	
18 USC 1902	Disclosure of crop information and speculation therein (Public Officers and Employees).	
18 USC 1903	Speculation in stocks or commodities affecting crop insurance (Public Officers and Employees).	
18 USC 1905	Disclosure of confidential information generally (Public Officers and Employees).	
18 USC 1906	Disclosure of information from a bank examination report (Public Officers and Employees).	
18 USC 1907	Disclosure of information by farm credit examiner (Public Officers and Employees).	
18 USC 1909	Examiner performing other services (Public Officers and Employees).	[Section pertains to national bank examiner or farm credit examiner performing any other service, for compensation, for any bank or loan association, or for any officer, director, or employee thereof, or for any person connected therewith in any capacity.]
18 USC 1910	Nepotism in appointment of receiver or trustee (Public Officers and Employees).	being a judge of any court of the United States, appoints as receiver, or trustee, any person related to such judge by consanguinity, or affinity.
18 USC 1911	Receiver mismanaging property (Public Officers and Employees).	
18 USC 1912	Unauthorized fees for inspection of vessels (Public Officers and Employees).	

Title & Section Numbers	Caption of Section (Chapter Headings)	Relates to any persons(s) who...
18 USC 1913	Lobbying with appropriated moneys (Public Officers and Employees).	
18 USC 1915	Compromise of customs liabilities (Public Officers and Employees).	
18 USC 1916	Unauthorized employment and disposition of lapsed appropriations (Public Officers and Employees).	violates the provision of Section 3103 of Title 5 that an individual may be employed in the civil service in an Executive department at the seat of Government only for services actually rendered in connection with and for the purposes of the appropriation from which he is paid.
18 USC 1917	Interference with civil service examinations (Public Officers and Employees).	
18 USC 1918	Disloyalty and asserting the right to strike against the Government (Public Officers and Employees).	
18 USC 1919	False statement to obtain unemployment compensation for Federal service (Public Officers and Employees).	
18 USC 1920	False statement or fraud to obtain Federal employee's compensation (Public Officers and Employees).	
18 USC 1921	Receiving Federal employees' compensation after marriage (Public Officers and Employees).	
18 USC 1922	False or withheld report concerning Federal employees' compensation (Public Officers and Employees).	
18 USC 1923	Fraudulent receipt of payments of missing persons (Public Officers and Employees).	

Title & Section Numbers	Caption of Section (Chapter Headings)	Relates to any persons(s) who...
18 USC 1924	Unauthorized removal and retention of classified documents or material (Public Officers and Employees).	
18 USC 1951	Interference with commerce by threats or violence (Racketeering).	
18 USC 1952	Interstate and foreign travel or transportation in aid of racketeering enterprises.	
18 USC 1953	Interstate transportation of wagering paraphernalia (Racketeering).	
18 USC 1954	Offer, acceptance, or solicitation to influence operations of employee benefit plan (Racketeering).	
18 USC 1955	Prohibition of illegal gambling businesses (Racketeering).	
18 USC 1956	Laundering of monetary instruments (Racketeering).	
18 USC 1957	Engaging in monetary transactions in property derived from specified unlawful activity (Racketeering).	
18 USC 1958	Use of interstate commerce facilities in the commission of murder-for-hire.	
18 USC 1959	Violent crimes in aid of racketeering activity.	
18 USC 1960	Prohibition of illegal money transmitting businesses (Racketeering).	
18 USC 1962	Prohibited activities (Racketeer Influenced and Corrupt Organizations).	receives any income derived from a pattern of racketeering activity or through collection of an unlawful debt in which such person has participated as a principal within the meaning of Section 2, Title 18 and uses or invests in acquisition of any interest in any enterprise which is engaged in interstate or foreign commerce.

Title & Section Numbers	Caption of Section (Chapter Headings)	Relates to any persons(s) who...
18 USC 1963	Criminal penalties (Racketeer Influenced and Corrupt Organizations).	violates any provision of section 1962 of this chapter.
18 USC 1991	Entering train to commit crime.	enters train with intent to commit murder, robbery, or unlawful violence.
18 USC 1992	Wrecking trains.	willfully derails, disables, or wrecks any train, engine, motor unit, or car used, operated or employed in interstate or foreign commerce by any railroad, or willfully sets fire to, or places any explosive substance on or near, or undermines any tunnel, bridge, viaduct, trestle, track, signal, station, depot, warehouse, terminal, etc.
18 USC 2071	Concealment, removal, or mutilation generally.	conceals, removes or mutilates any records and reports filed with any clerk or officer of any court of the U.S.
18 USC 2072	False crop reports.	being an officer or employee of the U.S. whose duties require compilation or report of statistics or information relating to the products of the soil, knowingly compiles for issuance, or issues, any false statistics or information as a report of the U.S. or any of its agencies.
18 USC 2073	False entries and reports of moneys or securities.	
18 USC 2074	False weather reports.	knowingly issues or publishes any counterfeit weather forecast or warning of weather conditions falsely representing such forecast or warning to have been issued or published by the Weather Bureau, or other branch of the Government service.
18 USC 2076	Clerk of United States District Court (Records and Reports).	being a clerk of a district court of the United States, willfully refuses or neglects to make or forward any report, certificate, statement, or document as required by law.

Title & Section Numbers	Caption of Section (Chapter Headings)	Relates to any persons(s) who...
18 USC 2101	Riots.	travels in interstate or foreign commerce or uses any facility of interstate or foreign commerce to incite a riot.
18 USC 2111	Special maritime and territorial jurisdiction.	takes or attempts to take from the person or presence of another anything of value within the special maritime and territorial jurisdiction of the U.S. by force and violence or by intimidation.
18 USC 2112	Personal property of the U.S.	robs or attempts to rob another of any kind or description of personal property belonging to the U.S.
18 USC 2113(a)	Bank robbery and incidental crimes.	by force and violence, or by intimidation, takes or attempts to obtain by extortion any property or money or other thing of value belonging to bank, credit union, or other savings and loan association.
18 USC 2113(b)	Bank robbery and incidental crimes.	takes or carries away, with intent to steal or purloin, any property or money or any other thing of value exceeding a specified amount belonging to bank, credit union, or other savings and loan association.
18 USC 2113(c)	Bank robbery and incidental crimes.	receives, possesses, conceals, stores, barters, sells, or disposes of any property or money or other thing of value which has been stolen from a bank, etc.
18 USC 2113(d)	Bank robbery and incidental crimes.	in committing or in attempting to commit any offense defined in subsections (a) and (b), assaults any person, or puts in jeopardy the life of any person.
18 USC 2113(e)	Bank robbery and incidental crimes.	in committing any offense defined in this section or in avoiding or attempting to avoid apprehension for the commission of such offense, or in freeing himself or attempting to free himself from arrest or confinement for such offense kills any person or forces any person to accompany him without the consent of such person.

Title & Section Numbers	Caption of Section (Chapter Headings)	Relates to any persons(s) who...
18 USC 2114(a)	Mail, money or other property of U.S. - Assault.	assaults any person having lawful charge, control, or custody of any mail, money, or property of the U.S. with intent to steal, rob or purloin such mail matter, money or property.
18 USC 2114(b)	Mail, money or other property of U.S. - Receipt, possession, concealment, or disposal or property.	receives, possesses, conceals, or disposes of any money or other property that has been obtained in violation of this section, knowing the same to have been unlawfully obtained.
18 USC 2115	Post Office.	forcibly breaks into or attempts to break into any post office, or any building used in whole or part as a post office with intent to commit larceny or other depredation.
18 USC 2116	Railway or steamboat post office.	by violence, enters a post office car or any part of any car, steamboat or vessel assigned to the use of mail service.
18 USC 2117	Breaking or entering carrying facilities.	breaks the seal of any lock of any railroad car, vessel, aircraft, motortruck, wagon or other vehicle or of any pipeline system or enters any such vehicle with intent in either case to commit larceny.
18 USC 2118(a)	Robberies and burglaries involving controlled substance.	takes or attempts to take from the person or presence of another by force or violence or intimidation any material or compound containing any quantity of controlled substance belonging to or in the care, custody, control, or possession of a person registered with the DEA.
18 USC 2118(b)	Robberies and burglaries involving controlled substance.	without authority, enters or attempts to enter or remains in the business premises or property of a person registered with the DEA.

Title & Section Numbers	**Caption of Section (Chapter Headings)**	**Relates to any persons(s) who...**
18 USC 2119	Motor vehicles.	with the intent to cause death or serious bodily harm, takes a motor vehicle that has been transported, shipped, or received in interstate or foreign commerce from the person or presence of another by force and violence or by intimidation or attempts to do so.
18 USC 2152	Fortifications, harbor defenses, or defensive sea areas (Sabotage).	wilfully trespasses upon, injures, or destroys any of the works or property or material of any submarine mine or torpedo or fortification or harbor defense system owned or constructed by the United States.
18 USC 2153	Destruction of war material, war premises, or war utilities.	
18 USC 2154	Production of defective war material, war premises, or war utilities.	
18 USC 2155	Destruction of national-defense materials, national-defense premises, or national-defense utilities.	
18 USC 2156	Production of defective national-defense materials, national-defense premises, or national-defense utilities.	
18 USC 2191	Cruelty to seamen.	being the master or officer of a vessel of the United States in any waters within the admiralty jurisdiction of the United States, flogs, beats, wounds, or without justifiable cause, imprisons any of the crew of such vessel.
18 USC 2192	Incitation of seamen to revolt or mutiny.	
18 USC 2193	Revolt or mutiny of seamen.	

Title & Section Numbers	Caption of Section (Chapter Headings)	Relates to any persons(s) who...
18 USC 2194	Shanghaiing sailors.	with intent that any person shall perform service or labor of any kind on board of any vessel engaged in trade and commerce among the several States or with foreign nations, procures or induces another by force or threats or by representations which he knows or believes to be untrue to go on board of any such vessel to perform service or labor thereon.
18 USC 2195	Abandonment of sailors.	
18 USC 2197	Misuse of Federal certificate, license or document (Seaman and Stowaways).	uses or attempts to use without being lawfully entitled, any certificate, license, or document issued to vessels or officers or seamen by any officer or employee of the U.S. authorized by law to issue the same.
18 USC 2199	Stowaways on vessel or aircraft.	
18 USC 2231	Assault or resistance (Searches and Seizures).	forcibly assaults, resists, opposes, prevents, impedes, intimidates, or interferes with any person authorized to serve or execute search warrants or to make searches and seizures.
18 USC 2232	Destruction or removal of property to prevent seizure.	
18 USC 2233	Rescue of seized property.	forcibly rescues, dispossesses, or attempts to rescue or dispossess any property, articles, or objects after the same have been taken, detained, or seized by any person authorized to make searches and seizures.
18 USC 2234	Authority exceeded in executing warrant (Searches and Seizures).	
18 USC 2235	Search warrant procured maliciously.	
18 USC 2236	Searches without warrant.	

Title & Section Numbers	Caption of Section (Chapter Headings)	Relates to any persons(s) who...
18 USC 2241	Aggravated sexual abuse.	in special maritime and territorial jurisdiction of the United States or in a Federal prison, knowingly causes another person to engage in a sexual act by force or threat or other means.
18 USC 2242	Sexual abuse.	
18 USC 2243(a)	Sexual abuse of a minor.	
18 USC 2243(b)	Sexual abuse of a ward.	
18 USC 2244	Abusive sexual contact.	
18 USC 2251	Sexual exploitation of children.	
18 USC 2251A	Selling or buying of children.	
18 USC 2252	Certain activities relating to material involving the sexual exploitation of minors.	
18 USC 2252A	Certain activities relating to material constituting or containing child pornography.	
18 USC 2257	Record keeping requirements.	procures any book, magazine, periodical, film, videotape, or other matter made after 1990 which contains one or more visual depictions of sexually explicit conduct must create and maintain individually identifiable records pertaining to every performer.
18 USC 2258	Failure to report child abuse.	
18 USC 2260	Production of sexually explicit depictions of a minor for importation into the United States.	

Title & Section Numbers	Caption of Section (Chapter Headings)	Relates to any persons(s) who...
18 USC 2261	Interstate domestic violence.	crosses a state line, with intent to injure, harass, or intimidate that person's spouse or intimate partner, or causes the crossing of a state line of a spouse or intimate partner by force, coercion, duress, or fraud.
18 USC 2262	Interstate violation of protection order.	
18 USC 2271	Conspiracy to destroy vessels (Shipping).	
18 USC 2272	Destruction of vessel by owner (Shipping).	
18 USC 2274	Destruction or misuse of vessel by person in charge (Shipping).	
18 USC 2275	Firing or tampering of vessel (Shipping).	sets fire to any vessel of foreign registry or any vessel of American registry entitled to engage in commerce with foreign nations.
18 USC 2276	Breaking and entering vessel (Shipping).	
18 USC 2277	Explosives or dangerous weapons aboard vessels (Shipping).	
18 USC 2278	Explosives on vessels carrying steerage passengers (Shipping).	
18 USC 2279	Boarding vessels before arrival (Shipping).	
18 USC 2280	Violence against maritime navigation (Shipping).	
18 USC 2281	Violence against maritime fixed platforms (Shipping).	
18 USC 2312	Transportation of stolen vehicles.	
18 USC 2313	Sale or receipt of stolen vehicles.	

Title & Section Numbers	Caption of Section (Chapter Headings)	Relates to any persons(s) who...
18 USC 2314	Transportation of stolen goods, securities, moneys, fraudulent State tax stamps, or articles used in counterfeiting.	
18 USC 2315	Sale or receipt of stolen goods, securities, moneys or fraudulent State tax stamps.	
18 USC 2316	Transportation of livestock (Stolen Property).	transports in interstate or foreign commerce any livestock knowing the same to have been stolen.
18 USC 2317	Sale or receipt of livestock (Stolen Property).	receives, conceals, stores, barters, buys, sells, or disposes of any livestock knowing the same to have been stolen.
18 USC 2318	Trafficking in counterfeit labels for phono records, copies of computer programs or computer program documentation or packaging, and copies of motion pictures or other audio visual works, and trafficking in counterfeit computer program documentation or packaging.	
18 USC 2319	Criminal infringement of a copyright.	
18 USC 2319A	Unauthorized fixation of and trafficking in sound recordings and music videos of live musical performances.	
18 USC 2320	Trafficking in counterfeit goods or services.	
18 USC 2321	Trafficking in certain motor vehicles or motor vehicle parts.	buys, receives, possesses, or obtains control of, with intent to sell, a motor vehicle or motor vehicle part knowing that an identification number for such has been removed, obliterated, tampered with, or altered.
18 USC 2322	Chop shops.	
18 USC 2332(a)	Criminal penalties (Terrorism).	kills a national of the U.S. while such national is outside the U.S.

Title & Section Numbers	Caption of Section (Chapter Headings)	Relates to any persons(s) who...
18 USC 2332(b)(1)	Criminal penalties (Terrorism).	attempts to kill, or engages in a conspiracy to kill, a national of the U.S. where the attempted killing is a murder as defined in this chapter.
18 USC 2332(b)(2)	Criminal penalties (Terrorism).	[Conspiracy by two or more persons to commit a killing that is a murder as defined in section 1111(a) if one or more of such persons do any overt act to effect the object of the conspiracy.]
18 USC 2332(c)	Criminal penalties (Terrorism).	engages, outside the U.S., in physical violence with intent to cause serious bodily injury, or the result is serious bodily injury to a national of the U.S.
18 USC 2332a	Use of weapons of mass destruction (Terrorism).	
18 USC 2332d	Financial transactions (Terrorism).	
18 USC 2339A	Providing material support to terrorism.	
18 USC 2339B	Providing material support or resources to designated foreign terrorist organizations.	
18 USC 2340A	Torture.	
18 USC 2342(a)	Unlawful acts (Trafficking in Contraband Cigarettes).	knowingly ships, transports, receives, possesses, sells, distributes, or purchases contraband cigarettes.
18 USC 2344(a)	Penalties (Trafficking in Contraband Cigarettes).	knowingly violates section 2342(a) of this title.
18 USC 2381	Treason.	

Title & Section Numbers	Caption of Section (Chapter Headings)	Relates to any persons(s) who...
18 USC 2382	Misprision of treason.	owing allegiance to the United States and having knowledge of the commission of any treason against them, conceals and does not, as soon as may be, disclose and make known the same to the President or to some judge of the United States.
18 USC 2383	Rebellion or insurrection (Treason).	incites, sets on foot, assists, or engages in any rebellion or insurrection against the authority of the United States.
18 USC 2384	Seditious conspiracy (Treason).	conspires to overthrow, put down, or to destroy by force the Government of the United States.
18 USC 2385	Advocating overthrow of Government (Treason).	
18 USC 2386	Registration of certain organizations (Treason).	
18 USC 2387	Activities affecting armed forces generally (Treason).	with intent to interfere with, impair or influence the loyalty, morale, or discipline of the military or naval forces of the United States advises, counsels, urges, or in any manner causes or attempts to cause insubordination, disloyalty, mutiny, or refusal of duty by any member of the military or naval forces of the United States.
18 USC 2388	Activities affecting armed forces during war (Treason).	
18 USC 2389	Recruiting for service against the United States (Treason).	
18 USC 2390	Enlistment to serve against United States (Treason).	
18 USC 2421	Transportation generally (Transportation for Illegal Sexual Activity and Related Crimes).	knowingly transports any individual in interstate or foreign commerce, or in any Territory or Possession of the U.S., with intent that such individual engage in prostitution, or in any sexual activity for which any person can be charged with a criminal offense.

Title & Section Numbers	Caption of Section (Chapter Headings)	Relates to any persons(s) who...
18 USC 2422	Coercion and enticement (Transportation for Illegal Sexual Activity and Related Crimes).	knowingly persuades, induces, entices, or coerces any individual to travel in interstate or foreign commerce, or in any Territory or Possession of the U.S., to engage in prostitution, or in any sexual activity for which any person can be charged with a criminal offense.
18 USC 2423(a)	Transportation of minors - Transportation with intent to engage in criminal sexual activity.	
18 USC 2423(b)	Transportation of minors - Travel with intent to engage in sexual act with a juvenile.	
18 USC 2424	Filing factual statement about alien individual.	fails to file a statement with the Commissioner of Immigration and Naturalization after commencing to keep, maintain, control, support, or harbor in any house or place for the purpose of prostitution, or for any other immoral purpose, any alien individual.
18 USC 2441	War crimes.	commits a grave breach of the Geneva Conventions, if the person committing such breach or the victim of such breach is a member of the Armed Forces of the United States or a national of the United States.
18 USC 2511	Interception and disclosure of wire, oral, or electronic communications prohibited.	
18 USC 2512	Manufacture, distribution, possession, and advertising of wire, oral, or electronic communication intercepting devices prohibited.	
18 USC 2701	Unlawful access to stored communications (Stored Communications Access).	intentionally accesses without authorization a facility through which an electronic communication service is provided.

Title & Section Numbers	Caption of Section (Chapter Headings)	Relates to any persons(s) who...
18 USC 3056(d)	Powers, authorities and duties of United States Secret Service.	knowingly and willfully obstructs, resists, or interferes with a Federal law enforcement agent engaged in the performance of the protective functions authorized by this section or by section 1752 of this title.
18 USC 3121	General prohibition on pen register and trap and trace device use; exception.	
18 USC 3146(b)(1)(A)	Penalty for failure to appear (Release and Detention Pending Judicial Proceedings).	being released in connection with a charge, or while awaiting sentence, surrender for service of sentence, or appeal or certiorari after conviction, fails to appear before court as required by the conditions of release.
18 USC 3146(b)(1)(B)	Penalty for failure to appear (Release and Detention Pending Judicial Proceedings).	being released for appearance as a material witness fails to appear before court as required by the conditions of release.
18 USC 3147	Penalty for offense committed while on release (Release and Detention Pending Judicial Proceedings).	
18 USC 3521	Witness relocation and protection (Protection of Witnesses).	
19 USC 283	Duty on saloon stores.	fails to make entries, report and pay duties.
19 USC 1304	Marking of imported articles and containers.	[Every article of foreign origin imported into the U.S. shall be marked legibly and permanently.]
19 USC 1341	Interference with functions of Commission (United States International Trade Commission).	prevent or attempt to prevent, by force, intimidation, threat, or in any other manner, any member or employee of the commission from exercising the functions imposed upon the commission by this subtitle.

Title & Section Numbers	Caption of Section (Chapter Headings)	Relates to any persons(s) who...
19 USC 1433	Report of arrival of vessels, vehicles and aircraft.	being in charge of the vehicle or vessel must report to customs officials immediately upon the arrival at any port, border, or airport within the U.S. or the Virgin Islands.
19 USC 1434	Entry; vessels.	within 24 hours after arrival at any port of the U.S., any foreign vessel or vessel carrying foreign merchandise must make formal entry to customs officials.
19 USC 1436	Penalties for violations of arrival, reporting, entry, and clearance requirements (Report, Entry, and Unlading of Vessels and Vehicles).	
19 USC 1459	Reporting requirements for individuals (Report, Entry, and Unlading of Vessels and Vehicles).	
19 USC 1464	Penalties in connection with sealed vessels and vehicles.	
19 USC 1586(c)	Unlawful unlading or transshipment.	
19 USC 1590	Aviation smuggling .	
19 USC 1620	Acceptance of money by United States officers.	
19 USC 1629	Inspections and preclearance in foreign countries.	willfully falsifies, conceals, or covers up by any trick, scheme or device a material fact, or makes any false, fictitious or fraudulent statements or representations in any matter before a foreign customs official stationed in the United States.
19 USC 1708(b)	Procuring lading with intent to defraud revenue laws; liability of citizen, master, and members of crew of U.S. vessel.	

Title & Section Numbers	Caption of Section (Chapter Headings)	Relates to any persons(s) who...
19 USC 1919	Penalties (Adjustment Assistance to Firms).	makes a false statement of a material fact knowing it to be false, or knowingly fails to disclose a material fact, or willfully overvalues any security for the purpose of influencing in any way the action of the Secretary of Commerce under this part, or for the purpose of obtaining money, property or anything of value under this part.
19 USC 2316	Penalties (Adjustment Assistance for Workers).	makes a false statement of a material fact knowing it to be false, or knowingly fails to disclose a material fact, for the purpose of obtaining or increasing for himself or for any other person, any payment authorized to be furnished under this part or pursuant to an agreement under section 2311 of this title.
19 USC 2349	Penalties (Adjustment Assistance for Firms).	makes a false statement of a material fact knowing it to be false, or knowingly fails to disclose a material fact for the purpose of influencing in any way a determination under this part.
20 USC 1069d	Penalties (Institutional Aid).	
20 USC 1097(a)	Criminal penalties - In general (Student Assistance Programs).	knowingly and willfully embezzles, misapplies, steals, obtains by fraud, false statement, or forgery or fails to refund any assets or property provided or insured under this chapter.
20 USC 1097(b)	Criminal penalties - Assignment of loans (Student Assistance Programs).	knowing and willfully makes any false statement, furnishes any false information or conceals any material information in connection with assignment of a loan.
20 USC 1097(c)	Criminal penalties - Inducements to lend or assign (Student Assistance Programs).	knowingly and willfully makes an unlawful payment to an eligible lender as an inducement to make or to acquire by assignment, a loan insured under that part.

Title & Section Numbers	Caption of Section (Chapter Headings)	Relates to any persons(s) who...
20 USC 1097(d)	Criminal penalties - Obstruction of justice (Student Assistance Programs).	conceals or destroys any record relating to the provision of assistance under this subchapter and part C of subchapter I of chapter 34 of Title 42 with intent to defraud the U.S. or to prevent the U.S. from enforcing any right obtained by subrogation under this part.
20 USC 4442	Administrative provisions (Native Hawaiians and Alaska Natives).	
20 USC 9007	Confidentiality (National Education Statistics).	
21 USC 63	Penalties; acts of agents deemed acts of principals (Filled Milk).	
21 USC 101	Suspension of importation of all animals.	[Providing importation of all animals may be suspended when necessary for the protection of animals in the U.S. against infectious diseases, and any importation of animals during such time of suspension is unlawful.]
21 USC 102	Quarantine of imported animals.	[Providing the Secretary of Agriculture is authorized, at the expense of the owner, to place and retain in quarantine all neat cattle, sheep and other ruminants, and all swine while in the U.S.]
21 USC 103	Importation except at quarantine ports, prohibited; slaughter of infected animals; appraisal; payment.	
21 USC 104	Importation of animals in general.	[Providing the Secretary of Agriculture may prohibit or restrict the importation or entry of diseased or infected animals to prevent the dissemination into the U.S.]

Title & Section Numbers	Caption of Section (Chapter Headings)	Relates to any persons(s) who...
21 USC 105	Inspection of animals.	[Providing the Secretary of Agriculture may inspect imported animals to ascertain whether they are infected with contagious disease or have been exposed to infection so as to be dangerous to other animals.]
21 USC 111	Regulation to prevent contagious diseases.	
21 USC 115	Transportation of diseased livestock and poultry prohibited.	
21 USC 117	Penalties for transportation of diseased livestock or live poultry.	
21 USC 120	Regulation of exportation and transportation of infected livestock and live poultry.	
21 USC 121	Shipments from areas suspected infected; control of animals and live poultry.	[Section pertains to whenever any inspector of the Bureau of Animal Industry issues a certificate showing such officer had inspected any cattle or livestock and found them free of disease, they may be transported or exported without further inspection.]
21 USC 122	Offenses; penalty.	violates the provisions of this Act.
21 USC 124	Transportation or delivery from quarantined State or Territory or portion thereof, of quarantined animals and live poultry, forbidden.	
21 USC 126	Moving quarantined animals and live poultry from State or Territory, under regulations.	[Providing quarantined animals and/or live poultry may be moved from a quarantined State or Territory or the District of Columbia only under and in compliance with the rules and regulations of the Secretary of Agriculture.]
21 USC 127	Transportation from quarantined State, Territory, etc.; penalties.	
21 USC 134a	Seizure, quarantine, and disposal of livestock or poultry to guard against introduction or dissemination of communicable disease.	

Title & Section Numbers	Caption of Section (Chapter Headings)	Relates to any persons(s) who...
21 USC 134b	Regulations for clean and sanitary movement of animals.	
21 USC 134c	Regulations for movement of animals affected or exposed to communicable disease.	
21 USC 134d	Inspections and seizures; issuance of warrant.	[Providing employees of the Department of Agriculture may stop and inspect with or without a warrant any person, means of conveyance, or premises for the prevention of the introduction or dissemination of any communicable disease.]
21 USC 134e	Enforcement provisions.	violates any regulation pursuant to the provisions of sections 134 through 134d.
21 USC 135a	Smuggling penalties.	
21 USC 141	Prohibition of importation without permit.	[Prohibits importation into the U.S. of milk and cream without a valid permit.]
21 USC 143	Inspection; certified statement in lieu thereof; waiver of requirements of section 142; regulations; suspensions and revocation of permit.	[Related to insuring that milk and cream are produced and handled as to comply with provisions of section 142 of this title.]
21 USC 144	Unlawful receiving of imported milk or cream.	
21 USC 145	Penalties.	violates any provision of sections 141 to 149 of this title.
21 USC 151	Preparation and sale of worthless or harmful products for domestic animals prohibited; preparation to be in compliance with rules at licensed establishments.	

Title & Section Numbers	Caption of Section (Chapter Headings)	Relates to any persons(s) who...
21 USC 152	Importation regulated and prohibited.	[Related to importation into the U.S. of any virus, serum, toxin, or analogous product for use in the treatment of domestic animals, and the importation of any worthless, contaminated, dangerous, or harmful virus, serum, toxin, or analogous product for use in the treatment of domestic animals is prohibited without a permit from the Secretary of Agriculture.]
21 USC 153	Inspection of imports; denial of entry and destruction.	[Related to viruses, serums, toxins and analogous products, for use in the treatment of domestic animals.]
21 USC 154	Regulation for preparation and sale; licenses.	[Related to viruses, serums, toxins and analogous products, for use in the treatment of domestic animals.]
21 USC 155	Permits for importation.	[Related to viruses, serums, toxins and analogous products, for use in the treatment of domestic animals.]
21 USC 156	Licenses conditioned on permitting inspection; suspension of licenses.	[Related to viruses, serums, toxins and analogous products, for use in the treatment of domestic animals.]
21 USC 157	Inspection.	[Providing any officer, agent, or employee of the Department of Agriculture duly authorized by the Secretary of Agriculture for the purpose may, at any hour during the daytime or nighttime, enter and inspect any establishment where any virus, serum, toxin, or analogous product for use in the treatment of domestic animals is prepared for sale, barter, exchange, or shipment as aforesaid.]
21 USC 158	Offenses; punishment.	violates any provision of this chapter.
21 USC 212	Offenses; punishment; duty to enforce provisions (Practice of Pharmacy and Sale of Poisons in Consular Districts in China).	

Title & Section Numbers	Caption of Section (Chapter Headings)	Relates to any persons(s) who...
21 USC 331	Prohibited acts.	adulterates or misbrands any food, drug, device or cosmetic in interstate commerce; introduces or delivers into, or receives in, interstate commerce any aforesaid items; manufactures any food, drug, device or cosmetic that is adulterated or misbranded; makes, sells, disposes of, or keeps in possession, control or custody any punch, die, plate, stone, or other thing necessary to create counterfeit drugs; does any act which causes a drug to be a counterfeit drug.
21 USC 333(a)(1)	Penalties - Violation of section 331 of this title; second violation; intent to defraud or mislead.	
21 USC 333(a)(2)	Penalties - Violation of section 331 of this title; second violation; intent to defraud or mislead.	commits such violation after a conviction of him under this section has become final.
21 USC 333(b)	Penalties - Prescription drug marketing violations.	knowingly imports a drug in violation of section 381(d)(1) of this title, or knowingly sells, purchases, or trades a drug or drug sample or knowingly offers to sell, purchase, or trade a drug or drug sample in violation of section 353(c)(1) of this title.
21 USC 376	Examination of seafood on request of packer; marking food with results; fees; penalties.	forges, counterfeits, simulates, or falsely represents, or without proper authority uses any mark, stamp, tag, label, or other identification devices authorized or required by the provisions of this section.

Title & Section Numbers	Caption of Section (Chapter Headings)	Relates to any persons(s) who...
21 USC 458	Prohibited acts.	(1) slaughter any poultry or process any poultry products which are capable of use as human food; (2) sell, transport, or receive for transportation, in commerce, any poultry products capable of use as human food and are adulterated or misbranded, or any poultry products required to be inspected under this chapter unless they have been so inspected; (3) do any act intended to cause such products to be adulterated or misbranded; (4) sell, transport, offer for sale or transportation or receive poultry from which the blood, feathers, feet, head, or viscera have not been removed in accordance with regulations promulgated by the Secretary, except as may be authorized by regulations of the Secretary; or (5) use to his own advantage, or reveal other than to the authorized representative of the U.S. government any information acquired under the authority of this chapter concerning any matter which is entitled to protection as a trade secret.
21 USC 459	Compliance by all establishments.	[Providing no establishment processing poultry or other poultry products for commerce shall process any poultry product except in compliance with the requirements of this chapter.]
21 USC 460	Miscellaneous activities subject to regulation.	
21 USC 461	Offenses and punishment (Poultry and Poultry Products Inspection).	
21 USC 463	Rules and regulations-storage and handling of poultry products; violations of regulations.	

Title & Section Numbers	Caption of Section (Chapter Headings)	Relates to any persons(s) who...
21 USC 466	Imports compliance with standards and regulations; status after importation.	[Section pertains to compliance regarding poultry, or parts or products thereof, with standards and regulations; status after importation; rules and regulations; destruction and exportation of refused imports; storage, cartage and labor charges for imports refused admission; domestic standards and processing facilities applicable; enforcement.]
21 USC 610	Prohibited acts.	[Section pertains to humane methods of slaughter; sales, transportation and other transactions; adulteration or misbranding; slaughtering animals or preparation of articles capable of use as human food.]
21 USC 611	Devices, marks, labels, and certificates; simulations - Devices to made under authorization of Secretary and other misconduct.	
21 USC 614	Clearance prohibited to vessel carrying animals for export without inspector's certificate.	
21 USC 617	Clearance prohibited to vessel carrying meat for export without inspector's certificate.	
21 USC 619	Marking, labeling, or other identification of kinds of animals of articles derivation; separate establishments for preparation and slaughtering activities.	
21 USC 620	Imports	[Section pertains to adulteration or misbranding prohibited, compliance with inspection, building construction standards, and other provisions; treatment as domestic articles subject to this chapter and food, drug, and cosmetic provisions; marking and labeling; personal consumption exemption; terms and conditions for destruction.]

Title & Section Numbers	Caption of Section (Chapter Headings)	Relates to any persons(s) who...
21 USC 622	Bribery of or gifts to inspectors or other officers and acceptance of gifts.	
21 USC 642	Record keeping requirements.	[Section pertains to record keeping requirements for meat processors and related industries.]
21 USC 643	Registration of business, name of person, and trade names.	[Section pertains to registration requirements for meat processors and related industries.]
21 USC 644	Regulation of transactions, transportation or importation of 4-D animals to prevent use as human food.	
21 USC 675	Assaulting, resisting, or impeding certain persons; murder; protection of such persons (Meat Inspection).	forcibly assaults, resists, opposes, impedes, intimidates, or interferes with any person while engaged in or on account of the performance of his official duties under this chapter.
21 USC 676	Violations (Meat Inspection).	[Section pertains to misdemeanors; felonies; intent to defraud and distribution of adulterated articles; good faith; and minor violations.]
21 USC 841(a)	Prohibited acts A - Unlawful acts (Drug Abuse Prevention).	manufactures, distributes, or dispenses, or possesses with intent to manufacture, distribute, or dispense, a controlled substance, or creates, distributes, or dispenses, or possesses with intent to distribute or dispense, a counterfeit substance.
21 USC 841(b)(1)	Penalties (Drug Abuse Prevention).	violates subsection (a).
21 USC 841(d)(1)	Offenses involving listed chemicals (Drug Abuse Prevention).	possesses a listed chemical with intent to manufacture a controlled substance except as authorized by this subchapter.

Title & Section Numbers	Caption of Section (Chapter Headings)	Relates to any persons(s) who...
21 USC 841(d)(2)	Offenses involving listed chemicals (Drug Abuse Prevention).	possesses or distributes a listed chemical knowing, or having reasonable cause to believe, that the listed chemical will be used to manufacture a controlled substance except as authorized by this subchapter.
21 USC 841(d)(3)	Offenses involving listed chemicals (Drug Abuse Prevention).	with intent of causing the evasion of the record keeping or reporting requirements of section 830 of this title, or the regulations issued under that section, receives or distributes a reportable amount of any listed chemical in units small enough so that the making of records or filing of reports under that section is not required.
21 USC 841(e)	Boobytraps on Federal property; penalties (Drug Abuse Prevention).	
21 USC 841(g)(1)	Wrongful distribution or possession of listed chemicals (Drug Abuse Prevention).	
21 USC 842(a)(1)	Prohibited acts B - Unlawful acts (Drug Abuse Prevention).	distributes or dispenses a controlled substance in violation of section 829 of this title.
21 USC 842(a)(2)	Prohibited acts B - Unlawful acts (Drug Abuse Prevention).	as a registrant distributes or dispenses a controlled substance not authorized by his registration to another registrant or other authorized person or manufactures a controlled substance not authorized by his registration.
21 USC 842(a)(9)	Prohibited acts B - Unlawful acts (Drug Abuse Prevention).	as a regulated person engages in a regulated transaction without obtaining the identification required by section 830(a) of this title.
21 USC 842(a)(10)	Prohibited acts B - Unlawful acts (Drug Abuse Prevention).	fails to keep a record or make a report under section 830 of this title.

Title & Section Numbers	Caption of Section (Chapter Headings)	Relates to any persons(s) who...
21 USC 842(b)	Manufacture (Drug Abuse Prevention).	being a registrant manufactures a controlled substance classified in schedule I or II not authorized by his registration.
21 USC 843(a)(1)	Prohibited acts C - Unlawful acts (Drug Abuse Prevention).	being a registrant distributes a controlled substance classified in schedule I or II in the course of his legitimate business, except pursuant to an order form as required by section 828 of this title.
21 USC 843(a)(2)	Prohibited acts C - Unlawful acts (Drug Abuse Prevention).	uses in the course of the manufacture or distribution of a controlled substance a registration number which is fictitious, revoked, suspended, or issued to another person.
21 USC 843(a)(3)	Prohibited acts C - Unlawful acts (Drug Abuse Prevention).	acquires or obtains possession of a controlled substance by misrepresentation, fraud, forgery, deception, or subterfuge.
21 USC 843(a)(4)(B)	Prohibited acts C - Unlawful acts (Drug Abuse Prevention).	presents false or fraudulent identification where the person is receiving or purchasing a listed chemical and the person is required to present identification under section 830(a) of this title.
21 USC 843(a)(6)	Prohibited acts C - Unlawful acts (Drug Abuse Prevention).	possesses any three-neck round-bottom flask, tableting machine, encapsulating machine, or gelatin capsule, or any equipment, chemical, product, or material which may be used to manufacture a controlled substance or listed chemical in violation of this subchapter of subchapter II of this chapter.
21 USC 843(a)(7)	Prohibited acts C - Unlawful acts (Drug Abuse Prevention).	manufactures, distributes, exports or imports any three-neck round-bottom flask, etc., knowing or intending that it will be used to manufacture controlled substances.
21 USC 843(a)(8)	Prohibited acts C - Unlawful acts (Drug Abuse Prevention).	creates a chemical mixture for the purpose of evading a requirement of section 830.

Title & Section Numbers	Caption of Section (Chapter Headings)	Relates to any persons(s) who...
21 USC 843(a)(9)	Prohibited acts C - Unlawful acts (Drug Abuse Prevention).	distributes, imports, or exports a list I chemical without the registration required by this subchapter, or subchapter II of this chapter.
21 USC 843(b)	Communication facility (Drug Abuse Prevention).	uses any communication facility in committing or in causing or facilitating the commission of any act or acts constituting a felony under any provision of this subchapter or subchapter II.
21 USC 843(d)	Penalties (Drug Abuse Prevention).	violates this section.
21 USC 844(a)	Penalties for simple possession - Unlawful acts; penalties (Drug Abuse Prevention).	
21 USC 846	Attempt and conspiracy (Drug Abuse Prevention).	attempts or conspires to commit any offense defined in this subchapter.
21 USC 848(a)	Continuing criminal enterprise - Penalties.	
21 USC 848(b)	Life imprisonment for engaging in continuing criminal enterprise.	
21 USC 848(e)	Continuing criminal enterprise - Death penalty.	
21 USC 849	Transportation safety offenses.	
21 USC 853	Criminal forfeitures (Drug Abuse Prevention).	
21 USC 854	Investment of illicit drug profits.	
21 USC 856	Establishment of manufacturing operations. (Drug Abuse Prevention).	maintains any place for the purpose of manufacturing, distributing, or using any controlled substance.
21 USC 858	Endangering human life while illegally manufacturing controlled substance.	

Title & Section Numbers	Caption of Section (Chapter Headings)	Relates to any persons(s) who...
21 USC 859	Distribution to persons under age twenty-one (Drug Abuse Prevention).	
21 USC 860	Distribution or manufacturing in or near schools and colleges (Drug Abuse Prevention).	
21 USC 861	Employment of persons under eighteen years of age in drug operation.	
21 USC 863	Drug paraphernalia.	sells, offers for sale, uses the mails or any other facility of interstate commerce to transport drug paraphernalia, or to import or export drug paraphernalia.
21 USC 952	Importation of controlled substances.	
21 USC 953	Exportation of controlled substances.	
21 USC 954	Transhipment and in-transit shipment of controlled substances.	
21 USC 955	Possession on board vessels, etc., arriving in or departing from U.S.	
21 USC 957	Persons required to register.	[Providing no person may import or export a controlled substance or list I chemical unless such person has a registration issued by the Attorney General under section 958 of this title.]
21 USC 959	Possession, manufacture, or distribution of controlled substance or listed chemical.	
21 USC 960(a)	Prohibited acts A - Unlawful acts.	imports or exports a controlled substance, brings or possesses on board a vessel, aircraft, or vehicle a controlled substance, or manufactures or distributes a controlled substance.
21 USC 960(b)	Penalties.	violates subsection (a) of this section.

Title & Section Numbers	Caption of Section (Chapter Headings)	Relates to any persons(s) who...
21 USC 960(d)(1)	Penalty for importation or exportation.	imports or exports a listed chemical with intent to manufacture a controlled substance.
21 USC 960(d)(3)	Penalty for importation or exportation.	imports or exports a listed chemical knowing, or having reasonable cause to believe, that the chemical will be used to manufacture a controlled substance in violation of this subchapter, or subchapter I of this chapter.
21 USC 960(d)(5)	Penalty for importation or exportation.	imports or exports a listed chemical with intent to evade the reporting or record keeping requirements of section 971 of this title.
21 USC 960(d)(6)	Penalty for importation or exportation.	imports or exports a listed chemical in violation of section 957 or 971 of this title.
21 USC 961	Prohibited acts B.	violates section 954 of this title or fails to notify the Attorney General of an importation or exportation under section 971 of this title.
21 USC 962	Second or subsequent offenses (Import and Export).	
21 USC 963	Attempt and conspiracy.	attempts or conspires to commit any offense defined in this subchapter.
21 USC 1041	Enforcement provisions (Egg Products Inspection).	
22 USC 277d-21	Attorneys' fees; penalties (International Boundary and Water Commission).	being an attorney, charges, demands, receives, or collects for services rendered in connection with such a claim any amount in excess of that allowed by the terms of this section.

Title & Section Numbers	Caption of Section (Chapter Headings)	Relates to any persons(s) who...
22 USC 286f	Obtaining and furnishing information to the Fund (International Monetary Fund and Bank for Reconstruction Development).	
22 USC 287c	Economic and communication sanctions pursuant to United Nations Security Council Resolution.	
22 USC 447	Financial transactions (Neutrality).	
22 USC 455	General penalty provision (Neutrality).	
22 USC 618	Enforcement and penalties (Registration of Foreign Propagandists).	
22 USC 703	Attendance of witnesses (Service Courts of Friendly Foreign Forces).	
22 USC 1623	Claims (Settlement of International Claims).	
22 USC 1631n	Penalties (Vesting and Liquidation of Bulgarian, Hungarian, and Rumanian Property).	
22 USC 1641p	Fees of agents, attorneys, or representatives (Claims Against Bulgaria, Hungary, Rumania, Italy, and the Soviet Union).	
22 USC 1642m	Fees of attorneys; limitation; penalty (Claims Against Czechoslovakia).	
22 USC 1643k	Fees for services; limitation; penalty (Claims Against Cuba and China).	
22 USC 1644l	Fees for services; limitation; penalty (Claims Against German Democratic Republic).	
22 USC 1645m	Fees for services; limitation; penalty (Claims Against Vietnam).	

Title & Section Numbers	Caption of Section (Chapter Headings)	Relates to any persons(s) who...
22 USC 1980(g)	Compensation for loss or destruction of commercial fishing vessel or gear - Penalty for false or misleading statements (Protecting of Vessels).	
22 USC 2197(n)	General provision relating to insurance, guaranty, financing, and reinsurance programs - Penalties for fraud.	makes any false statement or report, or willfully overvalues any land, property, or security for the purpose of influencing in any way the action of the Corporation with respect to any insurance, etc., under section 2194.
22 USC 2518	Seal and name (The Peace Corps).	uses the seal for which provision is made in this section, or any sign, insignia, or symbol in colorable imitation thereof.
22 USC 2712	Authority to control certain terrorism-related services (Department of State).	
22 USC 2778	Control of arms exports and imports.	
22 USC 2780	Transactions with countries supporting acts of international terrorism.	
22 USC 3105	Enforcement (International Investment and Trade in Services Survey).	fails to submit any information required under this chapter.
22 USC 3144	Access to information; confidentiality (Foreign Direct Investment and International Financing Data).	
22 USC 4199	Penalty for failure to give bond and for embezzlement (Powers, Duties and Liabilities of Consular Officers Generally).	
22 USC 4202	Exaction of excessive fees for verification of invoices; penalty (Powers, Duties and Liabilities of Consular Officers Generally).	
22 USC 4217	Embezzlement of fees or of effects of American citizens.	

Title & Section Numbers	Caption of Section (Chapter Headings)	Relates to any persons(s) who...
22 USC 4218	False certificate as to ownership of property (Powers, Duties and Liabilities of Consular Officers Generally).	
22 USC 4221	Depositions and notarial acts; perjury.	
23 USC 410	Alcohol-impaired driving countermeasures (Highway Safety).	
24 USC 154	Unlawful intrusion, or violation of rules and regulations (Battle Mountain Sanitarium Reserve).	
25 USC 202	Inducing conveyances by Indians of trust interests in lands (Protection of Indians).	
25 USC 450d	Criminal activities involving grants, contracts, etc.; penalties.	
25 USC 500m	Use of public lands; violation (Reindeer Industry).	
26 USC 999	Reports by taxpayers; determinations (International Boycott Determinations).	
26 USC 5214	Withdrawal of distilled spirits from bonded premises free of tax or without payment of tax.	
26 USC 5273(b)	Sale, use and recovery of denatured distilled spirits- Internal medicinal preparations and flavoring extracts.	

Title & Section Numbers	Caption of Section (Chapter Headings)	Relates to any persons(s) who...
26 USC 5273(c)	Sale, use and recovery of denatured distilled spirits- Recovery of spirits for reuse in manufacturing.	
26 USC 5291(a)	General - Requirement.	[Providing that every person disposing of any substance used in the manufacture of distilled spirits, or disposing of denatured distilled spirits or articles from which distilled spirits may be recovered, shall, when required by the Secretary, render a correct return, in such form and manner as the Secretary may by regulations prescribe, showing the name and address of the person to whom each disposition was made, with such details, as to the quantity so disposed of or other information which the Secretary may require as to each such disposition, as will enable the Secretary to determine whether all taxes due with respect to any distilled spirits manufactured or recovered from any such substance, denatured distilled spirits, or articles, have been paid.]
26 USC 5601(a)	Criminal penalties (Excise Taxes-Distilled Spirits, Wines, etc.).	
26 USC 5602	Penalty for fraud by distiller.	
26 USC 5603	Penalty relating to records, returns, and reports (Excise Taxes-Distilled Spirits, Wines, etc.).	
26 USC 5604(a)	Penalties relating to marks, brand, and containers-In general (Excise Taxes-Distilled Spirits, Wines, etc.).	
26 USC 5605	Penalty relating to return of materials used in the manufacture of distilled spirits, or from which distilled spirits may be recovered.	
26 USC 5606	Penalty relating to containers of distilled spirits.	
26 USC 5607	Penalty and forfeiture for unlawful use, recovery, or concealment of denatured distilled spirits, or articles.	

Title & Section Numbers	Caption of Section (Chapter Headings)	Relates to any persons(s) who...
26 USC 5608	Penalty and forfeiture for fraudulent claims for export drawback or unlawful relanding.	
26 USC 5661	Penalty and forfeiture for violation of laws and regulations relating to wine.	
26 USC 5662	Penalty for alteration of wine labels.	
26 USC 5671	Penalty and forfeiture for evasion of beer tax and fraudulent noncompliance with requirements.	
26 USC 5672	Penalty for failure of brewer to comply with requirements and to keep records and file returns.	
26 USC 5674	Penalty for unlawful production or removal of beer.	
26 USC 5681	Penalty relating to signs.	
26 USC 5682	Penalty for breaking locks or gaining access.	
26 USC 5683	Penalty and forfeiture for removal of liquors under improper brands.	
26 USC 5684	Penalties relating to the payment and collection of liquor taxes.	
26 USC 5685	Penalty and forfeiture relating to possession of devices for emitting gas, smoke, etc., explosives and firearms, when violating liquor laws.	
26 USC 5686	Penalty for having, possessing, or using liquor or property intended to be used in violating provisions of this chapter.	
26 USC 5687	Penalty for offenses not specifically covered.	

Title & Section Numbers	Caption of Section (Chapter Headings)	Relates to any persons(s) who...
26 USC 5691(a)	Penalties for nonpayment of special taxes.	
26 USC 5731	Imposition and rate of tax.	engaged in a business referred to in subsection (a) willfully fails to pay the tax imposed by subsection (a).
26 USC 5751(a)(1)	Purchase, receipt, possession, or sale of tobacco products and cigarette papers and tubes, after removal - Restrictions.	with intent to defraud the U.S., purchase, receive, possess, offer for sale, or sell or otherwise dispose of, after removal, any tobacco products or cigarette papers or tubes.
26 USC 5751(a)(2)	Purchase, receipt, possession, or sale of tobacco products and cigarette papers and tubes, after removal - Restrictions.	purchases, receives, possesses, offers for sale, or sells or otherwise disposes of, after removal, any tobacco products or cigarette paper or tubes, which are not put up in packages as required under section 5273 or which are put up in packages not bearing the marks, labels, and notices, as required under such section.
26 USC 5752	Restrictions relating to marks, labels, notices, and packages.	
26 USC 5762(a)(3)	Criminal penalties - Refusing to pay or evading tax.	
26 USC 5861	Prohibited acts - Firearms.	
26 USC 5871	Penalties - Firearms.	violates or fails to comply with any provision of this chapter.
26 USC 7201	Attempt to evade or defeat tax.	
26 USC 7202	Willful failure to collect or pay over tax.	
26 USC 7203	Willful failure to file return, supply information, or pay tax.	
26 USC 7204	Fraudulent statements or failure to make statement to employees.	being required under provision of section 6051 to furnish a statement willfully furnishes a false or fraudulent statement or fails to furnish a statement.

Title & Section Numbers	Caption of Section (Chapter Headings)	Relates to any persons(s) who...
26 USC 7205	Fraudulent withholding exemption certificate or failure to supply information.	
26 USC 7206(1)	Fraud and false statements - Declaration under penalties of perjury.	
26 USC 7206(2)	Fraud and false statements - Aid or assistance.	willfully aids or assists in, or procures, counsels, or advises the preparation or presentation under, or in connection with any matter arising under, the internal revenue laws, of a return, affidavit, claim, or other document, which is fraudulent or is false to any material matter, whether or not such falsity or fraud is with knowledge or consent of the person authorized or required to present such return, affidavit, claim, or document.
26 USC 7206(3)	Fraud and false statements - Fraudulent bonds, permits, and entries.	
26 USC 7206(4)	Fraud and false statements - Removal or concealment with intent to defraud.	
26 USC 7206(5)	Fraud and false statements - Compromises and closing agreements.	in connection with any closing agreement under section 7122, or offer to enter into any such agreement, willfully conceals property, or withholds, falsifies, or destroys records.
26 USC 7207	Fraudulent returns, statements, or other documents.	
26 USC 7208	Offenses relating to stamps.	[Section pertains to counterfeiting, mutilation or removal; use of mutilated, insufficient or counterfeit stamps; reuse of stamps; emptied stamped packages.]
26 USC 7209	Unauthorized use of stamps.	buys, sells, offers for sale, uses, transfers, takes or gives in exchange, or pledges any stamp, coupon, ticket, book, or other device prescribed by the Secretary under this title for the collection or payment of any tax imposed by this title.

Title & Section Numbers	Caption of Section (Chapter Headings)	Relates to any persons(s) who...
26 USC 7210	Failure to obey summons.	
26 USC 7211	False statements to purchasers or lessees relating to tax.	
26 USC 7212	Attempts to interfere with administration of internal revenue laws.	corruptly or by force or threats of force endeavors to intimidate or impede any officer or employee of the United States acting in an official capacity under this title.
26 USC 7213	Unauthorized disclosure of information (Internal Revenue Code).	
26 USC 7214	Offenses by officers and employees of the U.S.	
26 USC 7215	Offenses with respect to collected taxes.	
26 USC 7216	Disclosure or use of information by preparers of returns (Internal Revenue Code).	
26 USC 7231	Failure to obtain license for collection of foreign items (Internal Revenue Code).	
26 USC 7232	Failure to register, or false statement by manufacturer or producer of gasoline, lubricating oil, diesel fuel, or aviation fuel.	
26 USC 7512(b)	Separate accounting for certain collected taxes, etc.- Requirements.	
26 USC 9012(e)	Criminal penalties - Kickbacks and illegal payments (Presidential Election Campaign Fund).	
26 USC 9042(d)	Criminal penalties - Kickbacks and illegal payments (Presidential Primary Matching Payment Account).	

Title & Section Numbers	Caption of Section (Chapter Headings)	Relates to any persons(s) who...
27 USC 206	Bulk sales and bottling (Federal Alcohol Administration).	sell or offer to sell, contract to sell, or otherwise dispose of distilled spirits in bulk, except under regulations of the Secretary of the Treasury, for export.
28 USC 1826(c)	Recalcitrant witnesses.	escapes or attempts to escape from the custody of any facility or from any place in which or to which he is confined pursuant to this section or section 4243 of title 18, or rescues or attempts to rescue or instigates, aids, or assists the escape of such person.
28 USC 1864	Drawing of names from the master jury wheel; completion of juror qualification form.	willfully misrepresents a material fact on a juror qualification form for the purpose of avoiding or securing service as a juror.
28 USC 1866	Selection and summoning of jury panels.	fails to appear as directed for jury service.
28 USC 1867	Challenging compliance with selection procedures.	discloses contents of any record or paper used by the jury commission or clerk in connection with the jury selection process in violation of this subsection.
28 USC 2678	Attorney fees; penalty (Tort Claims Procedure).	being an attorney, charges, demands, receives, or collects for services rendered in connection with such claim any amount in excess of that allowed under this section.
28 USC 2902(e)	Discretionary authority of court; examination, report, and determination by court; termination of civil commitment.	escapes or attempts to escape while committed to institutional custody for examination or treatment, or rescues or attempts to rescue or instigates, aids, or assists the escape or attempt to escape of such a person.

Title & Section Numbers	Caption of Section (Chapter Headings)	Relates to any persons(s) who...
29 USC 162	Offenses and penalties (National Labor Relations).	resist, prevent, impede or interfere with any member of the Board or any of its agents or agencies in the performance of duties pursuant to this subchapter.
29 USC 186	Restrictions on financial transactions (Labor-Management Relations).	
29 USC 216	Penalties (Fair Labor Standards).	
29 USC 431	Report of labor organizations.	
29 USC 432	Report of officers and employees of labor organizations.	
29 USC 433	Report of employers.	
29 USC 439	Violations and penalties.	[Section pertains to violations and penalties of provisions of subchapter.]
29 USC 461	Reports - Trusteeships.	[Section pertains to filing and contents; annual financial report; penalty for violations.]
29 USC 463	Unlawful acts relating to labor organization under trusteeship.	
29 USC 501(c)	Fiduciary responsibility of officers of labor organizations - Embezzlement of assets; penalty.	
29 USC 502	Bonding of officers and employees of labor organizations; amount, form, and placement of bonds; penalty for violation.	
29 USC 503	Financial transactions between labor organization and officers and employees.	

Title & Section Numbers	Caption of Section (Chapter Headings)	Relates to any persons(s) who...
29 USC 504	Prohibition against certain persons holding office (Labor).	is an officer of a labor organization and has been a member of the Communist Party or has been convicted of, or served any part of a prison term resulting from his conviction of, robbery, bribery, extortion, embezzlement, grand larceny, burglary, arson, violation of narcotics laws, murder, etc.
29 USC 522	Extortionate picketing; penalty for violation (Labor).	
29 USC 530	Deprivation of rights by violence.	uses, or threatens to use, force or violence to restrain, or attempt to restrain, coerce, or intimidate any member of a labor organization for the purpose of interfering with or preventing the exercise of any right to which he is entitled under the provisions of this chapter.
29 USC 629	Criminal penalties (Age Discrimination in Employment).	forcibly resist, oppose, impede, intimidate or interfere with a duly authorized representative of the Equal Employment Opportunity Commission while it is engaged in the performance of duties under this chapter.
29 USC 666	Civil and criminal penalties (Occupational Safety and Health).	[Section pertains to willful or repeated violation; failure to correct violation; willful violation causing death to employee; false statements, representations, or certification.]
29 USC 1111	Persons prohibited from holding certain positions (Employee Retirement Income Security Program).	
29 USC 1131	Criminal penalties (Employee Retirement Income Security Program).	willfully violates any provision of part 1 of this subtitle or any regulation or order issued under any such provision.

Title & Section Numbers	Caption of Section (Chapter Headings)	Relates to any persons(s) who...
29 USC 1141	Coercive interference.	uses fraud, force, violence, or threat of the use of force or violence, to restrain, coerce, intimidate, or attempt to restrain, coerce, or intimidate any participant or beneficiary for the purpose of interfering with or preventing the exercise of any right to which he is or may become entitled under the plan, this subchapter, section 1201 of this title, or the Welfare and Pension Plans Disclosure Act.
30 USC 195	Enforcement (Mineral Lands and Mining).	organize or participate in any scheme, arrangement, plan or agreement to circumvent or defeat the provisions of this chapter or its implementing regulations.
30 USC 820	Penalties (Mine Safety and Health).	being an operator, willfully violates a mandatory health or safety standard, or knowingly violates or refuses or fails to comply with any order issued under section 814 of this title and section 817 of this title.
30 USC 933	Duties of operators in States not qualifying under workmen's compensation laws (Black Lung Benefits).	as an employer, fails to secure such benefits as required under this section.
30 USC 941	Penalty for false statements or representations (Black Lung Benefits).	
30 USC 1211	Office of Surface Mining Reclamation and Enforcement.	[Section pertains to conflict of interest; penalties; rules and regulations.]
30 USC 1232	Reclamation fee (Abandoned Mine Reclamations).	knowingly makes any false statement, representation, or certification required in this section.
30 USC 1267	Inspections and monitoring (Control of the Environmental Impacts of Surface Coal Mining).	

Title & Section Numbers	Caption of Section (Chapter Headings)	Relates to any persons(s) who...
30 USC 1268	Penalties (Control of the Environmental Impacts of Surface Coal Mining).	
30 USC 1294	Penalty (Administrative and Miscellaneous Provisions).	willfully resist, prevent, impede, or interfere with the Secretary or any of his agents in the performance of duties pursuant to this chapter.
30 USC 1461(3)	Prohibited acts (Deep Seabed Hard Mineral Resources).	refuses to permit any Federal officer or employee authorized to monitor or enforce the provisions of this chapter to board a vessel.
30 USC 1461(4)	Prohibited acts (Deep Seabed Hard Mineral Resources).	forcibly assaults, resists, opposes, impedes, intimidates, or interferes with any such authorized officer or employee in the conduct of any search or inspection described in paragraph (3).
30 USC 1461(5)	Prohibited acts (Deep Seabed Hard Mineral Resources).	resists a lawful arrest for any act prohibited by this section.
30 USC 1461(7)	Prohibited acts (Deep Seabed Hard Mineral Resources).	interferes with, delays, or prevents, by any means, the apprehension or arrest of any other person subject to this section knowing that such other person has committed any act prohibited by this section.
30 USC 1463	Criminal offenses (Deep Seabed Hard Mineral Resources).	commits any act prohibited by section 1461 of this title.
30 USC 1720	Criminal penalties (Federal Royalty Management and Enforcement).	
31 USC 783	Rules and regulations (Property Management).	
31 USC 1350	Criminal penalty (Appropriations).	
31 USC 1519	Criminal penalty (Appropriation Accounting).	

Title & Section Numbers	Caption of Section (Chapter Headings)	Relates to any persons(s) who...
31 USC 5111	Minting and issuing coins, medals, and numismatic items (Coins and Currency).	
31 USC 5313	Reports on domestic coins and currency transactions.	[Section pertains to when a domestic financial institution is involved in a transaction for the payment, receipt, or transfer of U.S. coins or currency, in an amount, denomination, or amount and denomination, or under circumstances the Secretary prescribes by regulation, the institution and any other participant in the transaction shall file a report on the transaction at the time and in the way the Secretary prescribes.]
31 USC 5314	Records and reports on foreign financial agency transactions.	
31 USC 5316	Reports on exporting and importing monetary instruments.	
31 USC 5322	Criminal penalties.	violates this subchapter or a regulation prescribed under this subchapter.
31 USC 5324	Structuring transactions to evade reporting requirement prohibited.	
33 USC 1	Regulations by Secretary of Army for navigation of waters generally).	
33 USC 2	Regulations for navigation of South and Southwest Passes of Mississippi River; penalties.	
33 USC 3	Regulations to prevent injuries from target practice (Navigable Waters).	
33 USC 403	Obstruction of navigable waters generally; wharves, piers, etc.; excavations and filling in.	

Title & Section Numbers	Caption of Section (Chapter Headings)	Relates to any persons(s) who...
33 USC 406	Penalty for wrongful construction of bridges, piers, etc.; removal of structures.	
33 USC 407	Deposit of refuse in navigable waters generally.	
33 USC 410	Exception as to floating loose timber, sack rafts, etc.; violation of regulations; penalty.	
33 USC 411	Penalty for wrongful deposit of refuse; use of or injury to harbor improvements, and obstruction of navigable waters generally.	
33 USC 441	Deposit of refuse prohibited; penalty (New York Harbor, Harbor of Hampton Roads, and Harbor of Baltimore).	
33 USC 443	Permit for dumping; penalty for taking or towing boat or scow without permit (New York Harbor, Harbor of Hampton Roads, and Harbor of Baltimore).	
33 USC 447	Bribery of inspector; penalty (New York Harbor, Harbor of Hampton Roads, and Harbor of Baltimore).	
33 USC 452	Taking shellfish or otherwise interfering with navigation in New York Harbor channels; penalty; arrest and procedure.	
33 USC 499	Regulations for drawbridges.	
33 USC 533	Penalties for violations (General Bridge Authority).	
33 USC 554	Duty of shipowners and officers to furnish information to person in local charge of improvement; penalty.	
33 USC 555	Duty of shipowners and officers to furnish information required by Secretary of Army.	

Title & Section Numbers	Caption of Section (Chapter Headings)	Relates to any persons(s) who...
33 USC 601	Mississippi River; regulation of reservoirs at headwaters.	
33 USC 682	Malicious injury to works; injury to navigable waters by hydraulic mining; penalty (California Debris Commission).	
33 USC 928	Fees for services (Longshore and Harbor Workers' Compensation).	
33 USC 931	Penalty for misrepresentation (Longshore and Harbor Workers' Compensation).	
33 USC 937	Certificate of compliance with chapter (Longshore and Harbor Workers' Compensation).	
33 USC 938	Penalties (Longshore and Harbor Workers' Compensation).	
3 USC 990	Offenses and penalties (Saint Lawrence Seaway).	with intent to defraud the Corporation, or to deceive any director, officer, or employee of the Corporation or any officer or employee of the United States, makes any false entry in any book of the Corporation.
33 USC 1227(b)	Investigatory powers (Navigation and Navigable Waters).	refuses to obey a subpoena issued by the Secretary in relation to an investigation under this section.
33 USC 1232(b)(2)	Criminal penalty.	in violation of this chapter or of any regulation issued hereunder, uses a dangerous weapon, or engages in conduct that causes bodily injury or fear of imminent bodily injury to any officer authorized to enforce the provisions of this chapter or the regulations issued hereunder.

Title & Section Numbers	Caption of Section (Chapter Headings)	Relates to any persons(s) who...
33 USC 1318	Records and reports; inspections.	as an authorized representative of the Administrator, knowingly or willfully publishes, divulges, discloses, or makes known in any manner or to any extent not authorized by law any information which is required to be considered confidential under this subsection.
33 USC 1319(c)(1)	Criminal penalties - Negligent violations.	negligently violates section 1311, 1312, 1316, 1317, 1318, 1321(b)(3), 1328, or 1345 of this title.
33 USC 1319(c)(2)	Criminal penalties - Knowing violations.	knowingly violates section 1311, 1312, 1316, 1317, 1318, 1321(b)(3), 1328, or 1345 of this title.
33 USC 1319(c)(3)	Criminal penalties - Knowing endangerment.	
33 USC 1319(c)(4)	Criminal penalties - False statements.	
33 USC 1321	Oil and hazardous substance liability.	
33 USC 1342	National pollutant discharge elimination system.	[Section pertains to permits for discharge of pollutants; suspension of Federal program under submission of State program; State permit programs; limitation on permit requirement; etc.]
33 USC 1344	Permits for dredged or fill material.	violates any condition or limitation in a permit issued by the Secretary under this Section.
33 USC 1415(b)	Criminal penalties.	violates any provision in this subchapter.
33 USC 1481	Violations; penalties (Pollution Casualties on High Seas).	violates any provision of this chapter or a regulation issued thereunder.

Title & Section Numbers	Caption of Section (Chapter Headings)	Relates to any persons(s) who...
33 USC 1907	Violations.	[Section pertains to general prohibitions, investigations, ship inspections, garbage disposal inspection, harmful substance or garbage disposal inspections, supplemental remedies and requirements.]
33 USC 1908	Penalties for violations.	
33 USC 2409	Penalties (Organotin Antifouling Paint Control).	
33 USC 2609	Penalties (Shore Protection).	
35 USC 186	Penalty (Secrecy of Certain Inventions and Filing Applications in Foreign Country).	
36 USC 728	Duration of regulations and licenses; publication of regulations; violations and penalties (Presidential Inaugural Ceremonies).	
38 USC 1987	Penalties (Veterans' Benefits).	make or cause to be made, or conspire, combine, aid, or assist in, agree to, arrange for, or in anywise procure the making or presentation of a false or fraudulent affidavit, declaration, certificate, etc., concerning any application for insurance under National Service Life Insurance or yearly renewable term insurance.
38 USC 5905	Penalty for certain acts (Veterans' Benefits).	directly or indirectly solicits, contracts for, charges, or receives any fee for compensation except as provided in section 5904 or 1984 of this title.

Title & Section Numbers	Caption of Section (Chapter Headings)	Relates to any persons(s) who...
38 USC 6101	Misappropriation by fiduciaries (Veterans' Benefits).	
38 USC 6102	Fraudulent acceptance of payments (Veterans' Benefits).	
40 USC 13m	Penalties; Supreme Court Building and grounds (Public Buildings, Property, and Works).	
40 USC 101	Laws of District extended to public buildings and grounds.	injure the buildings or shrubs or remove any stone, gravel, sand, or other property of the United States, or any other part of the public grounds or lots belonging to the United States in the District of Columbia.
40 USC 193h	Prosecution and punishment of offenses (Capitol Building and Grounds).	
40 USC 193s	Prosecution and punishment; Smithsonian grounds.	
40 USC 212a-2	Protection of Members of Congress, officers of Congress, and members of their families.	obstructs, resists, or interferes with a member of the Capitol Police engaged in the performance of the protective functions authorized by this section.
40 USC 318c	Penalties (The Public Property).	
40 USC 332	Violations; penalties (Contract Work Hours and Safety Standards).	
40 USC 883	Violations and penalties (Pennsylvania Avenue Development).	[Section pertains to larceny, embezzlement, or conversion; false entries, reports, or statements; rebates and conspiracies.]
40 App. USC 108	Personal financial interests (Appalachian Regional Commission).	

Title & Section Numbers	Caption of Section (Chapter Headings)	Relates to any persons(s) who...
41 USC 53	Prohibited conduct (Public Contracts).	provides, attempts to provide or offers to provide any kickback; solicits, accepts, or attempts to accept any kickback; or includes directly, or indirectly, the amount of any kickback prohibited by clause (1) or (2) in the contract price charged by a subcontractor to a prime contractor or a higher tier subcontractor or in the contract price charged by a prime contractor to the U.S.
41 USC 54	Criminal penalties.	engages in any conduct prohibited by section 53 of this title.
41 USC 423	Restrictions on disclosing and obtaining contractor bid or proposal information or source selection information (Office of Federal Procurement Policy).	
42 USC 261(a)	Penalties for introducing prohibited articles and substances into hospitals; escaping from, or aiding and abetting an escape from hospitals.	introduces any habit-forming narcotic drug or substance controlled under Controlled Substances Act, weapon, or any other contraband article or thing, or any contraband letter or message intended to be received by an inmate of a hospital at which addicts or other persons with drug abuse and drug dependence problems are treated and cared for.
42 USC 262	Regulation of biological products.	
42 USC 271	Penalties for violation of quarantine laws.	
42 USC 274e	Prohibition of organ purchases (Organ Transplants).	
42 USC 274k	National Registry (National Bone Marrow Donor Registry).	discloses the content of any record referred to in subsection (c)(5)(A) of this section without the prior written consent of the donor or potential donor.
42 USC 289g-2	Prohibitions regarding human fetal tissue.	

Title & Section Numbers	Caption of Section (Chapter Headings)	Relates to any persons(s) who...
42 USC 290cc-32	Prohibition against certain false statements (Projects for Assistance in Transition from Homelessness).	
42 USC 300a-8	Penalty for United States, etc., officer or employee coercing or endeavoring to coerce procedure upon beneficiary of Federal program.	
42 USC 300d-20	Prohibition against certain false statements (Formula Grants with Respect to Modifications of State Plans).	
42 USC 300e-17	Financial disclosure (Health Maintenance Organizations).	
42 USC 300h-2	Enforcement of program (Public Water Systems).	
42 USC 300i-1	Tampering with public water systems.	
42 USC 300j-23	Drinking water coolers containing lead.	sells in interstate commerce, or manufactures for sale in interstate commerce, any drinking water cooler which is not lead free.
42 USC 300w-8	Criminal penalty for false statements (Preventive Health and Health Services Block Grants).	
42 USC 300x-56	Prohibitions regarding receipt of funds (Block Grants Regarding Mental Health and Substance Abuse).	
42 USC 300aa-28	Manufacturer recordkeeping and reporting (Assuring a Safer Childhood Vaccination Program in United States).	destroys, alters, falsifies, or conceals any record or report required under paragraph (1) or (2) of subsection (a) of this section.
42 USC 300ee-19	Prohibition against certain false statements (Prevention of Acquired Immune Deficiency Syndrome).	
42 USC 405	Evidence, procedure, and certification for payments (Social Security).	

Title & Section Numbers	Caption of Section (Chapter Headings)	Relates to any persons(s) who...
42 USC 406	Representation of claimants before Commissioner of Social Security.	
42 USC 408	Penalties (Public Health and Welfare).	
42 USC 707	Criminal penalty for false statements (Maternal and Child Health Services Block Grant).	
42 USC 1306	Disclosure of information in possession of Social Security Administration or Department of Health and Human Services.	
42 USC 1307(a)	Penalty for fraud (Social Security).	makes or causes to be made any false representation concerning the requirements of this chapter.
42 USC 1307(b)	Penalty for fraud (Social Security).	with intent to elicit information as to the social security account number, date of birth, employment, wages, or benefits of any individual, falsely represents to the Commissioner of Social Security or the Secretary that he is such individual, or the wife, husband, widow, etc.; or falsely represents to any person that he is an employee or agent of the U.S.
42 USC 1320a-7b	Criminal penalties for acts involving Federal health care programs.	
42 USC 1320c-9	Prohibition against disclosure of information (Peer Review of Utilization and Quality of Health Care Services).	
42 USC 1320d-6	Wrongful disclosure of individually identifiable health information.	
42 USC 1383(d)(2)	Procedure for payment of benefits - Procedures applicable; prohibition on assignment of payments; representation of claimants (Public Health and Welfare).	

Title & Section Numbers	Caption of Section (Chapter Headings)	Relates to any persons(s) who...
42 USC 1383a(a)	Fraudulent acts; penalties; restitution (Public Health and Welfare).	makes or causes to be made any false statement or representation of a material fact in any application for any benefit under this chapter.
42 USC 1383a(b)	Fraudulent acts; penalties; restitution (Public Health and Welfare).	violates subsection (a) of this section and the violation includes a willful misuse of funds by the person or entity.
42 USC 1395nn(a)	Limitation on certain physician referrals - Prohibition of certain referrals.	[Provides if a physician or physician's immediate family member has a financial relationship with an entity specified in paragraph (2) the physician may not make a referral to the entity.]
42 USC 1395nn(b)(1)	Limitation on certain physician referrals - Physician's services.	[Provides subsection (a)(1) of this section shall not apply in the case of a physician's services provided personally by another physician in the same group practice as the referring physician.]
42 USC 1395nn(b)(2)	Limitation on certain physician referrals - In-office Ancillary Services.	[Provides subsection (a)(1) of this section will not apply in these cases.]
42 USC 1395nn(c)	Limitation on certain physician referrals - General exception related only to ownership or investment prohibition for ownership in publicly traded securities and mutual funds.	
42 USC 1395ss	Certification of medicare supplemental health insurance policies.	
42 USC 1713	Fraud; penalties.	for the purpose of causing an increase in any payment authorized to be made under this chapter, or for the purpose of causing any payment to be made where no payment is authorized hereunder, knowingly makes or causes to be made, or aids or abets in making of any false statement or representation of material fact.
42 USC 1714	Legal services (Compensation for Injury, Death, or Detention of Employees of Contractors with United States Outside United States).	

Title & Section Numbers	Caption of Section (Chapter Headings)	Relates to any persons(s) who...
42 USC 1760(g)	Criminal penalties (School Lunch Programs).	embezzles, willfully misapplies, steals or obtains by fraud any funds, assets, or property which are the subject of a grant or other form of assistance under this chapter or the Child Nutrition Act of 1966.
42 USC 1761(o)(1)	Violations and penalties (School Lunch Programs).	falsifies, conceals, or covers up by any trick, scheme or device a material fact, or makes any false, fictitious, or fraudulent statements or representations in connection with any application, procurement, record keeping entry, claim for reimbursement, or other document or statement made in connection with the program.
42 USC 1761(o)(2)	Violations and penalties (School Lunch Programs).	being a partner, officer, director, or managing agent connected in any capacity willfully embezzles, misapplies, steals, or obtains by fraud, false statement, or forgery, any benefits provided by this section.
42 USC 1973i(c)	False information in registering or voting; penalties.	
42 USC 1973i(d)	Falsification or concealment of material facts or giving of false statements in matters within jurisdiction of examiners or hearing officers; penalties.	
42 USC 1973i(e)	Voting more than once.	
42 USC 1973j(a)	Depriving or attempting to deprive persons of secured rights.	deprives or attempts to deprive any person of any right secured by section 1973, 1973a, 1973c, 1973e, or 1973h or violates section 1973i(a) of this title.
42 USC 1973j(b)	Destroying, defacing, mutilating, or altering ballots or official voting records.	
42 USC 1973j(c)	Conspiring to violate or interfere with secured rights.	

Title & Section Numbers	Caption of Section (Chapter Headings)	Relates to any persons(s) who...
42 USC 1973aa	Application of prohibition to other States; "test or device" defined.	[Provides no citizen shall be denied, because of his failure to comply with any test or device, the right to vote in any Federal, State or local election conducted in any State or political subdivision of a State.]
42 USC 1973aa-1a	Bilingual election requirements.	
42 USC 1973aa-3	Penalty.	deprives or attempts to deprive any person of any right secured by section 1973aa, 1973aa-1, or 1973aa-1a of this title.
42 USC 1973bb	Enforcement of twenty-sixth amendment.	
42 USC 1973gg-10	Criminal penalties.	intimidates, threatens, or coerces, or attempts to intimidate, threaten or coerce any person for registering to vote, or voting, or attempting to register to vote, urging or aiding any person to register to vote, or to attempt to register to vote, or exercising any right under this subchapter.
42 USC 1974	Retention and preservation of records and papers by officers of elections; deposit with custodian; penalty for violation (Federal Election Records).	
42 USC 1974a	Theft, destruction, concealment, mutilation, or alteration of records or papers; penalties (Federal Election Records).	
42 USC 1995	Criminal contempt proceedings; penalties; trial by jury (Civil Rights).	
42 USC 2000e-8	Investigations (Equal Employment Opportunities).	as an officer or employee of the Commission, makes public in any manner whatever any information obtained by the Commission pursuant to its authority under this section.

Title & Section Numbers	Caption of Section (Chapter Headings)	Relates to any persons(s) who...
42 USC 2000e-13	Application to personnel of Commission of sections 111 and 1114 of Title 18; punishment for violation of Title 18; punishment for violation of section 1114 or Title 18 (EEO).	
42 USC 2000g-2	Cooperation with other agencies; conciliation assistance in confidence and without publicity; information as confidential; restriction on performance of investigative or prosecuting functions; violations and penalties (Community Relations Service).	
42 USC 2000h	Criminal contempt proceedings; trial by jury, criminal practice, penalties, exceptions, intent; civil contempt proceedings (Civil Rights).	
42 USC 2077	Unauthorized dealings in special nuclear material.	
42 USC 2122	Prohibitions governing atomic weapons.	
42 USC 2131	License required.	[Making it unlawful to transfer or receive in interstate commerce, manufacture, produce, transfer, acquire, possess, use, import, or export any utilization or production facility except under and in accordance with a license issued by the Commission pursuant to section 2133 or 2134 of this title.]
42 USC 2272	Violation of specific sections (Atomic Energy).	violates any provision of sections 2077, 2122, or 2131 of this title.
42 USC 2273	Violations of sections.	violates sections 2095 or 2201(b), (i), or (o) of this title.

Title & Section Numbers	Caption of Section (Chapter Headings)	Relates to any persons(s) who...
42 USC 2274(a)	Communication of restricted data.	lawfully, or unlawfully, having possession of, access to, control over, or being entrusted with any document, writing, sketch, photograph, plan, model, instrument, appliance, note, or information involving or incorporating restricted data communicates the same to any individual or person with intent to injure the U.S. or with intent to secure an advantage to any foreign nation.
42 USC 2274(b)	Communication of restricted data.	communicates, transmits, or discloses the same to any individual or person, or attempts or conspires to do any of the foregoing with reason to believe such data will be utilized to injure the U.S. or to secure an advantage to any foreign nation.
42 USC 2275	Receipt of restricted data.	
42 USC 2276	Tampering with restricted data.	
42 USC 2278a(c)	Trespass upon Commission installations - Penalty for violation of regulations regarding enclosed property (Atomic Energy).	
42 USC 2278b	Photographing, etc., of Commission installations; penalty (Atomic Energy).	
42 USC 2283(a)	Protection of nuclear inspectors - Homicide.	kills any person who performs any inspections which are related to any activity or facility licensed by the Commission, and are carried out to satisfy requirements under this chapter or under any other Federal law governing the safety of utilization facilities required to be licensed under section 2133 or 2134(b) of this title, or the safety of radioactive materials.
42 USC 2283(b)	Protection of nuclear inspectors - Assault.	forcibly assaults, resists, opposes, impedes, intimidates or interferes with any person who performs inspections as described under subsection (a).

Title & Section Numbers	Caption of Section (Chapter Headings)	Relates to any persons(s) who...
42 USC 2284	Sabotage of nuclear facilities or fuel.	
42 USC 3220(a)	False statements; security overvaluation (Economic Development).	makes any statement knowing it to be false, or overvalues any security, for the purpose of obtaining for himself or for any applicant, any financial assistance under section 3131, 3141, 3142, or 3171 of this title.
42 USC 3220(b)	Embezzlement; misapplication of funds; false book entries; schemes to defraud; speculation (Economic Development).	
42 USC 3426	Penalties; false statements.	knowingly makes any false statement to the U.S. attorney in any petition under section 3412(a) of this title.
42 USC 3537a	Prohibition of advance disclosure of funding decisions (Department of Housing and Urban Development).	
42 USC 3611	Subpoenas; giving of evidence (Fair Housing).	
42 USC 3631	Violations; penalties.	by force or threat of force willfully injures, intimidates, or interferes with, or attempts to injure, intimidate or interfere with any person because of race, color, religion, sex, handicap, familial status, or national origin and because he is selling, purchasing, renting, financing, occupying, or contracting or negotiating for the sale, purchase, rental, financing, or occupation of any dwelling, or applying for or participating in any service, organization, or facility relating to the business of selling or renting dwellings.
42 USC 3791	General provisions (Justice System Improvement).	
42 USC 3795	Misuse of Federal assistance.	embezzles, willfully misapplies, steals, or obtains by fraud any funds, assets, or property which are the subject of a grant or contract or other form of assistance pursuant to this chapter.

Title & Section Numbers	Caption of Section (Chapter Headings)	Relates to any persons(s) who...
42 USC 4367	Reporting requirements of financial interests of officers and employees of Environmental Protection Agency.	
42 USC 4910	Enforcement (Noise Control).	violates paragraph (1), (3), (5), or (6) of subsection (a) of section 4909 of this title.
42 USC 4912	Records, reports, and information (Noise Control).	knowingly makes any false statement, representation, or certification in any application, record, report, plan, or other document filed or required to be maintained under this chapter.
42 USC 5157(a)	Misuse of funds.	misapplies the proceeds of a loan or other cash benefit obtained under this chapter.
42 USC 5410	Penalties (Manufactured Home Construction Safety and Standards).	
42 USC 5420	Failure to report violations; penalties (Manufactured Home Construction and Safety Standards).	
42 USC 6395	Enforcement (Energy Conservation).	willfully violates section 6394 of this title.
42 USC 6906	Financial disclosure (Solid Waste Disposal).	
42 USC 6927	Inspections (Hazardous Waste Management).	knowingly and willfully divulges or discloses any information entitle to protection under this subsection.
42 USC 6928(d)	Criminal penalties (Hazardous Waste).	transports or causes to be transported any hazardous waste identified or listed under this subchapter.
42 USC 6928(e)	Knowing endangerment.	knowingly transports, treats, stores, disposes of, or exports any hazardous waste identified or listed under this subchapter, knowing at that time that he thereby places another person in imminent danger of death or serious bodily injury.

Title & Section Numbers	Caption of Section (Chapter Headings)	Relates to any persons(s) who...
42 USC 6991d	Inspections, monitoring, testing, and corrective action (Regulation of Underground Storage Tanks).	knowingly and willfully divulges or discloses any information entitle to protection under this subsection.
42 USC 6992d	Enforcement (Demonstration Medical Waste Tracking Program).	omits material information or makes any false material statement or representation in any label, record, report, or other document filed, maintained, or used for purposes of compliance with this subchapter.
42 USC 7270b	Trespass on Strategic Petroleum Reserve facilities.	
42 USC 7413	Federal enforcement (Air Quality and Emissions Limitations).	
42 USC 8432	Criminal penalties (Powerplant and Industrial Fuel Use).	
42 USC 9113	Protection of submarine electric transmission cables and equipment.	break or injure, or attempt to break or injure, or in any manner procure, counsel, aid, abet, or be accessory to such breaking or injury, any submarine electric transmission cable or equipment being constructed or operated pursuant to this chapter.
42 USC 9151(2)	Prohibited acts (Ocean Thermal Energy Conservation).	refuses to permit any Federal officer or employee authorized to monitor or enforce the provisions of sections 9120 and 9153 of this title to enter or board an ocean thermal energy conservation facility or plantship or any vessel documented or numbered under the laws of the U.S., for purposes of conducting any search or inspection.
42 USC 9151(3)	Prohibited acts (Ocean Thermal Energy Conservation).	forcibly assaults, resists, opposes, impedes, intimidates, or interferes with any such authorized officer or employee in the conduct of any search or inspection described in paragraph (2) of this section.
42 USC 9151(4)	Prohibited acts (Ocean Thermal Energy Conservation).	resists a lawful arrest for any act prohibited by this section.

Title & Section Numbers	Caption of Section (Chapter Headings)	Relates to any persons(s) who...
42 USC 9151(5)	Prohibited acts (Ocean Thermal Energy Conservation).	interferes with, delays, or prevents, by any means, the apprehension or arrest of another person subject to this section knowing that the other person has committed any act prohibited by this section.
42 USC 9152(d)	Criminal penalties (Ocean Thermal Energy Conservation).	commits any act prohibited by section 9151 of this title.
42 USC 9603(b)	Penalties for failure to notify; use of notice or information pursuant to notice in criminal case (Hazardous Substances Releases, Liability, Compensation).	
42 USC 9603(c)	Notice to Administrator of EPA of existence of storage, etc., facility by owner or operator; exception; time, manner, and form of notice; penalties for failure to notify; use of notice or information pursuant to notice in criminal case (Hazardous Substances Releases, Liability, Compensation).	
42 USC 9603(d)	Record keeping requirements; promulgation of rules and regulations by Administrator of EPA; penalties for violations; waiver of retention requirements (Hazardous Substances Releases, Liability, Compensation).	
42 USC 9604	Response authorities (Hazardous Substances Releases, Liability, Compensation).	divulges or discloses any information entitled to protection under this subsection.
42 USC 9612	Claims procedure (Hazardous Substances Releases, Liability, Compensation).	gives or causes to be given any false information as a part of such claim.
42 USC 11045	Enforcement (Emergency Planning and Community Right-to-Know).	
42 USC 14072	FBI database.	

Title & Section Numbers	Caption of Section (Chapter Headings)	Relates to any persons(s) who...
43 USC 104	Disobedience to subpoena (District Land Offices).	
43 USC 362	Injury to signposts and filling up or fouling water supply (Discovery, Development, and Marking of Water Holes, etc., by Government).	
43 USC 942-6	Rights-of-way for Alaskan wagon roads, wire rope, aerial, or other tramways; reservations; filing preliminary survey and map of location; alteration, amendment, repeal, or grant of equal rights; forfeiture of rights; reversion of grant; liens.	
43 USC 1064	Violations of chapter; punishment (Unlawful Inclosures or Occupancy; Obstructing Settlement or Transit).	
43 USC 1350	Remedies and penalties (Submerged Lands).	
43 USC 1605	Alaska Native Fund.	expends, donates, or otherwise uses for the purpose of carrying on propaganda, or intervening in any political campaign on behalf of any candidate for public office, funds paid or distributed pursuant to this section to any of the Regional and Village Corporations established pursuant to this chapter.
43 USC 1619	Attorney and consultant fees (Alaska Native Claims Settlement).	receives any remuneration in addition to the amount allowed in accordance with this section.
43 USC 1733(a)	Regulations for implementation of management, use, and protection requirements; violations; criminal penalties (Public Lands).	
43 USC 1743	Disclosure of financial interests by officers or employees (Federal Land Policy and Management).	
43 USC 1864	Disclosure of financial interests by officers or employees of Department of the Interior.	

Title & Section Numbers	Caption of Section (Chapter Headings)	Relates to any persons(s) who...
45 USC 60	Penalty for suppression of voluntary information incident to accidents; separability of provisions (Railroads).	
45 USC 152	General duties (Railway Labor).	fails or refuses to comply with the terms of the third, fourth, fifth, seventh, or eighth paragraphs of this section.
45 USC 2311	Penalties (Railroad Retirement Act of 1974).	
45 USC 355	Claims for benefits (Railroad Unemployment Insurance).	
45 USC 359(a)	Failure to make report or furnish information; false or fraudulent statement or claim (Railroad Unemployment Insurance).	
46 USC 2302	Penalties for negligent operations (Vessels and Seamen).	
46 USC 2303	Duties related to marine casualty assistance and information (Vessels and Seamen).	
46 USC 2304	Duty to provide assistance at sea (Vessels and Seamen).	
46 USC 3102	Immersion suits (Inspection and Regulation of Vessels).	

Title & Section Numbers	Caption of Section (Chapter Headings)	Relates to any persons(s) who...
46 USC 3318	Penalties (Inspection and Regulation of Vessels).	manufactures, sells, offers for sale, or possesses with intent to sell, any equipment subject to this part, and the equipment is so defective as to be insufficient to accomplish the purpose for which it is intended.
46 USC 3501	Number of passengers (Inspection and Regulation of Vessels).	
46 USC 3718(b)	Penalties (Carriage of Liquid Bulk Dangerous Cargoes).	willfully violates this chapter, or a regulation prescribed under this chapter.
46 USC 4311	Penalties and injunctions (Recreational Vessels).	
46 USC 4507	Penalties (Uninspected Commercial Fishing Industry Vessels).	
46 USC 5116	Penalties (Load Lines of Vessels).	
46 USC 6306	Penalty (Investigating Marine Casualties).	attempts to coerce or to induce a witness to testify falsely in connection with a marine casualty.
46 USC 8503	Federal pilots authorized.	
46 USC 10908	Penalty for sending unseaworthy vessel to sea.	
46 USC 11110	Seamen's clothing (Protection and Relief).	detains a seaman's clothing.
46 USC 12309	Penalties (Numbering Undocumented Vessels).	
46 USC 12507	Penalties (Vessel Identification System).	
46 USC 31306	Declaration of citizenship (Commercial Instruments and Maritime Liens).	
46 USC 31330	Penalties (Commercial Instruments and Maritime Liens).	

Title & Section Numbers	Caption of Section (Chapter Headings)	Relates to any persons(s) who...
46 App. USC 143	Retaliation on denial of rights to United States vessels in British North America.	
46 App. USC 277	Inspection of documents (Regulation of Vessels in Domestic Commerce).	
46 App. USC 466c	Export of horses (Transportation of Passengers and Merchandise by Steam Vessels).	
46 App. USC 808	Vessels purchased, chartered, or leased; coastwise trade (Shipping Act).	
46 App. USC 835	Restrictions on transfer of shipping facilities during war or national emergency.	
46 App. USC 839	Approvals by Secretary (Shipping Act).	makes any false statement of a material fact to the Secretary of Transportation for the purpose of securing approval.
46 App. USC 1228	Fines and penalties; conviction as rendering persons ineligible to receive benefits of law (Merchant Marine Act, 1936).	
46 App. USC 1295f	Civilian nautical school (Maritime Education and Training).	
46 USC App. 1707a(f)(2)	Criminal penalties (Shipping).	willfully fails to pay a fee established under subsection (d) of this section.
46 USC App. 1903(a)	Vessels of U.S. or vessels subject to jurisdiction of the U.S. (Maritime Drug Law Enforcement).	knowingly or intentionally manufactures or distributes, or possesses with intent to manufacture or distribute, a controlled substance on board a vessel in the U.S. or on board a vessel subject to jurisdiction of the U.S.
46 USC App. 1903(g)	Penalties (Maritime Drug Law Enforcement).	commits an offense defined in this section.

Title & Section Numbers	Caption of Section (Chapter Headings)	Relates to any persons(s) who...
46 USC App. 1903(j)	Attempt or conspiracy to commit offense (Maritime Drug Law Enforcement).	conspires or attempts to commit an offense under this section.
47 USC 13	Violations; punishment; action for damages (Telegraphs).	
47 USC 21	Submarine cables; willful injury to; punishment.	
47 USC 22	Negligent injury to submarine cables; punishment.	
47 USC 24	Vessels laying cables; signals; avoidance of buoys (Submarine Cables).	
47 USC 25	Fishing vessels; duty to keep nets from cables (Submarine Cables).	
47 USC 27	Offending vessels to show nationality (Submarine Cables).	
47 USC 37	Violations; punishment (Submarine Cables).	commits, instigates, or assists in any act forbidden by section 34 of this title.
47 USC 220	Accounts, records, and memoranda (Common Carrier Regulation).	makes any false entry in the accounts of any book of accounts or in any record or memoranda kept by any such carrier, or willfully destroys, mutilates, alters, or by any other means or device falsifies any such account, record, or memoranda.
47 USC 223(b)(1)(A)	Obscene or harassing telephone calls in the District of Columbia or in interstate or foreign communications - Prohibited acts for commercial purposes; defense to prosecution.	knowingly within the U.S., by means of telephone, makes any obscene communications for commercial purposes to any person, regardless of whether the maker of such communication placed the call.

Title & Section Numbers	Caption of Section (Chapter Headings)	Relates to any persons(s) who...
47 USC 409	Hearings (Wire or Radio Communication) .	neglect or refuse to attend and testify, or to answer any lawful inquiry, or to produce books, papers, schedules of charges, contracts, agreements, and documents, in obedience to the subpoena of lawful requirement of the Commission.
47 USC 501	General penalty (Wire or Radio Communication).	willfully and knowingly does or causes or suffers to be done any act, matter, or thing, in this chapter prohibited or declared to be unlawful.
47 USC 508	Disclosure of payments to individuals connected with broadcasts (Wire or Radio Communication).	
47 USC 509	Prohibited practices in contests of knowledge, skill or chance (Wire or Radio Communication).	
47 USC 553	Unauthorized reception of cable service.	
47 USC 559	Obscene programming.	
47 USC 605	Unauthorized publication or use of communications.	
47 USC 606	War powers of President (Wire or Radio Communication).	
48 USC 1424c	Review of claims respecting land on Guam.	
49 USC 521	Civil penalties (Transportation).	knowingly and willfully violates any provision of subchapter III of chapter 311 or section 31502 of this title.
49 USC 522	Reporting and record keeping violations (Transportation).	

Title & Section Numbers	Caption of Section (Chapter Headings)	Relates to any persons(s) who...
49 USC 523	Unlawful disclosure of information (Transportation).	
49 USC 1155	Aviation penalties.	knowingly and without authority removes, conceals, or withholds a part of a civil aircraft involved in an accident.
49 USC 5124	Criminal penalty (Transportation of Hazardous Material).	
49 USC 11902	Interference with railroad car supply.	
49 USC 11903	Record keeping and reporting violations (Rail).	
49 USC 11904	Unlawful disclosure of information.	being a rail carrier providing transportation subject to the jurisdiction of the Board under this part, or an officer, agent, or employee of that rail carrier, or another person authorized to receive information from that rail carrier, knowingly discloses to another person information described in subsection (b) without consent of the shipper.
49 USC 11905	Disobedience to subpoenas (Rail).	
49 USC 11907	Punishment of corporation for violations committed by certain individuals.	[Provides acts or omissions that would be a violation of this part if committed by a director, officer, receiver, trustee, lessee, agent or employee of a rail carrier providing transportation or service subject to the jurisdiction of the Board under this part that is a corporation are also violations of this part by that corporation.]
49 USC 14903	Tariff violations.	
49 USC 14905	Penalties for violations of rules relating to loading and unloading motor vehicles (Motor Carriers, Water Carriers, Brokers, and Freight Forwarders).	

Title & Section Numbers	Caption of Section (Chapter Headings)	Relates to any persons(s) who...
49 USC 14909	Disobedience to subpoenas (Motor Carriers, Water Carriers, Brokers, and Freight Forwarders).	
49 USC 14912	Weight-bumping in household goods transportation (Motor Carriers, Water Carriers, Brokers, and Freight Forwarders).	
49 USC 16102	Recordkeeping and reporting violations (Pipeline Carriers).	
49 USC 16103	Unlawful disclosure of information (Pipeline Carriers).	
49 USC 16104	Disobedience to subpoenas (Pipeline Carriers).	
49 USC 21311	Records and reports (Rail Programs).	
49 USC 28302	Penalties (Rail Programs).	
49 USC 30307	Criminal penalties (National Driver Register).	
49 USC 32507	Penalties and enforcement (Bumper Standards).	
49 USC 32709	Penalties and enforcement (Odometers).	
49 USC 46306	Registration violations involving aircraft not providing air transportation.	
49 USC 46307	Violation of national defense airspace.	
49 USC 46308	Interference with air navigation.	
49 USC 46310	Reporting and recordkeeping violations (Air Commerce and Safety).	
49 USC 46311	Unlawful disclosure of information (Air Commerce and Safety).	

Title & Section Numbers	Caption of Section (Chapter Headings)	Relates to any persons(s) who...
49 USC 46312	Transporting hazardous material.	
49 USC 46313	Refusing to appear or produce records (Air Commerce and Safety).	
49 USC 46314	Entering aircraft or airport area in violation of security requirements.	
49 USC 46315	Lighting violations involving transporting controlled substances by aircraft not providing air transportation.	
49 USC 46502(a)	Aircraft piracy - In special aircraft jurisdiction.	
49 USC 46502(b)	Aircraft piracy - Outside special aircraft jurisdiction.	
49 USC 46504	Interference with flight crew members and attendants.	
49 USC 46505	Carrying a weapon or explosive on an aircraft.	
49 USC 46506	Application of certain criminal laws to acts on aircraft.	
49 USC 46507	False information and threats (Special Aircraft Jurisdiction of the United States).	
49 USC 47126	Criminal penalties for false statements (Airport Improvement).	
49 USC 47306	Criminal penalty (International Airport Facilities).	
49 USC 60123	Criminal penalties (Pipelines - Safety).	
49 USC 80116	Criminal penalty (Bills of Lading).	
49 USC 80501	Damage to transported property (Transportation).	

Title & Section Numbers	Caption of Section (Chapter Headings)	Relates to any persons(s) who...
50 USC 167k	Violations; penalties (War and National Defense - Helium).	
50 USC 192	Seizure and forfeiture of vessel; fine and imprisonment (Vessels in Territorial Waters of United States).	
50 USC 210	Penalties for unauthorized trading, etc.; jurisdiction of prosecutions (Insurrection).	
50 USC 217	Trading in captured or abandoned property (Insurrection).	
50 USC 783(b)	Receipt of, or attempt to receive, classified information by foreign agent.	
50 USC 783(c)	Penalties for violation (War and National Defense).	
50 USC 797	Security regulations and orders; penalty for violation (Control of Subversive Activities).	violates any regulation or order as, pursuant to lawful authority, shall be or has been promulgated or approved by the Secretary of Defense for the protection or security of military or naval aircraft, airports, vessels, harbors, bases, forts, posts, etc.
50 USC 855	Violations; penalties; deportation (Registration of Certain Persons Trained in Foreign Espionage Systems).	
50 USC 1705	Penalties (International Emergency Economic Power).	
50 USC 1809	Criminal sanctions (Electronic Surveillance).	engages in electronic surveillance under color of law except as authorized by statute.
50 USC 1827	Penalties (Physical Searches).	under color of law for the purpose of obtaining foreign intelligence information, executes a physical search within the United States except as authorized by statute.

Title & Section Numbers	Caption of Section (Chapter Headings)	Relates to any persons(s) who...
50 App. USC 12	Property transferred to Alien Property Custodian.	purchases property from the alien property custodian for an undisclosed principal, or for re-sale to a person not a citizen of the United States, or for the benefit of a person not a citizen of the United States.
50 App. USC 16	Offenses; punishment; forfeitures of property (Trading with the Enemy Act of 1917).	
50 App. USC 19	Print, newspaper or publication in foreign languages (Trading with the Enemy Act of 1917).	makes an affidavit containing any false statement in connection with the translation provided for in this section.
50 App. USC 327	Rules and regulations; penalties (Office of Selective Service Records).	
50 USC App. 462	Offense and penalties (Selective Service Act).	being a member of the Selective Service System or any other person charged as herein provided with the duty of carrying out any of the provisions of this title (sections 451 to 471(a) of this Appendix) or the rules or regulations made or directions given thereunder, knowingly fails or neglects to perform such duty.
50 App. USC 468	Utilization of industry (Military Selective Service Act).	fails or refuses to carry out any duty imposed upon him by subsection (b)of this section.
50 App. USC 473	Regulations governing liquor sales; penalties (Military Selective Service Act).	
50 App. USC 520	Default judgments; affidavits; bonds; attorneys for persons in service (Soldiers' and Sailors' Civil Relief Act).	makes or uses an affidavit required under this section knowing it to be false.
50 App. USC 530	Eviction of distress during military service; stay; penalty for noncompliance; allotment of pay for payment (Soldiers' and Sailors' Civil Relief Act).	takes part in any eviction or distress otherwise than as provided in subsection (a).

Title & Section Numbers	Caption of Section (Chapter Headings)	Relates to any persons(s) who...
50 App. USC 531	Installment contracts for purchase of property (Soldiers' and Sailors' Civil Relief Act).	resumes possession of property which is the subject of this section otherwise than as provided in subsection (1) of this section.
50 App. USC 532	Mortgages, trusts, deeds, etc. (Soldiers' and Sailors' Civil Relief Act).	makes or causes to be made any sale, foreclosure, or seizure of property, defined as invalid by subsection (3) hereof.
50 App. USC 534	Termination of leases by lessees (Soldiers' and Sailors' Civil Relief Act).	seizes, holds, or detains the personal effects, clothing, furniture, or other property of any person who has lawfully terminated a lease covered by this section.
50 App. USC 535	Protection of assignor of life insurance policy; enforcement of storage liens; penalties (Soldiers' and Sailors' Civil Relief Act).	
50 App. USC 1941d	Restriction on activities of members and employees after leaving Commission; penalty (Disposal of Government-Owned Rubber-Producing Facilities).	
50 App. USC 1985	Attorney's fees; penalty for overcharging (American-Japanese Evacuation Claims).	
50 App. USC 2009	Fee limitation for representing claimants; penalties (War Claims).	
50 App. USC 2017m	Fees of attorneys and agents (War Claims).	
50 App. USC 2073	Penalties (Defense Production Act of 1950).	
50 App. USC 2155	Investigations; records; reports; subpoenas; right to counsel (Defense Production Act of 1950).	
50 App. USC 2160	Employment of personnel; appointment policies; nucleus executive reserve; use of confidential information by employees; printing and distribution of reports (Defense Production Act of 1950).	

Title & Section Numbers	Caption of Section (Chapter Headings)	Relates to any persons(s) who...
50 USC App. 2410	Violations (Export Regulation).	violates or conspires to or attempts to violate any provision of this Act (sections 2401 to 2420 of this Appendix) or any regulation, order, or license issued thereunder.

APPENDIX D

MEMBERS OF THE TASK FORCE

Professor John S. Baker, Jr.

Louisiana State University Law Center
Baton Rouge, LA

John S. Baker, Jr., J.D., University of Michigan (1972), is a Professor of Law at Louisiana State University Law Center where he teaches Constitutional Law, Criminal Law, Federal Courts, and Jurisprudence. Professor Baker has served as a law clerk in Federal District Court, as an Assistant District Attorney in New Orleans, and as a consultant to the Justice Department, the U.S. Senate Judiciary Subcommittee on Separation of Powers, and the Office of Planning in the White House. He has argued constitutional and criminal issues in various courts, including the U.S. Supreme Court. In addition to numerous articles, his writing includes: THE INTELLIGENCE EDGE (with FRIEDMAN, FRIEDMAN & CHAPMAN (Crown Books/Random House, 1997); HALL'S CRIMINAL LAW: CASES AND MATERIALS (with BENSON, FORCE & GEORGE; 5th ed. Michie, 1993); AN INTRODUCTION OF THE UNITED STATES (ed., with LEVASSEUR; University Press of American, 1992).

Professor Sara Sun Beale

Duke University School of Law
Durham, NC

Professor Sara Sun Beale is Professor of Law at Duke University School of Law, where she also recently served as Senior Associate Dean for Academic Affairs. She was Assistant to the Solicitor General, United Sates Department of Justice, Washington, D.C.(1977-1979). Professor Beale held the position of Attorney Adviser, Office of Legal Counsel at the Justice Department in 1976 and 1977. Most of Professor Beale's research and writing for the past 18 years has dealt with federal criminal law. Other activities include Associate Reporter of the Workload Subcommittee of the Federal Courts Study Committee (1989-1990), member of the Criminal Law Advisory Board, Journal of Criminal Law and Criminology (1995-present), and Reporter for the Three Branch Working Group on the Principles to Govern the Federalization of Criminal Law, convened by Attorney General Janet Reno.

Judge Susan A. Ehrlich
Arizona Court of Appeals
Phoenix, AZ

Since 1989, Susan A. Ehrlich has served as a Judge on the Arizona Court of Appeals. After receiving a B.A. from Wellesley College, she worked as a research analyst in the Civil Rights Division of the United States Department of Justice reviewing cases of alleged racial discrimination in target companies. After receiving her J.D. from Arizona State University College of Law, she served as a Law Clerk for Chief Justice Jack D. H. Hays, Arizona Supreme Court. She was in private practice from 1976-77 in Phoenix, Arizona. During 1978-80, she was an attorney with the Appellate Section, Civil Division, United States Department of Justice in Washington, D.C., and has handled cases in every federal circuit. From 1981-89, she was an Assistant United States Attorney, Chief of Appellate Section, District of Arizona. She is a member of the American Law Institute.

Colonel Reuben M. Greenberg
Chief, Charleston Police Department
Charleston, SC

Reuben M. Greenberg was appointed Chief of Police of the Charleston Police Department in 1982. He was formerly the Undersheriff of the San Francisco County Sheriff's Department; a Major with the Savannah, Georgia Police Department; Chief of Police in Opa-Locka, Florida; Chief Deputy Sheriff of Orange County, Florida Sheriff's Department; Director of Public Safety of Mobile, Alabama, and a Deputy Director of the Florida Department of Law Enforcement.

He was Assistant Professor at California State University, Hayward, where he taught Sociology. He taught Political Science at the University of North Carolina at Chapel Hill and Criminal Justice at Florida International University. He has conducted law enforcement seminars and training sessions in numerous countries. He is the current President of the South Carolina Law Enforcement Officers' Association.

The Honorable Howell Heflin
Former U.S. Senator
Law Offices of H. Thomas Heflin, Jr.
Tuscumbia, AL

Howell Heflin is a former United States Senator. He received a B.A. degree from Birmingham Southern College and a J.D. from the University of Alabama School of

Law. He possesses 14 honorary degrees, is a former Chief Justice of Alabama, an Honorary Fellow, American Bar Foundation, Fellow, American College of Trial Lawyers, International Academy of Trial Lawyers, and the International Society of Barristers. He is a former president of the Alabama State Bar Association and former president, National Conference of Chief Justices. He has received both the Justice Award and Harley Award from the American Judicature Society. He is a former faculty member of William and Mary College, University of Alabama, and the University of North Alabama.

Professor Philip B. Heymann
James Barr Ames Professor of Law
Harvard Law School
Cambridge, MA

Philip Heymann served as Deputy Attorney General from 1993 to 1994, when he returned to Harvard University to resume teaching at Harvard Law School and at the Kennedy School of Government.

He is the James Barr Ames Professor at Harvard Law School, Director of its Center for Criminal Justice, and Professor at Harvard's Kennedy School of Government, where he directs the Program for Senior Managers in Government. He was Assistant Attorney General in charge of the Criminal Division from 1978-1981; Associate Watergate Special Prosecutor from 1973-1975; and, in the prior decade, held the following posts in the U.S. Department of State: Executive Assistant to the Undersecretary of State, Deputy Assistant Secretary of State for International Organizations, and head of the Bureau of Security and Consular Affairs. After clerking for Justice John Harlan of the U.S. Supreme Court, Professor Heymann served in the Solicitor General's Office from 1961-1965.

Victor S. Johnson III
District Attorney General
Nashville, TN

Victor S. (Torry) Johnson III received a J.D. from Vanderbilt University in 1974, and served as a Law Clerk for the late William E. Miller, Judge of the United States Court of Appeals for the Sixth Circuit, Cincinnati, Ohio. From 1975-81 he was Assistant District Attorney and Director of Special Prosecution Unit. He was in private practice with Farris, Warfield and Kanaday in Nashville, TN from 1981-84. During 1984-87 he served again as an Assistant District Attorney. In 1987 he was appointed District Attorney General of Metropolitan Nashville-Davison County, TN, by the Governor to fill an unexpired term. In August 1988 and 1990 he ran unopposed and was elected

District Attorney General of Nashville-Davidson County, TN. He was elected again to an eight year term beginning September 1, 1998.

Mr. Johnson served as Vice President of the National District Attorneys Association (1994-96). He was Chairman of the Tennesse Supreme Court Advisory Commission on Rules of Criminal Procedure (1992-96) and continues to be a member (1989-).

The Hon. Robert W. Kastenmeier
Former U.S. Representative

Robert W. Kastenmeier was first elected to the U.S. House of Representatives in 1958. When he left Congress on January 3, 1991, he had served 32 years and was among the top 10 in seniority in the House of Representatives. From 1969, he was chairman of the Judiciary Subcommittee on Courts, Intellectual Property, and the Administration of Justice. From 1985-1991, Mr. Kastenmeier was a member of the Select Committee on Intelligence.

Robert S. Litt, Esq.
Principal Associate Deputy Attorney General
United States Department of Justice
Washington, D.C.

Robert S. Litt is currently Principal Associate Deputy Attorney General, Department of Justice. He has previously served as a Deputy Assistant Attorney General in the Criminal Division of the United States Department of Justice. Mr. Litt graduated from Harvard College in 1971 and Yale Law School in 1976. He clerked for Judge Edward Weinfeld in the United States District Court for the Southern District of New York and Justice Potter Stewart on the United States Supreme Court. From 1978 to 1984 Mr. Litt served as an Assistant United States Attorney in the Southern District of New York, prosecuting fraud, racketeering and official corruption cases, among others. From 1984 to 1993 he was an associate and (from 1988) a partner at the firm of Williams & Connolly in Washington, D.C. He served as Special Advisor to the Assistant Secretary of State for European and Canadian Affairs from April 1993 to June 1994, and then joined the Department of Justice. Mr. Litt served on the Task Force in an individual capacity and the views he expressed in the work of the Task Force do not necessarily represent the views of the Department of Justice.

Mr. Litt succeeded **Paul J. Fishman**, formerly Principal Associate Deputy Attorney General at the Department of Justice, who served on the Task Force in its initial phases.

Edwin Meese III, Esq.
Ronald Reagan Distinguished Fellow in Public Policy
The Heritage Foundation
Washington, D.C.

Edwin Meese III currently holds the Ronald Reagan Chair in Public Policy at The Heritage Foundation, a Washington-based public policy research and education institution. He is also a Distinguished Visiting Fellow at the Hoover Institution, Stanford University, and a Distinguished Senior Fellow at the Institute of United States Studies, University of London. He served as Chair of the Federalization Task Force.

Mr. Meese served as the 75th Attorney General of the United States from February 1985 to August 1988. Prior to that service, he held the position of Counsellor to the President from 1981 to 1985. He also served as a member of the National Security Council, as chairman of the National Drug Policy Board, and as chairman of the Domestic Policy Council. Prior to entering the federal government, Mr. Meese was a professor of law at the University of San Diego and director of its Center for Criminal Justice Policy and Management. He served as Vice Chairman of California's Organized Crime Control Commission and was a county Deputy District Attorney. He is co-editor of MAKING AMERICA SAFER: WHAT CITIZENS AND THEIR STATE AND LOCAL OFFICIALS CAN DO TO COMBAT CRIME (1997).

Dr. Barbara S. Meierhoefer

Dr. Barbara Meierhoefer has served as director of a federal pilot program aimed at the identification and effective supervision of drug dependent federal defendants, a joint-agency project funded by the U.S. Department of Justice and administered by the Administrative Office of the U.S. Courts. She was formerly a member of the research staffs of the U.S. Parole Commission and the Federal Judicial Center. For the past 20 years, Dr. Meierhoefer has investigated and written in the areas of criminal sentencing, probation and parole supervision, and judicial workload in the federal district and appellate courts. She also served as an original member of the Oklahoma Truth in Sentencing Commission, and has evaluated local programs designed to prevent youth gang involvement, delinquency, and substance abuse. Dr. Meierhoefer served as statistical consultant to the Task Force.

James F. Neal, Esq.
Neal & Harwell
Nashville, TN

James F. Neal has a B.S. degree from the University of Wyoming (1952); L.L.B. Vanderbilt University School of Law (1957); L.L.M. Georgetown University School of Law (1960). He was Special Assistant to the Attorney General of the United States; United States Attorney for the Middle District of Tennessee; Chief Trial Counsel, Watergate Special Prosecution Force; Lecturer in Law, Vanderbilt University School of Law; Chief Counsel, Senate Select Committee to Study Undercover Operations of the Department of Justice; and presently is a partner with Neal & Harwell in Nashville, Tennessee.

Judge Jon O. Newman
U.S. Court of Appeals for the Second Circuit
Hartford, CT

Senior Judge Newman is a graduate of Princeton University and Yale Law School. He is the immediate past Chief Judge of the United States Court of Appeals for the Second Circuit (Conn., N.Y., and Vt.) and has served as a member of the Court since June 25, 1979. He was the United States Attorney for the District of Connecticut and he served as a United States District Judge for that district from January 17, 1972, until his appointment to the Court of Appeals.

Judge Newman is a member of the American Law Institute and the International Society for the Reform of Criminal Law. He is a Fellow of the American Bar Foundation. He served on the American Bar Association's Action Commission on Tort Liability and was one of the American Law Institute's advisers on the Restatement of the Law of Unfair Competition.

Otto G. Obermaier, Esq.
Weil, Gotshal & Manges
New York, NY

Otto G. Obermaier is a partner at Weil, Gotshal & Manges in New York City. He served as United States Attorney for the Southern District of NY (1989-93). He was Chairman of the New York-New Jersey High Integrity Drug Trafficking Area (HIDTA) and New York-New Jersey Organized Crime Drug Enforcement Task Force (OCDETF). He served as Chief Trial Counsel, New York Regional Office, United States Securities and Exchange Commission (1968-70), and as an Assistant United

States Attorney for the Southern District of New York (1964-68).

He has written and lectured widely on issues of criminal justice, including recent articles on aspects of the federalization issue.

Donald Santarelli, Esq.

Bell, Boyd & Lloyd
Washington, D.C.

Donald E. Santarelli, a member of Bell, Boyd & Lloyd, practices law in Washington D.C. He serves as Chairman, National Committee on Community Corrections 1989-); Chairman, Federal City Council Committee for Corrections for the District of Columbia (1996-); Vice Chair for CLE/Professional Development, American Bar Association Criminal Justice Section (1994-96); National District Attorneys Association American Prosecutors Research Institute Director (1989-).

Mr. Santarelli was Administrator (Chief Executive) of the Law Enforcement Assistance Administration, U.S. Department of Justice (1972-74); Associate Deputy Attorney General, U.S. Department of Justice (1969-72); Special Counsel to the Senate Judiciary Subcommittee on Constitutional Rights (1968-69); Minority Counsel to the U.S. House of Representatives Committee on the Judiciary (1967-68); Assistant United States Attorney for the District of Columbia (1966-67); and Law Clerk to United States District and Fourth Circuit Judge Thomas J. Michie (1964-65).

Professor James A. Strazzella

James G. Schmidt Chair in Law
Temple University School of Law
Philadelphia, PA

Professor James A. Strazzella holds the James Schmidt Chair in Law at Temple University Law School, teaching criminal law, criminal procedure, and appellate procedure. He has taught at the University of Pennsylvania Law School, Georgetown, in Tel-Aviv and Rome, and for several years was acting dean at Temple and vice-dean at the University of Pennsylvania Law School. A member of the American Law Institute and the author of numerous publications, he edited a volume on *The Federal Role in Criminal Law* (1996). He is a former Assistant United States Attorney in Washington, D.C., and has remained active in litigation and court-related work. He served as the Reporter for this Task Force.

For many years, he chaired the committee that devised the criminal procedure rules for Pennsylvania courts and he has chaired a long list of other groups involved with justice improvement, including the Pennsylvania Attorney General's Task Force on Family

Violence, as well as the Criminal Law Section of both the Pennsylvania State Bar and the Federal Bar Association, and the Federal Merit Selection Panel for U.S. Magistrate-Judges (E.D.PA). In 1970, he served as chief counsel to the Presidential Commission's investigation of the Kent State shootings.

William W. Taylor, III, Esq.

Zuckerman, Spaeder, Goldstein, Taylor & Kolker, L.L.P.
Washington, D.C.

William W. Taylor, III, is a 1966 graduate of the University of North Carolina and a 1969 graduate of Yale University Law School. Following a clerkship for the Honorable Caleb M. Wright, Chief Judge, United States District Court for the District of Delaware (1969-70), Mr. Taylor served as Staff Attorney and Special Assistant for Training at the Public Defender Service for the District of Columbia (1970-75). Since 1975, Mr. Taylor has been in private practice as a civil and criminal litigator and is a partner with Zuckerman, Spaeder, Goldstein, Taylor & Kolker, LLP, Washington, D.C. He served as the 1996-97 Chair of the Criminal Justice Section of the ABA, and initiated this Task Force.

John Van de Kamp, Esq.

Dewey Ballentine
Los Angeles, CA

John K. Van de Kamp graduated from Stanford Law School in 1959, and served as an Assistant U.S. Attorney from 1960-66 and as U.S. Attorney for the Central District of California from 1966-67. He then served in Washington, D.C., as Director of the Executive Office of U.S. Attorneys under Deputy Attorney General Warren Christopher. In 1972, he became the Central District's first appointed Federal Public Defender. In 1975, he was appointed Los Angeles County District Attorney. As District Attorney, he established the office's first Victim Assistance Program and chaired the state committee establishing such programs throughout California. Mr. Van de Kamp was elected California's Attorney General in 1982 and served two terms. He is presently of counsel in the law firm of Dewey Ballentine in Los Angeles, California.

ACKNOWLEDGMENTS

The Task Force appreciates the assistance of the many individuals and organizations who, in one way or another, supplied important information, views, support, and effort to the project.

Dr. Barbara Meierhoefer's expertise in analyzing statistical data concerning the justice system proved invaluable. Information, including statistical data about the actual prosecution of federal crimes and federal court dockets, was gleaned from a number of sources, including material helpfully made available by the U.S. Sentencing Commission, the Administrative Office of U.S. Courts, the Federal Judicial Center, the Judicial Conference of the United States, and organizations representing state judges and others involved in law enforcement issues. Many interested organizations and individuals, representing a cross-section of experience with federalization, were invited to submit views to the Task Force. The views of the members of the American Bar Association Criminal Justice Section (over 7,000 in number) and many law professors active in the field were also solicited.

In chairing the Task Force, Edwin Meese III provided experienced, knowledgeable leadership and fostered a collegial atmosphere for the many Task Force discussions. Former ABA Criminal Justice Section Chair William W. Taylor, III, initiated the Task Force and was actively involved in all phases of its work. His valuable judgment and energetic support were essential to the success of the project. His successors as Chair of the Section, Ronald Goldstock and Myrna Raeder, assured continued support and encouragement. ABA administrative liaison was afforded by ABA staff members Thomas C. Smith (Criminal Justice Section Executive Director), Kenneth Goldsmith, Elizabeth Harth, Adele Meyer, and Mabel Muldrow. The Washington, D.C., firm of Zuckerman, Spaeder, Goldstein, Taylor & Kolker, L.L.P., donated valuable research and clerical assistance, and we had the helpful cooperation of many persons at Temple University Law School. In particular, the efforts of Kimberly A. Boyer, John Cuddihy, Jeffrey Davidson, Pamela J. Eaton, Rosetta Ellis, Shirley Hall, Lori Hamlin-Bias, James E. Huggett, Belinda Jones, Tammi A. Markowicz, Sherry F. Scruggs, and Elizabeth Weathers contributed to the Report.

This Report also draws on points made in the thoughtful studies reviewed by the Task Force (APPENDIX A) and the Task Force acknowledges its debt to this literature.

J.A.S.